DEVELOPING WEB-BASED INSTRUCTION

PLANNING, DESIGNING, MANAGING, AND EVALUATING FOR RESULTS

EDITED BY ELIZABETH A. DUPUIS

NEAL-SCHUMAN PUBLISHERS, INC.
NEW YORK   LONDON

The New Library Series

No. 1 – *Finding Common Ground: Creating the Library of the Future without Diminishing the Library of the Past.* Edited by Cheryl LaGuardia and Barbara A. Mitchell.

No. 2 – *Recreating the Academic Library: Breaking Virtual Ground.* Edited by Cheryl LaGuardia.

No. 3 – *Becoming a Library Teacher.* Edited by Cheryl LaGuardia and Christine K. Oka.

No. 4 – *Teaching the New Library to Today's Users: Reaching International, Minority, Senior Citizens, Gay/Lesbian, First-Generation College, At-Risk, Graduate and Returning Students, and Distance Learners.* Edited by Trudi E. Jacobson and Helene C. Williams.

No. 5 – *Designing, Building, and Teaching in the Electronic Library Classroom.* By Cheryl LaGuardia and John Vasi.

No. 6 – *Digital Reference Service in the New Millennium: Planning, Management, and Evaluation.* Edited by R. David Lankes, John W. Collins III, and Abby S. Kasowitz.

No. 7 – *Developing Web-Based Instruction: Planning, Designing, Managing, and Evaluating for Results.* Edited by Elizabeth A. Dupuis.

Published by Neal-Schuman Publishers, Inc.
100 William Street, Suite 2004
New York, NY 10038

Printed and bound in the United States of America.

The paper used in this publication meets the minimum requirements of American National Standard for Information Sciences—Permanence of Paper for Printed Library Materials, ANSI Z39.48—1992 ∞

ISBN 1-55570-428-X

Cataloging-in-Publication data for this book is available from the Library of Congress

For all things Austin and Tamalpais

Table of Contents

Part III: Design and Development

List of Figures

Series Editor's Foreword

Cheryl Laguardia

"The New Library" is shorthand for the fascinating phenomenon of the perpetually rapid changes in the physical space and virtual reality of today's professional workplace environment. Every day, students and educators, practicing librarians, library managers, and other information industry professionals encounter the challenges, clashes, opportunities, and pressures of bridging the gap between information and its potential users. Integrating current and projected developments in electronic resources into a solid base of established library knowledge, *The Neal-Schuman New Library Series* sketches, summarizes, and charts the exciting future of information management.

As the editor of this series, I'm always on the lookout for innovative ideas and projects in librarianship to translate into books. Developing useful Web-based instruction is one of the most interesting responses to the revolution created in libraries by the combination of digital communication and the power of the Internet. Web-based instruction is still an area in the nascent stages of development so I wasn't sure I could find someone capable of writing a book exploring the sensible yet cutting-edge world of today's Web-based instruction. One problem was finding someone with both practical experience in the field along with the vision and literary powers to come up with a good book. So I was ready to settle for one — or the other.

Until I found Elizabeth Dupuis, that is. I became fascinated with Elizabeth's work when a message went out over library instruction lists announcing the availability of the Texas Information Literacy Tutorial created at University of Texas-Austin.

A visit to the award-winning site convinced me, along with the rest of the library world, that the creators had come up with a very good idea and put it into practice beautifully. A call to Elizabeth to discuss what she and her colleagues had done convinced me that here was the right person to write the book I was looking for. A few e-mails later this book was underway.

As head of instructional services at a large university, may I make a confession? All of the lofty purposes and principles that motivated the commission of this book are true, but in the background, there is a bottom line truth. I wanted Elizabeth Dupuis to do this book because I've wanted to read it and use it in my own work. Period.

When Elizabeth gathered together the cadre of authors writing in these pages, I was impressed at the diversity of experiences and backgrounds they brought to the project. These are some of the most interesting, and credible, practitioners and writers about library instruction in the world today. Having a collection of what they have done, and what they know, in this volume makes it even more valuable—to me and to others. (Noticed that self-serving leitmotif again, did you?)

Like other books in the series, *Developing Web-Based Instruction: Planning, Designing Managing, and Evaluating for Results* is aimed as much at solving the daily problems of practicing librarians as it is at meeting the long-term planning needs of administrators and managers. Elizabeth and the other authors here have both first-hand knowledge of what they write, and the ability to step back and make it broadly applicable to many libraries with different clientele and issues.

Developing Web-Based Instruction is about "how to do it good" anywhere, in any library setting. The planning, management, evaluation, assessment, design, and development guidelines presented here comprise an excellent blueprint for Web-based instruction in libraries anywhere. If we all follow the advice in this book, we'll have solid, effective, responsive online tutorials and other Web-based instruction projects.

To combine the practical with the theoretical in a single volume is one feat; to do so in a stimulating manner accessible to all is a feat multiplied by magnitudes. So this book is a wonder indeed. I must add that the knowledge conveyed in this book is highly transferable to a wide variety of situations. Although Elizabeth could have chosen to describe how "they did it good" with TILT at UT and the other authors could have just told how they are "doing it good" at their respective libraries, they took the longer, wider path.

This longer, wider path leads to higher ground. Accepted as the father of the library science movement in India, Dr. S. R. Ranganathan's expansive and poetic thoughts about libraries have shaped the institution everywhere. Over seventy years ago, his "Five Laws of Library Science" was widely accepted as a definitive statement of the ideal of library service. The laws are:

- Books are for use.
- Every book is its reader.
- Every reader his book.
- Save the time of the reader.
- A library is a growing organism.

I think *Developing Web-Based Instruction: Planning, Designing, Managing, and Evaluating for Results* embodies all five of Ranganathan's principles in very meaningful ways. Heaven knows this book will be used, and useful, to its readers; it will have plenty of readers (and each one will consider it hers/his); it will help its readers' libraries grow; and perhaps most importantly, it will save the time of the reader. After reading this book, we instruction librarians won't have to reinvent the wheel, just spin it a bit for a "fit" on our particular library wagons.

Thank you, Elizabeth and Company.

Cheryl LaGuardia
Head, Instructional Services
Harvard College Library
Harvard University
Cambridge, Massachusetts
and
Editor, *The New Library Series*

Preface

Elizabeth A. Dupuis

Developing Web-Based Instruction: Planning, Designing, Managing, and Evaluating for Results examines the entire process of creating Web-based library instruction. Today, Web-based instruction is discussed variously as hybrid learning, blended learning, e-learning, distance learning, distributed learning, Web-based training, remote education, and so on. Regardless of the specific label, quality online instruction takes its cues from quality face-to-face instruction—with a focus on the learner and learning, not the instructor or the teaching. To that end, this guide emphasizes instructional design and educational technologies chosen in terms of instructional goals. Rather than emphasizing specific technologies or software, the authors offer suggestions for determining the technologies, instructional approaches, and media useful for various types of projects.

This book was written for students, librarians, and other educators who are creating, revising, or studying online instructional models from stand-alone, short tutorials to full online courses. *Developing Web-Based Instruction: Planning, Designing, Managing, and Evaluating for Results* has been designed to address many different types of libraries and other educational institutions and organizations with training programs, undertaking Web-based instruction projects.

The genesis of the idea for this book began in 1996 at the University of Texas at Austin, when my first step of discovery in Web-based instruction turned into one of the most exciting adventures of my professional life. Nearly three years later, Brent Simpson, Clara Fowler, and I had completed our first

Web-based instruction project, TILT (Texas Information Literacy Tutorial, available at http://tilt.lib.utsystem.edu/), an interactive opportunity for students to begin exploring and researching in the online world. The complete tale of the TILT journey is full of comedy, intrigue, and suspense . . . but that is another story. *Developing Web-Based Instruction* is inspired by our experiences with and lessons learned from TILT, but translated into principles and recommendations to aid other libraries and educational organizations developing similar types of learning environments.

One of the most compelling insights I had during the process of creating TILT was about the power of true collaboration. When approached to write this book, I thought it fitting to seek out other talented librarians and educators to contribute their thoughts and perspectives, creating a more diverse collection of chapters offering advice, opinions, and insights drawn from their considerable experience with a range of Web-based instructional projects. Transforming my role from sole author to editor, I sought chapter authors who would bring diverse experiences and professional backgrounds, and who were willing to contribute to a book that read as a coherent whole rather than separate chapters about individual successes.

I was fortunate to find fourteen excellent partners in this endeavor. The chapter authors are an aggregation of librarians, distance learning coordinators, faculty, administrators and instructional technologists, representing institutions of various sizes and diverse student populations. Collectively, they have developed short online assignments, stand-alone tutorials, credit-bearing courses delivered over the Internet, and an impressive range of other Web projects for a wide variety of audiences. Many of the chapter authors have been recognized by professional organizations for their excellence and accomplishments.

As editor, it was my role to ensure the final chapters complemented each other in a way that guaranteed that all significant topics were addressed, without unnecessary repetition of ideas—a complex task with fourteen people, spread across the country, and working on an intense schedule. Throughout the project, collegiality and creativity were hallmarks of our collaboration. To provide the general framework, I authored overviews to begin each new section, or stage, of the book. The chapters outline and explain the important elements of the multifaceted and iterative process of creating a Web-based instructional project from inception to completion. Chapters are organized in three broad stages: Part I, "Planning and Management"; Part II, "Evaluation and Assessment"; and Part III, "Design and Development." Each chapter offers theory along with practical approaches, framing the issues so they will be useful for a wide range of projects.

Please note: Acknowledging the variety of terminology used in various environments, some words are used interchangeably such as audience, users, learners, and students.

Part I, "Planning and Management," discusses considerations for project planning and management. Chapter 1, "Scope, Timeline, and Budget," by Susan Carol Curzon includes a series of questions and tips for designing the foundational elements of project planning. Chapter 2 by Deborah A. Murphy covers aspects of gathering and managing "Teams and Partners" who are crucial for the project development. Chapter 3 by Clara S. Fowler offers suggestions for understanding the needs and interests of the "Audience and Stakeholders," two important but different groups the project is designed to serve. Chapter 4 by Nancy H. Dewald articulates theories related to the differences between teaching children and adolescents and teaching adults in "Pedagogy and Andragogy"—especially those issues in terms of online instruction. Chapter 5 by Scott Macklin offers insight into choosing "Educational Technology" responsive to the needs of learners, proving that technology does not have to be the driving force in your Web-based instruction.

Part II, "Evaluation and Assessment," highlights various methods for evaluating and assessing your project and student learning. While it is unusual to place evaluation before design, I chose this order to stress the importance of considering what and how you will measure various aspects of the project through quantitative and qualitative methods. Chapter 6 by Trudi Bellardo Hahn discusses "Statistics and Metrics" based upon electronic data from individual computers and servers. Chapter 7 by Pat Davitt Maughan offers tips for "Focus

Groups," from preparation to analysis of data. Chapter 8 by Jerilyn R. Veldof suggests tips for "Usability Testing," including effective methods for organizations without access to formal usability labs. Chapter 9 by Trudi E. Jacobson discusses "Assessment of Learning" through myriad examples of instructional design approaches that offer formative and summative assessments of student learning.

Part III, "Design and Development," encompasses aspects of Web and instructional design and development. Chapter 10 by Craig Gibson covers "Goals and Objectives" from traditional (behaviorist and cognitivist) and constructivist views, emphasizing the need for metacognitive approaches for competencies and content that require higher-order cognitive skills. Chapter 11, "Interactivity," by Susan Sharpless Smith offers an overview of categories, frameworks and technologies for interactivity, emphasizing that interaction—whether with a computer or other humans online—is an important element of active learning in online environments. Chapter 12 by Sarah McDaniel builds on earlier chapters to offer strategies for "Content Organization and Development" for both traditional and constructivist approaches. Chapter 13 by Nancy O'Hanlon provides an overview of "Site Design" options for overall architecture, navigation, and page design. Chapter 14 by Dennis Glenn uses a discussion of principles and elements of design to offer suggestions for "Putting Content Online," including text, audio, and video.

Two practical appendices complete the book. The first explains recommended elements for a project proposal. The second is a list of selected resources on related subjects.

Readers with experience know that developing Web-based instruction and teaching online are exciting and rewarding challenges. For those embarking on a new journey developing educational Web sites—or considering sending others down this path—I welcome you to this exciting collaborative endeavor. I trust both newcomers and seasoned librarians will find information that is inspiring and useful. My hope is that *Developing Web-Based Instruction: Planning, Designing, Managing, and Evaluating for Results* will become one of your best guides, and companions, along the way.

Part I

Planning and Management

The beginning of a project is always exciting, perhaps in part because of the mystery of what lies ahead. Planning a Web-based instructional project requires you to draw from educational theory, management theory, and your own creativity to create a product that meets the needs of your intended audience. The final product will be a result of the unique mix of project goals, team members, ideas, and choice of implementation. And yet, every project—regardless of scale, duration, innovation, or complexity—follows essentially the same process that starts with planning.

Planning entails considering possibilities, gathering information, assessing needs and resources, balancing priorities, articulating goals, and outlining an overall process. Unfortunately, in many cases, planning is considered frivolous, an impediment to getting the actual work done. In fact, many problems await the project team that overlooks this step and jumps into development too early.

While there are many ways to proceed, project management has become a recognized method for moving any type of project through the stages from beginning to end. Historically, project management has focused on balancing the triple constraints of time, cost, and quality. Most project teams are under pressure to produce quality at a low cost and in a short period. To create a product of high quality on a small budget, you are likely to need more time to reach completion. Similarly, to create a product of high quality in a short amount of time, you are likely to need a larger budget to supply more equipment and perhaps contract with additional staff. Although it can be difficult to work within all three constraints, it is important to be conscious of the relevance of each of these elements throughout the planning, development, and evaluation stages.

Over the past decade, an additional, important element has been recognized within the study of project management. Rather than focusing simply on schedules and expenses, emphasis is increasingly placed on the involvement and satisfaction of the "customers" or people involved. The fourth element, now recognized as core to project management, emphasizes participation, communication, and team dynamics within the project team, and between the team, stakeholders, and target audience.

Perhaps most importantly, the project manager must ensure the project chosen is worth the organization's and the team's investment. As you plan, be realistic about your constraints. Although you may envision the ideal project, an assessment of the skills and resources available might suggest you undertake a less extensive project. Prioritizing and scaling back the dimensions of a project can be difficult. Even the most visionary leader will benefit from the collective expertise of others involved, especially the core team members and the most influential stakeholders, to make these decisions. To ensure your final proposal will remain viable, never lose sight of the project as a whole and your initial reasons for undertaking it.

Certainly, overplanning is a waste of time. However, without a great deal of luck, inadequate planning may lead to a product that does not address the original need or, in the worst case, never gets completed. To avoid these scenarios, initial planning and ongoing management and review are important. Common reasons a Web-based instructional project might fail include:

- Lack of administrative support or interest outside of the project team.
- Dysfunctional communication between project team members.
- Misconceptions about institutional and audience needs.
- Poor choice of instructional approach and educational technology.

- Omission of ongoing reviews and prototyping on a smaller scale.
- Refusal to revisit issues after initial planning.

Proactive measures can be taken to negotiate around these obstacles. When initiating the project, ensure the project proposal is well defined in philosophy, scope, and language. Appendix A outlines elements for a project proposal in more detail. Once the appropriate stakeholders endorse the proposal, the project manager can begin to translate those ideas into an action plan with more specific timelines and assignments.

At the beginning of the project, articulate criteria to define success for your project. Ideally this list will be developed and approved by all members of the project team, as well as the primary stakeholders in the project. Consider elements such as time, budget, administrative support, audience needs, project reliability, level of quality, level of use, institutional awareness, and impact on related programs and services. For example, what functionality must be included in the final product? What groups will need to be involved in planning from the start? How will you confirm that the instruction designed is appropriate for the intended audience? What methods will you incorporate to ensure you remain on target with your project goals? Similarly, what methods will you use to determine whether development of a Web-based instructional project is an effective approach for this content? Along with the list of elements, develop some initial methods for measuring how well the project is going and how closely the team is meeting their original expectations. If you remain true to the original goals of the project, changes in the initial framework and perceptions of success are acceptable and indicate the project team is learning from their experiences.

The effectiveness of the project team itself should also be considered. In some cases a project team will elect to terminate a project during development due to changes in audience needs, introduction of new technologies, or organizational priorities. In these cases, the management of the project may still be considered successful even if the project itself failed—an important distinction for groups that may be asked to contribute to similar projects in the future. To assess the effectiveness of the team,

it is also useful to develop criteria, which characterize successful project management for your organization. Consider elements such as leadership, organization, communication, deci-
sion-making, delegation, creativity, commitment, conflict reso-
lution, flexibility, and assessment. By regularly, if even informally, evaluating the management of the project you will be
contributing to the effectiveness of your organization as well.

When there are few other models to follow, it can be difficult to know if a project is on the right track or if doubts are
founded. The more complete and well researched your project
proposal, the better prepared you are to evaluate any concerns
and make decisions. Success of the project should not be determined solely by completion of the project, but also by whether
the project is in concert with your institution's readiness for a
project of this type and scale so it will be sustainable. With tech-
nology-related projects, there is an increased tension between
meeting specific requirements and accepting large amounts of
uncertainty and risk. Experience is the best guide, but often
project managers are new to the type of initiative they have been
asked to lead. Without experience, you must next rely on intu-
ition, listen to others, inform yourself about the possibilities, and
have contingency plans.

Planning is important, but do not be controlled by it. Accept that no matter how determined you are to create a perfect
timeline, the project will never go exactly as planned and you
will not be able to predict all of the problems or obstacles ahead.
It is useful to develop an overall strategy for development, but
remain flexible in your timeline, process, approach, and implementation. If you are too rigid, the project will become frustrating and stressful for all involved. Instead, see decisions and al-
terations to your original plan as part of the process and not
changes to it.

Without micromanaging each aspect of the project, the manager must find ways to monitor and enable the work. Regular
meetings—at which each team member is encouraged to discuss
their progress, problems, and ideas—are extremely valuable for
keeping on task and maintaining strong communication. Built-
in checkpoints and deliverables (such as prototypes, reports, or
completion of smaller components) are other positive strategies

for ensuring constant progress and resolving problems early. By distributing work among all team members, drawing from or supporting development of their expertise, and involving members of the target audience, a project manager can gain commitment for the process and ensure relevance of the final product.

Some will find their projects are not so much like work as like an adventure, with unexpected obstacles and rewards. As with a trip, when it concludes some parts will stand out and others will be completely forgotten. Whether you choose to extensively document your plans, or prefer to make brief notes, the basic elements of planning should be considered before beginning any work. Since you or others in your organization may repeat the process for future projects, it can be beneficial to keep a log or journal during the process. Not only will it help guide others in the future, but it can be an interesting souvenir when your project is completed.

Planning and management occur throughout the process of creating Web-based instruction. Fortunately, many problems can be avoided or resolved if adequate time is devoted in the planning stage to the scope and timeline, team and partners, audience and stakeholders, pedagogical approach, and educational technology. Each of these areas is discussed in greater detail in the chapters that follow.

Chapter 1

Scope, Timeline, and Budget

Susan Carol Curzon

A successful Web-based instruction project begins with successful planning. Three of the key components of planning—scope, timeline, and budget—create a road map that illustrates where you are going with a project. Your goal in this initial step of the project is to ensure that you have a well-defined scope that addresses a genuine need, a reasonable timeline that allows for unpredictable factors, and an adequate budget that provides the necessary resources for the development and maintenance of the project. All three components are vital and must be managed effectively throughout the entire process in order to bring the project to conclusion. When these components are not successfully managed, the project may be underfunded, understaffed, and misunderstood, which results in unnecessary pressure and turmoil. This chapter explores the triple dimensions of scope, timeline, and budget.

SCOPE

Why is the development of the scope a primary consideration? Many projects suffer because development starts before the project team has sufficiently analyzed what needs the project is being designed to address. It is important to invest time in understanding scope at the beginning, as this is the conceptual phase of the project in which you will take time to understand what you are trying to do. Scope defines the extent and aim of

7

a project. Understanding scope allows you to set the project goals, work within your limits, meet the instructional needs, and recognize when you have achieved success. When you invest time to initially define the project scope, you will have clarity about your purpose, more efficiency in the development of the project, and an improvement in the overall quality. The reason for this is simple: clear directions are established and everyone involved in the project is working toward the same end, reducing the likelihood of the project getting out of control with conflicting goals, delayed deadlines, and cost overruns. To determine the scope of your instruction project, address these three questions:

- What is the purpose of the project?
- Are you capable of completing the project?
- Does this project merit your effort?

What Is the Purpose of the Project?

To develop a finished product that addresses an actual problem or need, one should carefully analyze the reasons for embarking on such an endeavor and develop justification for committing the necessary resources to such a project. This analysis helps to define the scope of the project which, in turn, will help to establish the goals. There can be a wide range of reasons why one would undertake Web-based instruction. Let's review a few that are most common.

Impart new knowledge or skills

Educational institutions and public organizations nationwide are focusing on the importance of ensuring people of all ages develop the necessary skills to seek, evaluate, manage, and create information. If you have determined that members of your audience—such as students, staff, instructors, patrons, researchers, or clients—might benefit from instruction on a particular topic, then a Web-based instruction project may be a meaningful addition to your offerings.

Maximize limited resources

Good instruction requires careful thought and often a significant commitment of time from the instructor. This is no less true for quality online instruction. However, by using a Web-based product you can still reach a large number of your target audience in a short time span, without concerns about limitations of classroom space or a high number of in-person sessions. Using this model, you can ensure all audience members are introduced to the same content online and allow them to seek additional assistance only as needed.

Support distance learning initiatives

Many campuses are launching significant distance or distributed learning efforts. These efforts to offer classroom instruction available remotely must be matched by the delivery of online library instruction. If such an initiative is underway on your campus, you have good reason to launch a Web-based instruction project designed in concert with the goals of those programs. If distance learning initiatives are not yet substantial for your organization, you may consider taking the lead by making online library instruction available alone or in partnership with another interested library or agency.

Transform connections with curriculum

Some educational institutions have library instruction or information literacy requirements built into the curriculum. In these cases, Web-based instruction may offer a solution to providing consistent and meaningful instruction to a number of courses that address similar audiences or topics. In the absence of these initiatives, any traditional partnership—such as with a schoolteacher, faculty member, training coordinator, or community organization—may provide opportunities for integrating library instruction, research skills, or even use of specific resources if developed as online components or modules. Developing Web-based alternatives with these partners may encourage them to creatively redesign the instruction or training program they currently offer.

Encourage independent learning

Some library users seek resources they can use independently. If your audience is comprised of many people who have restrictive schedules, who are technologically savvy, who prefer personalized online services, or who would benefit from similar just-in-time learning experiences as others, a Web-based instruction project might be one way to address their interests and needs. Some people may prefer this on-demand model especially in cases where the content can be addressed as well online, by incorporating integrated interactions.

Are You Capable of Completing This Project?

The desire, in itself, will not ensure that the project can be completed. A suitable environment, ample resources, and strong motivation must coexist to accomplish any goal. To ascertain whether your project can be accomplished, analyze the strengths and weaknesses of your library and institution and address these questions:

Can you gather people with the right skills to accomplish the project?

Not only will this project require time from all members of the project team, it will also require staff with the necessary skills and shared motivation to see the project through to completion. Ask yourself if you can gather the expertise needed to start and finish the project.

Does the timing complement other library goals?

The development of a Web-based instruction project will consume many resources. If there are other major, concurrent initiatives in the library, consider whether the timing is right to launch this project. An organization juggling too many goals often means that few may be accomplished. On the other hand, if your project truly addresses a problem or need, then its development may simultaneously address some of those other initiatives and you are likely to find administrators and other stakeholders offering the needed support.

Is there the money for the project?

Later in this chapter the budget will be discussed more completely, but it is important at this stage to confirm that funding is available. If the budget is tight for the library and there is little discretionary money, you may want to defer the project. Inadequate funding means that there is a great likelihood that the project will not be finished which, in turn, will mean that the funding that was spent will be wasted. Rather than relying on your institution's budget, you may consider applying for a grant to fund your planning and development.

Is your audience ready for technology-based learning?

Learning through instructional technologies and Web sites not only requires technological competencies, but also patience, discipline, and a capacity for independent learning. Ideally your instruction will employ strong pedagogical practices that will engage the learner in the process of acquiring and forming new knowledge from the instructional framework. Even still, part of the success of the project will be determined by how well you match that framework to the needs, interests, and abilities of your target audience.

Are your potential partners and stakeholders supportive?

Enthusiasm for, and adoption of, this new instructional model will rely in part on how well the scope defines this project in terms that partners and stakeholders—such as administrators, instructors, faculty, colleagues, and training staff—understand and believe is in alignment with their goals. In researching the current state of your organization, seek out other models of Web-based instruction that have been proposed or successfully completed. If models do not already exist, browse strategic plans and other documents to determine if there are ways to propose new collaborations to further everyone's goals.

Does This Project Merit Your Effort?

After defining the project's purpose and confirming the availability of basic resources, you need to decide if the project is worth the time, money, and personnel. In determining if the project is worthy of the effort, consider these questions:

Does this project complement the library and organization's goals?

Most libraries have a strategic plan in which the major initiatives and directions are clearly defined. Similarly many institutions and agencies have broader expectations or goals related to student learning, company efficiency, or public accountability. Consider these and articulate how the proposed Web-based library instruction complements the goals of both the library and the larger organization. This is not only important politically for the library but also may be an avenue of funding. If a clear connection is not obvious, you may want to reconsider your scope and timing.

Can you achieve your goals another way?

A Web-based instruction project will likely require a substantial commitment of institutional resources to complete and maintain, particularly if no one at your institution has the required skills and experience with the process. Remembering that technology is not a panacea, carefully consider whether an online model is the best solution for your goals or if there are other alternatives that more efficiently and effectively address your problem or need.

Can the project be sustained?

It is one thing to develop a project, but another to sustain it for many years. Your scope should outline an approach to the planning, design, and content that strives to ensure the final product will not be unused or quickly become outdated. The less constant the need for updates, especially with technical and programming skills, the more likely the organization will be able to continue to hire staff to handle the project. Similarly, sustaining online instruction is not only a task that comes at the end of the process. In truly engaging online projects, there may be elements that allow learners to communicate with others and with the librarian or instructor. These facets will demand ongoing commitment as well.

What are the long-range consequences?

Think through possible consequences of the project. Will Web-based instruction increase or decrease demand for other types of library instruction or library services? Will the project require different types of personnel to be hired in the short-term or in the long-term? Will the library need to invest in servers and networking? Brainstorm a list of potential consequences before deciding to proceed.

What are the risks?

There are two key risks related to a project like this. The first relates to the endorsement of and investment in this type of instruction for your institution; the second relates to the utility of the final product. When considering whether or not to do a project, reverse thinking may help. Consider what will happen if you do not do the project. What will be the consequences? What will be the missed opportunities? Addressing these questions may bring your project into sharper focus.

When developing the scope of the project, remember these tips:

1. Articulate good reasons to commit resources to this project. Good reasons do not include "because other li-

braries are creating projects like this" or "because this will cost less than hiring staff." First, your rationale should be based on the needs and goals of your institution and your audiences. It is possible that Web-based instruction is not appropriate for your organization at the current time. Second, undertaking development of Web-based instruction is rarely less expensive than traditional means of teaching and learning. The project will still require work from a wide range of staff and is likely to transfer costs to other parts of the organization, particularly toward programmers and system administrators. A successful project demands a long-term commitment and recognition of the impact it will have on the organization.

2. Dedicate time to developing a sound scope with the project team. Without a complete understanding of what the project is intended to accomplish, it will be difficult—if not impossible—to assess the success of the finished product. At a minimum your scope statement should describe the purpose of your project, the target audience, the instructional approach and educational technologies you intend to use, and a brief description of the content that will be covered or learning outcomes targeted.

3. Watch out for "scope creep." During the progress of a project there will be many small adjustments. Obviously, the project team will need to be flexible on many issues, but they should also be aware that changes should be made consciously and carefully so the final product is not substantially different than the initial intent.

TIMELINE

With the scope defined, you can begin to create your project timeline. Unfortunately, many people believe this component of planning simply delays the start of the project. Projects that overlook development of a timeline are often delayed or abandoned, as a result of more pressing daily demands. Not only a commitment to the final due date, when used well, the timeline is a valuable planning tool that aids in managing simultaneous projects, controlling workflow for project team members, and allowing periodic review to catch any problems before they become pervasive. Similarly, with smaller project deadlines throughout the process, everyone can focus on little successes and feel a sense of accomplishment when they see the results of their efforts.

The project team should be involved in creating and adjusting the initial timeline. As specialists, they will have insights about the ordering of the tasks and the amount of time needed for each phase of the work. Additionally, participating in the creation of the timeline will give them early ownership of the project.

When establishing a timeline, start first by thinking about the completion date and then work backwards to the present date. If there are not enough weeks between the two dates to complete all of the phases, then you know that your timeline is unrealistic. If your project team lacks any type of similar experience to draw from, you might consider first planning for a smaller pilot project and some time at the end to review any lessons the group has learned before embarking on the project as a whole. A good timeline will take into account areas where there are likely to be delays, and will include time for review, comments, and necessary changes along the way.

A timeline has ten general phases. Phase One through Phase Four—project definition, research, requirements, and setup—relate to the planning and management stages of the project. Phase Five and Phase Six—development and testing—relate to the design and development stages and may seem like an endless cycle between creation, testing, changes, and more testing. Phase Seven through Phase Ten—production, publicity, assessment, and enhancement—relate to the production and evaluation stages, which continue after all initial design and review has been completed.

Phase One: Project definition

During this initial phase, you should define your project by developing the project scope and establishing clear project goals. The success of the project rests on the clarity of these goals. Consider conducting focus groups with members of your target audience at this point to ensure from the beginning that you understand their needs and interests.

Phase Two: Research

Investigate what other libraries, educational institutions, and instructors have created. Listen for hints about what made other projects succeed, and what pitfalls they encountered. View their projects and ask them what they would do differently. Look beyond libraries to other educational units, organizations, and associations for projects, models, principles, and expertise. In other words, learn from people who have done something similar to what you want to accomplish.

Phase Three: Requirements

Explicitly state the features of the instruction you are designing. This is a difficult phase because the concepts and goals must now become reality. Spend as much time as needed to ensure that you have widespread agreement with the major partners in the project about how the site will look, how the instruction will be segmented, how other programs will relate to this site, what statistics will be available to evaluate the project, and so on. Everything flows from the requirements, so give it the time that it needs. Consider additional surveys or focus groups with other possible project partners to ensure you have taken into account all the necessary features.

Phase Four: Setup

With the project clearly defined, you need to gather resources. This includes everything from readying the office space for group work and meetings to purchasing and installing necessary hardware and software. It may also include hiring additional personnel or introducing all members of the project team. Allow time for delays in all these aspects. The goal is to create an environment with all the tools and resources nearby and operational so that the work goes smoothly.

Phase Five: Development and ongoing testing

Development and testing are inextricably linked and together comprise the most time-consuming activity. The length of time depends upon the variety of features, complexity of the project, and scope of the activity. Be sure also to allow extra time in case the development team has a learning curve with new software or hardware. In order to do a quality job the designers need time for creative thought and intense computer work. Never rush development. As you develop one component or prototype of your project, you should incorporate some element of testing at that point. That testing might involve colleagues reviewing the initial content, project partners discussing the framework of the instructional model, or usability tests with your target audience.

Phase Six: Final testing

Once you have the entire project developed, take time for a thorough final testing. Make sure all aspects of the project work from the library site and remotely with a variety of browsers and platforms. Ask members of the target audience and library personnel not involved with the project to help with usability testing. These testers are likely to approach parts of the site in unintended ways that can be more informative than if you guide them through the site. Then and only then, when you are sure that the Web-based instruction is doing what you want it to do, are you ready to move to the next phase.

Phase Seven: Production

Production means that the project is going live and is now ready for prime time. All of the users should be able to use it in the way that you intended. Staff should be informed about the project so they will be able to answer any questions at reference desks or in related classes. If possible choose a memorable URL for the project, and then be sure it is linked to all relevant places on your organization's Web site.

Phase Eight: Publicity

It is important to put publicity on the timeline. This is the period of time in which you create awareness of the Web-based instruction. Notice that the phase of publicity is deliberately after the phase of production. Often, it is tempting to publicize a service immediately, but it is better to wait a few weeks to ensure all final bugs have been identified and fixed. Be certain of the project's success before advertising it.

Phase Nine: Review

Depending upon the scale of the project, at three, six, or twelve months after production you should carry out a formal review of the site to assess the project as well as student learning. Gather feedback from users about the design, features, and content of the Web-based instruction. Review statistics and e-mail comments you have collected since the initial release date. Although some of this information may reveal flaws in the initial site, use all of this information—positive and negative—toward your goal of creating an effective, user-centered instructional project.

Phase Ten: Enhancement

Feedback from users and statistics alike will help you determine what changes are needed. These enhancements may require fine-tuning of select features, or may require a radical overhaul. In either case, go back through these phases to guide your process of redesign.

When developing your timeline, remember these tips:

1. A timeline is a guideline, not a rule. Try to stick to it but do not obsess over it. Unanticipated things will inevitably arise, so build your timeline to accommodate emergencies. In creating the timeline, be mindful of other work that the project team is handling at the same time and design the schedule to accommodate those needs. Take into consideration that additional time might be needed if

more than one person is using the same piece of equipment. The ideal completion date may not be possible. Rather than push a project through too quickly, be considerate of the pace of the project for members of the team.

2. Adjust the timeline in light of holidays and vacations. Not only are project team members probably hoping to rest, but groups you may hope to involve in testing are likely to be away as well. Overlooking this issue may throw your project off by weeks.

3. Create time for the project team to learn to work together. This could add some days to the project as people adjust to each other's styles but will be invaluable later.

4. Establish milestones in the timeline in which reports and updates can be given so that the administrators know the status of the project. Their comfort level about the progress of the project is important for current and future resources.

5. Keep a log related to the project: meetings, expenses, problems, and so on. This will help you with future planning and also with enhancements.

6. Celebrate when you are done. Wait until you are successfully in production as technology-based projects can offer many last-minute surprises, but then celebrate. Your project represents clever, creative, hard work that should be recognized.

BUDGET

No project is possible without the budget to garner and manage the resources needed to accomplish the goal. A budget is not just an allocation and expense sheet but a commitment to the goal and an indication of the organization's willingness to support the project.

The budget for a Web-based instruction project depends largely upon three factors. First, consider the learning curve for the project team. If experienced people are working on Web-based instruction, then the personnel time will be less. Second, take into account the existing internal resources of the library.

If the library already has the equipment and software needed, then funding will not need to be allocated for these expenses. Third, consider the amount of innovation required. If the project is at a high technological level, the cost—particularly in terms of personnel time—will go up.

Here are the budget elements that should be considered in every project.

Personnel and Labor

Consider personnel costs for all members of the project team and all support units that will be contributing to aspects of the project, including clerical assistance and publicity. Chapter 2 discusses membership of the project team in more detail. Include notations about temporary hires needed for aspects of the project, or leave time requested for specific people. Additionally, consider whether you will need to hire someone on a contract basis for elements of the project.

Facilities and Supplies

You may already have a workspace in mind for the project. More than likely the project will be done in office spaces you already have set aside for that purpose. Although you need not spend a great deal of money for new facilities, the addition of small elements such as dry erase boards or more comfortable seating may make your project group time more effective and more creative. Similarly, you probably have most supplies on hand, though special items such as books for group use may be helpful. Consider special arrangements that may be needed for large amounts of photocopying or mailings during review and testing phases. Include all items in the budget even if no funding is allocated, so that you will know the true cost of the project.

Hardware and Software

List all hardware and software you expect to use such as the computer, scanner, and digital camera, and Web authoring and graphics applications. Consider how you will manage workflow if more than one person needs to use a particular station, or if it is necessary to acquire multiple stations for the project. Again, even if some equipment is already available, show it on the budget but with zero allocation.

Overhead

Consider any additional costs you will have associated with project management, photocopying, traveling to other sites, or even communicating with others by phone or fax. These expenses may be particularly acute during the planning phases, when you may need to contact various groups to gain support for your project, and during the testing phase, when you may choose to distribute surveys, focus groups, usability tests, or other processes. With testing, you may have charges for rooms, refreshments, rented equipment, photocopying, as well as any payment for those who volunteer to assist with testing.

Publicity

Publicity may include brochures, flyers, and even promotional mouse pads or other gifts. Allow for costs for graphic design, printing, mailing, and personnel to assist if there is a great deal of labeling. Also, publicity may draw requests for demonstrations, which may incur charges for room reservations and refreshments.

When developing the budget, remember these tips:

1. Be realistic about the budget. Be careful about assuming that some costs are fixed or one-time. In most cases, expenses are variable and recurring. Hardware and software in particular may need additional upgrades during the project as additional features are developed. Although you may be pressed to cut corners, doing so may damage the project in the long run.
2. Ask others who have developed projects about their costs. Their budgets will help to serve as a benchmark for yours.
3. Have a contingency fund. The unexpected should always be expected.

4. Report the budget to the administrators on an agreed schedule. If there is any possibility that you have under-estimated the project and may need additional resources, early notice to them is critical.

CONCLUSION

As you read through the chapters of this book, you will learn much about how to develop Web-based instruction. Each of the authors provides you with details about important elements and concepts so you will have a firm foundation when you are ready to create your own project. However, all projects should begin with the development of the scope, the timeline, and the budget.

Effective management of scope, timeline, and budget are the cornerstones upon which every successful Web-based instruction project is built. With these three elements, you will know what you are doing, when you are going to do it, and what it will cost. Having a handle on scope, timeline, and budget will enable you to bring the project to a successful conclusion.

Chapter 2

Teams and Partners

Deborah A. Murphy

"Alliance, partnership, networking, relationship, teamwork, collaboration, coordination, cooperation, liaison, building bridges" (Cook, 2000: 19) are all current terms used in education, business, and library literature. These terms highlight the more active role librarians and other educators have assumed as they employ technologies to expand access to library resources and reach populations within the community, K–12 schools, and higher education in new and innovative ways.

The combination of experience, programming skills, and subject expertise needed for most projects are seldom found in a single individual. "The benefits of effective cross-functional teams are great, and the nature of work in the next century will require even greater collaboration as organizations evolve." (Smart and Barnum, 2000: 21) A team or a partnership is more than just a group of people working together or engaged in a common activity. It is a group that shares a mission and goals, a group that has a common vision of the shape and dimensions of what they are developing (Lippincott, 2002). Katzenbach and Smith define a team as "a small number of people with complementary skills who are committed to a common purpose, performance goals, and approach for which they hold themselves mutually accountable." (1999: 45)

Web development teams can take many forms. Depending on the project, members may come from an existing single unit or may already be connected by similar interests. More challenging are teams comprised of diverse members with differing experiences and backgrounds. This chapter addresses the process of finding the right people to make a collaborative Web-based instruction project a reality.

SELECTING MEMBERS

A wide range of expertise—such as project management, instructional design, graphic design, programming, database development, assessment, and testing—is necessary for development of Web-based instruction. Many of these skills may be found in members of your current staff who may have experience developing Web resources, working on teams, and creating instructional materials. In many cases, though, the need for additional expertise will require you to develop partnerships with others. In the early stages of team creation it is important to bring together the right mix of people to match the needs of the project being developed. Think carefully about your project scope and dimensions and the intended audience when pulling together a good team. Consider including people that offer a range of perspectives, experiences, and cross-disciplinary expertise. This may encourage you to invite artists or graphics staff, subject experts, members of your target audience, faculty, programmers, and administrators to play various roles in the development of the project.

Members of the team may participate in different ways and with varying commitments of time. To contribute to this project, some may be adding responsibilities into their existing workload, some may have specific time scheduled for the project, and some may be able to devote as much time as they wish. Depending on the skill sets available within your institution and the limited availability of some key expertise, you may choose to hire contractors for aspects of the project, which will require different types of management.

Though size of the group may differ depending on your project or the availability of staff, most successful teams range between "two and twenty-five people." (Katzenbach and Smith, 1999: 45) Smaller teams are more nimble and more likely to be able to interact constructively and reach agreement than larger groups. Large groups are less likely to reach consensus on specifics (such as common goals, approach, and mutual accountability) and tend to become more hierarchical and logistically unwieldy. While it is important to keep all team members involved in the planning and ongoing communication about the project, consider selecting a core team of three to five people who will have the largest ongoing commitment and who will be continuously involved in all aspects of planning, development, and assessment. Additional team members should also be involved in the initial planning and selected meetings throughout, but could primarily contribute to smaller, more focused aspects of the project development that best utilize their expertise. Team leaders often mistakenly believe " . . . that without 'just the right set of people at the start' an effective team will not be possible." (Katzenbach and Smith, 1999: 120–121) In fact, a team does not need to have all technical, social, and collaborative skill sets represented in its membership at the start of a project. Teams can identify gaps as they progress, inviting new members or supporting existing members as they develop the needed expertise. In making selections of key members, look for people who have regular contact with your target audience, who show potential and interest in learning new skills as needed, and who demonstrate a willingness to commit their time, creativity, and energy.

TEAM BUILDING

Once you gather your initial team members, there are several steps you can take to start the process of evolving from a group of individuals to groups of partners working constructively. Your first discussions and meetings should cover the following:

Meeting Ground Rules

Creating a good team is as much about communication and group dynamics as it is about project development. Though they may seem obvious, basic guidelines for meeting format and conduct can help ensure that members work together respectfully. The opportunity for each member to speak and the expectation that they will listen when others share their opinions are key characteristics of successful teams. Total agreement or consensus of opinions is not necessary, but there should be a shared interest in learning from others in the group. Members should honor and appreciate differences. The ability to look beyond parochial departmental goals, turf wars, and territorial boundaries is critical. True conflict can arise and paralyze the team if these issues are not clearly discussed and ground rules agreed upon at the start. A set of guidelines might include:

- Agree upon regular meeting dates and duration.
- Determine how meeting agendas will be decided.
- Provide an agenda prior to each meeting.
- Require prompt arrival at meetings, and prior notification if unable to attend.
- Encourage open, productive, confidential discussions.
- Respect and listen to the opinions of other members.
- Direct constructive criticism toward the project, not individual team members.
- Ensure shared understanding by explaining terminology and jargon.
- Determine methods for reaching agreement (such as voting, prioritizing alternatives, continuing discussion, and delegating to a sub-group).
- Keep action minutes, noting responsibilities and timelines.
- Designate a team member responsible for each action or activity.
- Distribute and archive minutes.

Shared Purpose and Project Definition

Groups need to develop a sense of ownership for their project. A lack of consensus on a common purpose may prevent a team identity from forming. The project manager should share the draft project proposal and rough project scope in a way that inspires team members as they embark on the project. Members should understand how their expertise and perspective adds to those of others in the group and is necessary for a successful conclusion. The phrase "the whole is greater than the sum of its parts" can be used to define a team that has come together in this key phase.

Goals and Accountability

Teams should set specific project goals for themselves in order to maintain momentum and energy. Even small goals can help "concretize work efforts and maintain a timeline." (Katzenbach and Smith, 1999: 45–81) Project management and calendaring are essential not only to meet deadlines, but also to let members see their progress towards project completion. As discussed in Chapter 1, designing a project timeline with a series of smaller projects and deadlines allows team members to hit milestones and celebrate their achievements throughout the process. By developing and sharing the timeline with the group, team members will more easily see how missing their deadlines will negatively impact the work of others.

Procedures and Processes

Establishing a team contract, even if done informally, is often a good approach to ensuring an effective working environment for team members. Procedures and team structure need to be discussed. Members should agree on how to get the "real work" done. Meeting tasks—such as scheduling, taking minutes, and organizing work—and project tasks related to each member's expertise need to be clearly defined and assigned. "Effective teams always have members who assume important social, as well as leadership, roles such as challenging, interpreting, supporting, integrating, remembering, and summarizing. Members may assume different roles at different times and . . . these roles evolve over time to meet varying needs." (Katzenbach and Smith, 1999: 45–81)

MEMBER ROLES AND LEADERSHIP

Roles and responsibilities within a Web development team can emerge in different ways. Members are often selected because of specific skills or subject expertise they bring. Some roles are specific and easy to label, whereas other roles—though equally important—are less easily articulated. Barnum describes roles that "are product-oriented and are often easy to understand," and roles that are process-oriented roles which "tend to keep harmony and good will, ease tensions and build cohesiveness." (2000: 328) Eventually a team becomes a solid working unit, though every team is unique in how it allows this process to happen. Many team members may find that their role evolves as they develop expertise, learn new skills, and adapt with the needs of the project. But there are some key facets of teamwork skills that apply to all teams:

- Team members respect and follow the meeting ground rules.
- Project goals are shared and understood.
- Team members are treated as equal partners.
- All members actively participate and contribute meaningfully to the work.
- Issues are clarified and conflicts are resolved.
- Supportive reinforcement and constructive criticism is offered and received by all team members.
- Credit and recognition is shared as a group.

One of the key members of the team will be the project manager or leader whose role is to keep people and process moving towards the goal of successfully completing the project. A team leader or manager may be appointed or be selected by team members. In some cases, there may be shared leadership. Although it may seem that managing the *project* is the main work of a leader, in reality the most important role of the team leader is managing the *team*. Some team members may confuse leadership with complete control or decision making. It is up to the team leader to convey the message that real leadership depends on believing in the project and the capabilities of the team members. The success of the project will depend on how well the group works together.

A good team leader "brings a team together, learns and understands the skills and desires of the team members, and harmonizes disparate ideas." (Veldof and Nackerud, 2001:16) Good team leaders help members see that they share a common goal and that they are all mutually accountable for reaching that goal. They possess good communication skills and spend as much or more time listening rather than speaking, know when to delegate or do things themselves, and take risks when necessary. It requires a careful hand to balance "providing guidance and giving up control, between making tough decisions and letting others make them, and between doing difficult things alone and letting others learn how to do them." (Katzenbach and Smith, 1999: 132)

Katzenbach talks about six areas that are necessary to provide good team leadership:

- Keep the purpose, goals, and approach relevant and meaningful.
- Build commitment and confidence by providing constructive reinforcement while avoiding intimidation.
- Strengthen the mix and level of skills by encouraging members to acquire new skills, or finding those skills outside the team as needed.
- Manage relations with those outside the team by communicating the team's goals and progress, as well as negotiating outside obstacles.
- Create new opportunities for members by stepping back occasionally and letting others have the chance to lead initiatives or make presentations.
- Most importantly, contribute real work within the team and be available to help with both the large and small tasks. (1999:138)

COMMUNICATION

One of the most important features of a successful team is effective communication. Though the need for good communication may seem obvious, without proper attention it is easy to stop or impede the flow of information. Interpersonal styles, terminology, and assumptions about technical skills can all be barriers to information exchange and collaboration. It is important to keep all group members in mind when establishing how communication is shared. Burdman describes several common causes of poor communication:

- Differing disciplines and lack of mutual terminology.
- Personality conflicts and fear.
- Hidden agendas.
- Ineffective meetings.
- Unspoken assumptions about project goals or other team members.
- Unmanaged solo efforts of team members. (1999: 76)

The key to addressing such problems is to establish a sense of trust around the sharing and understanding of communication between all team members. Start by acknowledging that communication preferences and styles vary. E-mail allows faster and more frequent communication, and as such is an excellent medium for sharing factual information or reaching quick decisions. However, e-mail lacks the contextual clues shared in face-to-face meetings. Face-to-face meetings are useful for brainstorming, idea development, and discussions. Rather than choose one over the other, you may want to use various methods.

Communication is also dependent on members being able to understand one another. This means that terminology and jargon need to be explained and understood by all in a respectful and supportive environment. As members begin to speak the same language, the mutual knowledge base of the team grows and develops as well. Sharing expertise will also promote good communication. For example, not all members need to be able to do HTML coding, but sharing some concepts will allow conversations to proceed with all members as participants.

Good communication also means establishing an infrastructure for sharing and archiving information. Are all members satisfied with the way information is shared? Smaller team size means that there is the potential for all members to be up-to-date on issues. However, this does not preclude the necessity of assigning responsibility to create meeting agendas, maintain project calendars, archive e-mail, or keep and distribute meeting minutes. The availability of online resources such as group calendars, project management software, listservs, and Web archives can make most of these tasks easier to initiate and more productive.

CONFLICT MANAGEMENT

Conflict is probably one of the greatest problems team members face. Unmanaged conflict can paralyze a team. Few people enjoy addressing the "problem participant," and members often work under the false assumption that group consensus is the only way to avoid confrontation. This is not true. In fact, it is a poor team that does not have conflict. Well-managed conflict can provide a new perspective and discussions that can bring about changes or shifts in thinking and approaches. "Conflict is a necessary part of becoming a real team. [The] challenge is to make it constructive instead of just enduring it." (Katzenbach and Smith, 1999: 110)

Frank and open communication must be encouraged and supported. This means providing a supportive environment where members can trust that their comments can be heard without misunderstandings or animosity. As noted above, not all conflict is bad. However, it is important to be able to determine if conflict is helping or hurting the process. Barnum describes two kinds of negative conflict: "*Affective*, interpersonal disagreement and emotional reactions, and *Procedural*, disagreements about how a group should be run." (2000: 329) Members will look toward the team leader to aid in resolving these types of conflict. For example, team leaders can meet privately with individuals or collectively remind members of the group's guidelines. In addition to these two types of conflict, there is a third healthy type of disagreement which is *Substantive* and "deals with disagreement about content, context and concepts." (Barnum, 2000: 329)

The best way to head off most negative conflict is to have in place a clear set of guidelines around behavior and meeting conduct. Revisiting these periodically during the project will remind members of their original agreement. It is also important to agree on the concepts of flat and hierarchical structure. Members may need to be reminded that colleagues are equal partners within the team structure even though they may hold differing levels of power in the usual working environment. Team members do not have to be close friends, but they do need to be able to work with one another in a respectful and professional manner, and be able to compromise.

CHARACTERISTICS OF SUCCESSFUL TEAMS

The literature on successful teams offers many recipes for creating a productive team. In fact, many of us might find it easier to list what makes an unsuccessful team. Poor leadership, bad communication, unmanaged conflict, lack of project management, and lack of trust are all examples of how to ensure a team's frustration and failure.

Describing a successful team synthesizes the entire process of team selection, building, role development, and conflict management. As Barnum notes, "Successful teams define tasks and resolve problems before they get out of hand. They value group cohesion and social interaction." (2000: 331)

Successful teams can be characterized as having many of the following traits:

- *Roles are agreed on,* though members may rotate these roles as the team evolves.
- *Technical and social roles are equally valued* as key contributions to the work of the team.
- *Individuals are clear about their commitments* of time, skills, and energy. Though members may vary in the amount of their contributions, all are equal partners in the process.
- *Procedures and structures are clearly understood* and agreed on regarding communication, meeting formats, and conflict management.
- *Effective leadership is on hand,* requiring a balance between guiding and letting go of control.
- *Conflicts are an important part of teamwork* and are resolved in a constructive and productive manner.
- *Members promote working together respectfully* and professionally and are self-monitoring on issues such as meeting deadlines, sharing information, and positive reinforcement.

KEEPING THE TEAM GOING

Teams and partnerships may go through many cycles depending on the nature of the project. Some projects may require ongoing commitments from initial team members, while others may need to invite new members to the group to sustain the project. All teams go through productive and unproductive cycles of work during a Web-development project. Sometimes teams must let go of long-held ideas that are not working, face major redesign issues, or loss of key members. Maintaining cohesion and communication is key to keeping the team's momentum going during difficult times. By being aware of these issues, you can contribute to keeping members involved in a number of ways:

Don't Lose Touch

Maintaining personal contacts within and outside of the meeting environment can keep interest alive. Sometimes all it takes is the acknowledgment of how intense the work has been.

Recognize Contributions

Honoring examples of members' work, giving credit to the entire team, and providing positive feedback are also crucial to keeping members active and involved.

Share Results

Teams may also find new energy from planning on how to share their results via conference papers, articles, or books.

Rethink Team Membership

Being able to discuss the addition of new members and other plans for change can invigorate and enliven discussions. New members can bring a fresh outlook on issues and contribute new perspectives. Or your project may have moved on to a point that no longer requires input from all members. In this case, attrition can occur as members choose to leave, participate as needed, or transition to a consulting basis. Remaining members may want to consider the opportunity of transition to a smaller team to allow faster, more efficient updates and revisions.

CASE STUDY

The following project is one example of how using many of the guidelines outlined in this chapter can lead to the creation of a successful and effective Web-based product that continues to be an active collaborative project.

In the spring of 1997, a campus-wide conference on undergraduate education at the University of California, Santa Cruz (UCSC) started a conversation among a group of librarians, computer center staff, and faculty—a good example of how diverse segments of the campus population were drawn together by a shared interest. This group became the pool from which a self-selected, interested team coalesced with the goal of developing a prototype for UCSC's first campus-wide Web-based online literacy tutorial.

Representation on the committee came from academic staff, administrators, and faculty members from a variety of divisions such as the Computing Center, Humanities, Sciences, Social Sciences, and the Library. The diverse opinions and perspectives brought to the discussions were key to the project's success. The team was comprised of eight members, a size that allowed for quick responses to development needs. Overall leadership was given by the Director of Campus Computing, but all members were equal partners in the development process with aspects of the leadership role rotating through the membership as different project areas were addressed. For example, Computing Services directed the process of hiring outside consultants to design an overall look for the Web site, with all members having input on the final decision.

Regular meetings, e-mail, and subgroups were initiated from the start and were key in keeping the team on track. This foundation of strong communication in both electronic and face-to-face formats created environments for independent and group decisions. Later in the project, individual content authors handled development of specific tutorials and directed layout and design. Conflicts were resolved in a manner that ultimately benefited the project by affecting change at crucial points.

The development team leveraged the successful initial introduction of the tutorial NetTrail (http://nettrail.ucsc.edu) to obtain additional funding for continued development. A smaller number of team members will refine and update modules as needed.

CONCLUSION

Teams have become increasingly necessary, as Web-based instruction demands more diverse and more specialized kinds of expertise. Although the creation and ongoing development of the team is unique to each project, there are strategies to ensure a successful partnership. Clearly articulate the nature of the Web project, goals, purpose, audience, and scope—this is the foundation from which all else derives. Look for potential members who are good communicators, and who show a willingness to learn and teach what they know. Agree on responsibilities and leadership roles, but allow flexibility for members to move among roles as the project evolves. Use managed conflict as a productive tool. And finally, keep momentum going by sharing information, positive reinforcement, and occasional reviews of the group's membership.

"The essence of effective teamwork is to create a product through a collective effort that exceeds the quality of any individual endeavor." (Smart and Barnum, 2000: 19) Ultimately, a team is much more than the project it develops—the process of becoming partners changes each member and their perceptions of one another. Partnerships, like those described in this chapter, can have a long lasting impact.

REFERENCES

Barnum, Carol M. 2000. "Building a Team for User-Centered Design." In *Proceedings of the IEEE International Professional Communication Conference 2000: Technology and Teamwork (September 24–27, 2000)*, 325–332. Piscataway, NJ: IEEE.

Burdman, Jessica R. 1999. *Collaborative Web Development: Strategies and Best Practices for Web Teams*. Reading, MA: Addison Wesley.

Cook, Doug. 2000. "Creating Connections: A Review of the Literature." In *Collaborative Imperative: Librarians and Faculty Working Together in the Information Universe,* edited by Dick Raspa and Dane Ward, 19–38. Chicago: Association of College and Research Libraries.

Katzenbach, Jon R., and Douglas K. Smith. 1999. *The Wisdom of Teams: Creating the High-Performance Organization.* New York: Harper Business.

Lippincott, Joan K. 2002. "Cyberinfrastructure: Opportunities for Connections and Collaboration." In *Proceedings for the 11th Biennial Conference of the Victorian Association for Library Automation: E-volving Information Futures (February 6–8, 2002)*, 437–450. Croydon, Victoria, Australia: VALA. Available: www.vala.org.au/vala2002/2002pdf/31Lipnct.pdf.

Smart, Karl L., and Carol Barnum. 2000. "Communication in Cross-Functional Teams." *Technical Communication* 47, no.1 (February): 19–21.

Veldof, Jerilyn R., and Shane Nackerud. 2001 "Do You Have the Right Stuff? Seven Areas of Expertise for Successful Web Site Design in Libraries." *Internet Reference Services Quarterly* 6, no.1: 13–38.

Chapter 3

Audience and Stakeholders

Clara S. Fowler

Creating Web-based instruction projects that meet users' educational needs requires communicating with individuals beyond the immediate project team. The two groups of people whom you will have the most contact with are your audience and stakeholders.

The audience is your target group of learners; by analyzing their characteristics you can ensure that the instruction is appropriate and relevant. Stakeholders are the influential individuals, such as administrators, who have an investment in the success of the project. By convincing your stakeholders of a project's importance they can alleviate potential resistance and roadblocks usually caused by political friction in an organization. Understanding the needs and motivations of the audience and the stakeholders will assist you in communicating effectively with each group, garnering administrative support, and developing and implementing a usable product.

AUDIENCE

Learners are the main audience for Web-based instruction and you may be familiar with the groups for which you are developing your project. You may already teach these students in the classroom or they may be patrons you assist at the reference desk. If you do not know who your target audience will be for this project, it is important to make a clear determination of this group during the initial planning stage. Without this information it is difficult to create appropriate content for the group you wish to teach.

Many instruction projects will have multiple potential groups of learners. A clear scope will identify the target audience for your project. Determining the skill level, affiliations, motivations, and values of these end users should directly impact the content and design of the project. You should find general characteristics of the target audience as well as the preferences of representative individuals. The following are some characteristics to discover about your intended audience.

- **Age**
  Are the learners children, teenagers, adults, or seniors? Each age group will have different experience with online content. A younger audience most likely has been learning with computers for most of their education, while an older audience may be less likely to have interacted with online instruction environments. Age level directly impacts the type of information, sophistication of language, and tone of the content. It also will strongly influence the popular culture references you can expect the audience to understand. For example, the Information Cycle tutorial (www.libraries.psu.edu/instruction/infocyle. htm) developed by Instructional Programs at Penn State University Libraries, effectively uses the 2000 Columbine high school shooting to illustrate how information is created and distributed. Since many of today's college students share this point of reference, its use demonstrates a compelling way to teach finding appropriate resources based on information need.
- **Affiliation**
  If the audience is affiliated with the same school, organization, or geographical area, it may be easier to tailor your content to address the uniqueness of that institution or region. Commonalties in affiliation could point to an approachable theme to use for the project. For example, if the target audience is from the same state, you could choose to use an event from state history; a tutorial on finding primary source material created in Texas might

use the Alamo to illustrate research techniques. Or, if the audience is from the same company, using corporate logos and having the CEO discuss an aspect of the instruction will provide a recognizable link for the employees. You may determine that your audience has diverse affiliations, however there will be some common characteristic that brings them together to learn the content you are presenting.

- **Internet access**

  Access to a computer with an Internet connection is becoming increasing commonplace. However, if your audience is from an economically disadvantaged or rural area, then their access may be limited. Access to technology will determine the time requirements you can place on an assignment since some people may need to go to their public or school library in order to use a computer with Internet connections. Even those with Internet access at home may be limited to slow dial-up connections. This will impact the bandwidth that your project can use which may have implications for the site design, graphics, and interactivity in the instruction.

- **Technological skills**

  What are the most common activities your target audience engages in on the Internet? The Internet has a wide variety of uses from communication and social interaction to information and research. Each use may require a different technological skill. Users who download music on a regular basis will probably be able to download additional plug-ins necessary for advanced interactivity. Frequent users of chat may prefer using a chat module in online instruction. Students who have experience with distance education courses may be able to navigate Web-based instruction with ease, while novice users of technology will need more contextual help within the instructional environment and might require a person to contact for assistance by phone, e-mail, or in person.

- **Educational need**

  Will they be participating in the instruction for staff training? Will the instructional project be tied to an existing course? If there are prerequisites that the audience must take before your instruction, then you can build on what they have previously learned. Or, you may wish to measure what they already know and build the instruction from that point. When looking at educational need and background, you may also want to determine the learning styles of your audience to determine the best methods for conveying the information online.

- **Culture**
Will you have a diverse audience with representatives from different countries and cultures? Knowing the nationality of your target audience and testing the site with a few representatives of this culture will alleviate many potential problems. Though your audience's primary language may be English, it is easy to unintentionally lose your international users' interest or even offend through seemingly benign cultural references. Choices such as colors for the site design and graphics can have dramatic cultural significance. In the *Journal of Interactive Instruction and Development*, Linda Loring uses the example, "Euro-Disney tried the color purple for advertising, which was perceived as morbid by potential customers in the European Catholic sector." (2002: 25)

    Many Web-based designs created for an international audience have selected icon representatives that are neutral across cultures such as the paper clip in Microsoft Word. In Research Tutor (http://researchtutor.sdsu.edu/), the designers chose cartoon sea creatures such as fish, whales, and octopi to represent students, professors, and librarians. These illustrations are gender and ethnically neutral and are entertaining images to teach college students about the research process.

- **Interests**
Using popular authors, hot topics, and recognized experts will make the instructional experience more relevant for the audience. If you are addressing business professionals, then using examples such as the Enron bankruptcy may be compelling for that audience. If children or teenagers are your primary audience, you may find they are

interested in particular television shows or after-school activities. Determining the interests of your audience may point to a theme to use throughout the project.

In any group, there will be a wide variety of likes and dislikes but the larger your audience and the more similarities in age and background the more likely you will find some patterns. Obviously it is best to avoid what your audience really dislikes and to capitalize on what they prefer. College-age audiences, for example, may react strongly to language that "tries too hard" using colloquial expressions and current slang. If your learners have a number of common interests, you may be able to tailor sections of the Web-based instruction to personalize the experience.

- **Motivation**
  Determining what motivates your target audience to learn will help you design a project that fills an immediate educational need. Linking the instructional project to an existing course and requiring its completion will be the strongest motivator for students. However, there are other reasons that people are motivated to learn. If the instruction will have a clear economic impact such as securing a new job or streamlining a business process, then the learner will be more likely to invest the necessary time and effort.

- **Expectations**
  If your audience has previous experience with online instruction, they are likely to have developed preferences and expectations for those types of learning environments. Students who have used a learning management system in courses, such as WebCT or Blackboard, will have gained familiarity with communication tools, such as chat and threaded discussion boards, and with document management tools to collaboratively share and edit documents online. Due to systems and tools such as these, learners are likely to expect greater control of the instructional experience, picking and choosing the content that is most relevant and interesting to them.

  If your audience is hesitant about using technology

or libraries, you may need to emphasize development of a supportive learning environment. If they are early adopters of technology and love to tinker with new products, then they might be receptive to a cutting-edge instructional experience.

You have a number of strategies that you can use to determine the demographics and needs of your audience including surveys, focus groups, and one-on-one discussions with audience members. Surveys distributed to a representative sample are the best method for identifying demographic information such as age, affiliation, background, Internet access, and cultural background. To find information about expectations, motivations, and attitudes it will be necessary to talk to people from your target audience. You probably have representative members of your audience, such as students, working in or frequently visiting your library or institution. This group is an excellent source of information since they understand your mission and may have a level of trust that makes them willing to share their likes, dislikes, and attitudes. However, they should not be the only audience members you contact. Identify representatives across a broad spectrum of your audience and bring them in for a focus group, discussed more completely in Chapter 7. This will be the best way to find out what the audience's needs are and their characteristics that impact the instructional product.

It is important that the project team has an opportunity to talk with the audience and ask questions early in the project timeline. Make sure that they see the results of the focus group sessions and are involved in constructing questions for the surveys, since they will each bring unique concerns and perspectives to the planning process. Audience representatives should also be involved in the design and evaluation phases of the project. They will be your best source for feedback about the project's effectiveness. In your project timeline, allow adequate time to make changes based on their input.

It is easy to develop a general idea of your audience if you work with the population on a daily basis. Try to avoid too many generalizations when assessing the audience and don't make assumptions about the group or it will undermine the final product's effectiveness. Spending time with a thorough audience assessment will be a good investment, which will be especially evident when you are making decisions about design and content.

STAKEHOLDERS

For any instructional project, there are always external groups that will have a stake in the success of the project. Common stakeholders for instructional projects include:

- Faculty, librarians, and other partners.
- Administrators in the library and at your institution.
- Administrators and staff from other divisions or schools in the system.
- Interested parties at the local and state government level.
- Representatives from library consortiums or districts.

Stakeholders can be your best allies during your project. They have a vested interest in your success as well as a unique perspective on the environment and how it may impact your progress. As a group, they are not the easiest to manage. They are busy with many projects and concerns, have diverse interests, and are usually under time constraints. The following four steps may help you effectively identify people to include in the group and provide tips for communicating with them with care.

1. Identify your stakeholders.

Determining who your stakeholders are requires an understanding of the environment at your institution. If you need help identifying your stakeholders, talk to influential people in your organization who have managed large projects or are involved in broad initiatives. These people will be your connection to the stakeholders and may garner administrative support. Identify stakeholders who have a philosophy that complements the project, such as a commitment to teaching or a belief that online instruction is effective and worthwhile. They will be able to translate these ideas for the group that they represent or manage, and may provide insight for convincing people resistant to the project to see its merits.

2. Analyze the needs and concerns of your stakeholders.
Stakeholders are indirect customers of your project. Since they are usually the budget keepers, the technology managers, and the political figures, they are people whom you will have to please when developing an implementing online instruction. Determining the values and motivations of this group will help you spin your project to meet their demands. Talk to people in the organization who are successful in working with people from across the institution and ask them for insight.

3. Convince stakeholders to support you.
During your initial contacts with the stakeholders, it is important to convince them of the impact that the project will have on the audience and to generate enthusiasm among the group. Create a project summary that concisely communicates your vision. Present the project as a solution to a known problem.

Some aspects of developing online instructional projects may be considered contentious to stakeholders. Time investments by staff for development, expenditures for software or hardware, computer security, and management required to handle large numbers of students, changes in current programs due to implementation of the project—these are all complicated issues and potential roadblocks for stakeholders. Identify and address these issues up front, spinning your responses in favor of the project before the issues become problematic. By responding to stakeholder concerns, you will communicate that you are prepared to handle the impact that the project will have on the organization.

Once they are on board, you can define their role in the project as well as their responsibilities and rights. Allowing stakeholders to take too much control may derail the project from its original goals, and may lead to low morale for the project team. Clearly communicating what you expect, while sometimes an uncomfortable situation, will alleviate many potential problems you could encounter when dealing with people in positions of power within the organization.

4. Maintain relationships with stakeholders.

Project managers have a responsibility to communicate the status of the project throughout the planning, development, and implementation. The manager should be open to comments from stakeholders and willing to address their issues at any time. Use the methods of communication that are most comfortable for the individuals. Some may prefer to receive brief e-mail updates, others may prefer private meetings, or you might find it effective to hold meetings with groups of stakeholders. It is important that the project manager or a member of the project team be a visible representative. Do not allow others to present the project without your preparation, data, and approval. Project managers should also use the formal processes and organizational structures to develop instructional initiatives. To attempt to bypass these steps will open the project to criticism from people from whom you need acceptance for successful project development and implementation. Including key administrators and librarians in your group of stakeholders will assist the project moving through these stages. Since Web-based instruction usually requires an allocation of resources such as people, time, and money, influential stakeholders can also smooth any political friction within the organization.

A project manager in any organization will spend a significant amount of time addressing the stakeholders' concerns. However, by being attentive to these individuals, you will cultivate partners that will help make the Web-based instruction project a reality.

CONCLUSION

Your clearly articulated scope will define your target audience. Consulting with people in your institution who have successfully completed large projects will help you identify your stakeholders. The audience and stakeholders are the primary groups you should focus on throughout the development of the Web-based instruction project. Determining what motivates them and then capitalizing on it, to garner their support or capture their attention, will help you reach your instructional objectives. Making informed decisions about your audience and the stakeholders early in the planning stage will ensure that the project development runs smoothly and there will be fewer problems with implementation.

REFERENCE

Loring, Linda. 2002. "Six Steps to Preparing Instruction for a Worldwide Audience." *Journal of Interactive Instruction Development* 14, no.3 (Winter): 24–29.

Chapter 4

Pedagogy and Andragogy

Nancy H. Dewald

New technologies are seductive in that their new way of approaching tasks can make us think this will be the answer to whatever problem we want to solve. Stephen C. Ehrmann points out that over the years the latest technology has repeatedly been hyped as the ultimate answer to education's limitations (1995). But he emphasizes that the medium is not the message, and technology will only improve instruction if the educational strategy behind it is thoroughly planned and matched to an appropriate supporting technology. One need not use the latest software or hardware, but the technology selected does need to be appropriate for the educational aims desired (Ehrmann, 1995).

Various theories of learning have shaped computerized instruction over the past half century. Two overarching educational movements are pedagogy and andragogy. Pedagogy, as generally used, simply means the art of teaching. In 1970, Malcolm Knowles differentiated pedagogy, which he said refers to the teaching of children and adolescents and focuses on teacher-centered methods, from andragogy, which refers to the teaching of adults and focuses on learner-centered methods. (Imel, 1989; Carlson, 1989) Knowles made these distinctions because he saw adult learning as very different from learning by children. Figure 4–1 outlines the differences between the pedagogical and andragogical models.

Although Knowles originally considered only adults to have andragogical learning characteristics, he has come to believe

| Figure 4–1. Knowles' Comparison of Two Models ||
Pedagogical Model	Andragogical Model
The learner is dependent on the teacher to decide what will be taught and how it will be taught.	The learner prefers to be self-directed, so the learner and teacher should plan together what will be learned.
The learner has little experience to contribute to the learning effort, so the goal is to transmit knowledge through lectures, assigned readings, and presentations.	The learner brings a wealth of experience to the learning situation, and therefore learning should include elements such as experiments, discussion, case studies, and simulations.
Learning is organized by the logic of the subject matter.	Learning is organized around a task to be completed or problem to be solved.
Learners are considered ready to learn when they attain prescribed ages.	Learners are considered ready to learn when they have a need to know something, and learners want to be able to apply what they learn to their lives.
Motivation is inspired by external rewards such as punishment, grades, and pressure from teachers and parents.	Motivation is inspired by internal incentives such as self-confidence, better quality of life, and curiosity.
The teacher is responsible for content design, determining coverage, and efficient transmittal methods.	The teacher, as facilitator, is responsible for process design, creating the climate for learning, and making resources available.

(Knowles, 1995: 1–4, 89–90)

these are "innate tendencies . . . that emerge as people mature." (Feuer and Geber, 1988: 33) Knowles' model of learning generated much discussion, and not everyone agreed with his assertions, but educators at all levels see advantages to moving toward learner-centered education. (39) Increasingly, educators are using both learner-centered and teacher-centered methods as appropriate to each teaching-learning situation, with learners of all ages. (Imel, 1989) For example, when a student of any age "is entering into a totally new content area, he or she will be dependent on a teacher until enough content has been acquired to enable self-directed inquiry to begin." (Knowles, 1995: 89) While most students have experienced teacher-directed learning in all or nearly all educational situations, many educators see an advantage in encouraging self-directed and task-oriented learning in their classes in order to create lifelong independent learners and critical thinkers. (Feuer and Geber, 1988: 38)

Both pedagogy and andragogy have been influenced by three movements in educational psychology: behaviorism, cognitivism, and constructivism. These movements are not exclusive of each other. They build on, react to, and/or overlap each other, and all have elements that are useful in planning online instruction.

BEHAVIORISM

Although behaviorism has roots in the early twentieth century, it was during the 1950s that it led to the development of programmed instruction by B. F. Skinner. Skinner studied negative and positive reinforcement, with immediate feedback to the learner, in order to modify the learner's behavior. Behavioral objectives are used as the outline for instruction, and the learner is allowed to learn at his or her own pace, gradually mastering the task. Behaviorism's influence on instructional technology "led to the design of piecemeal instruction with immediate feedback and reinforcement, drill and practice procedures, and self-paced programmed instruction." (McNeil, 2000a)

Also in the behavioral camp was an effort to measure learning outcomes, classified as "intellectual behaviors." (Lee, 1999) In 1956 a group of college examiners headed by Benjamin Bloom produced the *Taxonomy of Educational Objectives*. (1956) The objectives in the cognitive domain were: Knowledge, Comprehension, Application, Analysis, Synthesis, and Evaluation, describing in ascending order (from simpler to more complex) the desired cognitive behaviors of the learner. The higher the learner progresses in the taxonomy, the better learning has been achieved. Since the development of the *Taxonomy*, educators have used this description of intellectual behaviors in instructional design and in analyzing instructional outcomes. (McNeil, 2000b)

COGNITIVISM

Whereas behaviorism focuses on the learner's external behavior, cognitivism focuses on the learner's internal cognitive processes, before any behavior is observable. The learner is seen as more active in cognitivism because, rather than simply responding to stimuli provided by the instructor, the learner is actively processing information—either by assimilating new information into his/her existing understanding or by accommodating his/her understanding to new information. (Furth, 1970: 15–19) The cognitive approach involves finding ways to build on learners' previous knowledge, such as with analogies, metaphors, outlines, concept mapping, and advance organizers. This approach is seen as more effective for complex learning, such as problem solving, while the behavioristic approach is useful for the acquisition of simple learning, such as memorization. (Ertmer and Newby, 1993: 59)

Learning Styles

In considering how learners perceive and process information, the concept of learning styles developed. There are many learning style theories, and here we will only consider those that have been used to address online learning. Jonathan L. Ross and Robert A. Schulz analyzed several learning style theories and applied them to the design of supplementary course materials and activities on the Web (1999).

Visual/Auditory/Kinesthetic Learning Styles

A well-known method of classifying learning styles is by the sensory preferences students have for perceiving and processing information. For the visual learner who primarily uses sight, Ross and Schulz recommend animated graphs, hypertext diagrams, or video clips as appropriate to the content to be conveyed. For the auditory learner who primarily uses sound, they recommend taping class summaries to place on the Web, or using various sound resources, again when content appropriate. For the kinesthetic learner who primarily uses bodily movement, touch, and experience, and who prefers practice over theory, Ross and Schulz recommend interactive Web programming to engage students in activities in which, for instance, they use the mouse to manipulate items on the screen. (1999: 125)

Social Learning Styles (Grasha-Reichmann)

Anthony F. Grasha and Sheryl Reichmann described various social learning styles: competitive/collaborative, avoidant/participant, and dependent/independent. (Grasha, 1996: 128) Ross and Schulz write that the collaborative learner can benefit from a class listserv, bulletin board, conferencing, and chat rooms to expand opportunities for collaboration, while also allowing those less interested in collaboration to be less active in this regard. David P. Diaz and Ryan B. Cartnal used Grasha and Reichmann's learning style inventory to compare students in the same course, which they could take either in a traditional classroom environment or via distance learning. (1999) They found the distance students to be more independent learners, more self-directed, while the traditional class students were more dependent on the instructor for guidance, which may not be surprising given that these students self-selected into the versions of the class. "Self-direction and independence were facilitated in the online course by offering students flexible options to shape their learning environment" such as self-pacing and a menu selection of online assignments. (Diaz and Cartnal, 1999: 134) They also found that the online students were "willing and able to participate in collaborative work if they have structure from the teacher to initiate it" such as through "threaded discussion" areas. (Diaz and Cartnal, 1999: 134) Diaz and Cartnal did not find any significant correlations with the competitive or avoidant/participant aspects of the Grasha-Reichmann styles between traditional and online students.

Concrete/Abstract/Sequential/Random Learning Styles (Gregorc)

Ross and Schulz describe Anthony F. Gregorc's delineation of adults' preferences for perceiving in concrete situations or in abstract situations, and preferences for ordering or arranging information in sequential (linear) or random (nonlinear, multidimensional) fashion. (1999: 126, 128) Gregorc characterized learners by their preferences for one of four categories using these two dimensions: concrete-sequential, abstract-sequential, concrete-random, and abstract-random, and Ross and Schulz suggest ways that online learning can help these four categories of learners. They recommend flexibility in navigation so that sequential learners have a structure to follow but random learners can select their own paths. For the concrete learners, examples of successful work, virtual labs, video case studies, or other ways to clarify material for the concrete thinker is helpful. Abstract thinkers can benefit from links to outside sources of information so they can construct their own understanding of concepts and further investigate topics as they wish (Ross and Schulz, 1999: 128–129).

Learning Style Inventory (Kolb)

David A. Kolb described the experiential learning model—a cycle of learning that begins with a concrete experience on which the learner makes observations and reflections. These reflections lead to the formation of abstract concepts and generalizations, which are tested in new situations, and lead to yet another concrete experience. (Kolb, 1981: 235) He described learners as needing four different types of abilities for successful learning: concrete experience, reflective observation, abstract conceptualization, and active experimentation. (236) Liam Rourke and Linda Lysynchuk studied the relationship of Kolb's learning style in students to their success in hypertext courses. They found that those who prefer concrete experience and active experimentation ("accommodators") performed less well than the other styles of learners. Because accommodators perform best through interaction with peers and the instructor, Rourke and Lysynchuk recommend the use of computer-mediated communication to benefit these learners. (2000: 8) Brian Dille and Michael Mezack studied community college students taking telecourses using Kolb's Learning Style Inventory (1991). They too found that those who showed a preference for concrete experience had less success in telecourses than those who did not need concrete experiences. (Dille and Mezack, 1991: 31) This is a problem of the telecourses which Web-based learning is finding ways to address, as will be discussed later.

All of these learning style theories grew from a desire to understand the process of learning within the student, recognizing the process as variable depending on the characteristics each individual brings to the learning situation. A further emphasis on learners bringing different past experiences to the learning situation, coupled with a different philosophy of knowledge, led to Constructivism.

CONSTRUCTIVISM

Constructivism grew out of cognitivism in its emphasis on the internal processes of the learner's mind. Constructivism sees the learner constructing his or her own understanding of knowledge, but to a greater degree than in cognitivism. When cognitivism sees the learner accommodating or assimilating his or her understanding to new knowledge, the assumption exists that knowledge is in the world for humans to acquire. Constructivism sees the learner not *acquiring* knowledge, but *creating* it. (Jonassen, 1991:10; Ertmer and Newby, 1993: 62) In reaction to behaviorism, constructivists believe instructional objectives are not to be imposed on the learner but negotiated with the learner, and evaluation is "more of a self-analysis tool." (Jonassen, 1991: 12) In addressing educational methods for instructional systems technology, David H. Jonassen explains that "at best, teachers and designers constrain learning, but in order to maximize individual learning, we may have to yield some control and instead prepare learners to regulate their own learning by providing supportive rather than intervening learning environments." (1991: 13) Constructivist theory recommends placing learners in environments that, in order to facilitate the creation of knowledge, will allow them to interact with a variety of resources in realistic situations relevant to their experience. (Ertmer and Newby, 1993: 63) Constructivism is a radical departure from traditional pedagogies, and it is not for every learning situation, but is most appropriate to "tasks demanding high levels of processing" (1993: 68) or when multiple learning outcomes are acceptable. (1993: 66) Summarizing the application of behaviorism, cognitivism, and constructivism to instructional design, Ertmer and Newby write:

> [A] behavioral approach can effectively facilitate mastery of the content of a profession (knowing what); cognitive strategies are useful in teaching problem-solving tactics where defined facts and rules are applied in unfamiliar situations (knowing how); and constructivist strategies are especially suited to dealing with ill-defined problems through reflection-in-action. (1993: 68)

APPLICATION

What do all of these learning theories have to tell us about planning educationally-sound online learning? Much of the application of learning theories to online education has focused on full courses, while the isolated tutorial has not as often been addressed. In the traditional classroom environment in higher education, librarians may teach credit courses, but far more often they provide library and information literacy instruction one or more times for courses by other faculty. Online this translates to: isolated tutorials that can be used in the context of an online course or as a supplement to traditional classroom instruction; librarian involvement in class online discussions; and/or librarians acting as consultants by e-mail. The discussion below will suggest strategies for full library courses and options with limited librarian involvement.

Since 1987, undergraduate education has been guided by the *Seven Principles for Good Practice in Undergraduate Education*, written by Arthur Chickering and Zelda Gamson and published by the American Association for Higher Education, and that seminal work was later applied to educational technology by Chickering and Stephen C. Ehrmann. (2002) Here is a summary of their suggestions for using technologies according to the *Seven Principles*, with additional suggestions for Web-based instruction that apply to a range of purposes and audiences.

1. Good Practice Encourages Contacts Between Students and Faculty

Asynchronous communication through e-mail, computer conferencing, and the Web has been very successful in increasing student-faculty communication, offering more opportunities for students to express themselves than just in the classroom. (Chickering and Ehrmann, 2002) This increased communication helps learners who need personal connections and concrete experiences for most effective learning (Kolb's accommodators).

In Web tutorial situations, there is not an ongoing student-librarian connection, either in person or online. However, if the larger course or context in which the tutorial is being used has some type of asynchronous communication set up, the librarian can arrange with the other instructors to be a part of that. This could involve:

- Assignments integrated into the tutorial which are sent to the librarian for review and returned to each student.
- Online discussions which the librarian monitors or manages.
- E-mail availability of the librarian for assistance as needed.

The newest reference models are using enhanced chat programs to offer personal, synchronous assistance to students as needed (supported by networks of librarians). In addition, if the tutorial is supplementing traditional courses, the librarian can visit the classroom to introduce the instruction and follow up the tutorial by revisiting to help students apply the tutorial lessons to a project. The object is to make a personal connection between librarian and students.

2. Good Practice Develops Reciprocity and Cooperation Among Students
Having students experience the give-and-take of ideas with peers can likewise be accomplished with either asynchronous or synchronous communication. In full courses, this can involve "study groups, collaborative learning, group problem solving, and discussion of assignments." (Chickering and Ehrmann, 2002) Diaz and Cartnal found that students who self-selected into online courses usually had an independent learning style, but that structured online discussions encouraged them to collaborate. (1999: 134)

When there is not a full library course, students can be assigned by an instructor to use a library tutorial in pairs to help each other with assignments or ungraded quizzes included in the tutorial. Or in course-integrated library instruction, the librarian can help design library-related online assignments that involve small groups helping each other.

3. Good Practice Uses Active Learning Techniques
Chickering and Ehrmann include the above communication strategies in active learning, but under this principle they add "learning by doing," such as with simulations and "apprentice-like activities." (2002) Knowles' andragogical model emphasizes activities such as experiments, case studies, and simulation by students who also can bring their own past experiences to bear on learning tasks. Bloom's *Taxonomy* includes Application, Analysis, Synthesis, and Evaluation in the higher-learning categories, all forms of active learning. Constructivism assumes learners construct their own knowledge through active involvement with the material to be learned. In the online environment, active learning means interactivity. Learners should not simply scroll or click through linear Web pages,

but Web-based learning must ask of the learner thought and action, particularly with Bloom's goals of Application, Analysis, Synthesis, and Evaluation.

Kolb's model assumes an equally strong role for all four aspects of his learning cycle, and yet the concrete experience aspect is not easy to place in online learning. In "Experience-Based Pedagogical Designs for e-Learning" Albert Ip and Som Naidu describe several experience-based designs, such as simulations, case studies, and problem-based learning, and how these learning tools, long used in face-to-face education, can be used on the Web and in computer-mediated communication (2001). They describe:

- Goal-based scenarios where an actor explains the scenario and learners "make an informed judgment on action that is required."
- Role-play simulations which are games online, where peers are "competitors, partners, or collaborators" and the moderator is "an angel providing just-in-time support."
- Rule-based simulations where the computer provides preprogrammed responses to different actions by the student.
- Case studies which provide the focus of online discussion and analysis by students.
- Problem-based learning where a problem is presented online and students draw on their own and the group's experience to solve it gradually over a period of time.
- Critical-incident-based collaborative learning, where a learner presents an actual experience (such as from the workplace) for reflection and sharing with peers, "bringing theory to bear upon practice." (Ip and Naidu, 2001)

The experience-based learning designs described by Ip and Naidu can apply not only to full courses but also, in some cases or with some modification, can be used in individual tutorials.

4. Good Practice Gives Prompt Feedback

Chickering and Ehrmann mention e-mail, simulations, video observation of student performance, and editing features of word-processing programs as examples of ways to use technology to give students prompt feedback.

Long ago B. F. Skinner's programmed instruction included immediate feedback and reinforcement to a learner's self-paced steps through a tutorial. New technologies can make the feedback more interesting and instructive than the early computer attempts, such as with games that test knowledge. But while there is still a limited place for programmed instruction, that should not be the model for an entire tutorial. Feedback can be provided through more creative active learning techniques and more emphasis on Bloom's activities of Application, Analysis, Synthesis, and Evaluation. In constructivist environments, a realistic context provides an opportunity in which to practice learned skills, and self-evaluation becomes an important part of feedback.

5. Good Practice Emphasizes Time on Task

Technologies can entice students to spend more time on a project than they might have otherwise, but among more tech-savvy learners, the technology has to be well done to keep their interest. This is where context plays a part. When students can relate the task to something they want to accomplish, their interest follows. If possible, have the library task be based in an information need or assignment need the student already has. If this is not possible, a few choices for topics within a tutorial can be given. Or simulations, scenarios, or games can interest a student to spend the time thinking about and applying library and information literacy topics rather than simply clicking through pages of explanation.

6. Good Practice Communicates High Expectations

Chickering and Ehrmann recall Bloom in writing, "[s]ignificant real-life problems, conflicting perspectives, or paradoxical data sets can set powerful learning challenges that drive students to not only acquire information but sharpen their cognitive skills of analysis, synthesis, application, and evaluation." (2002) Students in a full library course can be encouraged to use real-life information needs of their own as they learn to apply new information-seeking skills.

Full courses have the time to develop Bloom's full range of cognitive skills, but individual tutorials can also encourage higher learning levels. For example, when a tutorial not only presents criteria for Web evaluation but also asks students to apply those criteria to Web sites they have found on their own course topics, students are doing Analysis and Application as well as Evaluation. Similarly, when scenarios dealing with the ethical use of information ask students to decide whether a given activity is ethical, students are again using Analysis, Application, and Evaluation. At the other extreme, when a tutorial only asks students to memorize a list, expectations and achievement will be low.

7. Good Practice Respects Diverse Talents and Ways of Learning

Technologies offer a variety of approaches to learning for students of different learning styles. The discussion of learning styles above outlined a number of recommendations for helping various types of students, both on the Web and with computer-mediated communication. Chickering and Ehrmann add that technologies:

> can supply structure for students who need it and leave assignments more open-ended for students who don't. Fast, bright students can move quickly through materials they master easily and go on to more difficult tasks; slower students can take more time and get more feedback and direct help from teachers and fellow students. (2002)

The simple addition of a menu bar, always visible on the side of a tutorial, plus lists of tasks to complete, allows for some of this flexible structure within a stand-alone tutorial.

In a study of one hundred research reports on online learning, Marion Coomey and John Stephenson found four common features that were found to be "essential to good practice": dialogue, involvement, support, and control. They write "Most 'lessons learnt' focused on the importance of structuring the learning activity and designing the materials in order to promote dialogue, secure active involvement of the learner, provide personal or other support and feedback and enable the learner to exercise the degree of control expected." (2001: 38) These elements have been discussed in the *Seven Principles*, and the seventh principle above alludes to the issue of control by the student. Modern educational theory is moving in the direction of offering the learner increasing opportunities to manage his or her own learning, that is, the andragogical model. However, students often come to the learning situation expecting to sit back and be "taught" because that has been their prior experience. Note that Coomey and Stephenson mention "the degree of control expected." That is, students will benefit from having more control over their learning, but they are not always ready to assume that control. Instructors can provide structure and guidance in the learning situation while encouraging gradually increasing levels of involvement and control by students, so that those who are ready to exercise some management of their own learning will be comfortable doing so, but those who are not comfortable with it will have adequate structure to guide them. Referring to full online courses, Coomey and Stephenson state that "control can cover responses to exercises, pace and timing, choice of content, management of learning activities, learning goals and outcomes, overall direction and assessment of performance." (2001: 40) In a tutorial, pace and timing is certainly up to a student, and tutorials or assignments that offer several possible exercises or activities give students a measure of control. Returning to the menu example, when students can select which items in a tutorial to view or review, they have navigational control.

Chickering and Ehrmann add an important caveat for the use of technology, writing that instructors "need to eschew materials that are simply didactic, and search instead for those that are interactive, problem-oriented, relevant to real-world issues, and that evoke student motivation." (2002) An excellent example of a learning environment with all these characteristics is described by Jan Herrington and Peter Standen of Edith Cowen University in Australia. What began as a set of multimedia business research skills tutorials in what they describe as an "instructivist" (behaviorist) model was transformed by the addition of "an overarching constructivist shell to provide a meaning to the lessons that comprised the original program." (Herrington and Standen, 2000) Although multimedia formats, self pacing, frequent feedback, animations, and some degree of learner control were expected to interest and engage students, the authors realized that the material did not sufficiently interest students to stay with the program because it was only theoretical, with no real-world application. They created a video in which they presented a realistic scenario of an employer asking students to create a business report to solve a problem, with the understanding that there may be more than one way to approach the problem. The "constructivist shell" further provided not only the tutorials as resources, but a wealth of other resources from which to choose as needed, including information from "other employees" (on video) and access to the instructor as a coach and guide. The original tutorials were not required except as the students, who worked in pairs or small groups to help each other, felt the need for such information to accomplish the task at hand. The assessment, likewise, was not based on individual quizzes for each tutorial, but on the resulting reports, as it would be in a real business situation. Herrington and Standen's creation, unfortunately, is not available online. (P. Standen, personal communication, September 17, 2002)

QUESTIONS TO ASK

When does one use these educational theories? What questions can one ask to determine which instructional design elements to include? In addition to the tips for following the *Seven Principles for Good Practice in Undergraduate Education*, below are more suggestions for planning online instruction.

Is the information basic or required before the learner can proceed?

In Bloom's taxonomy the basic level of understanding is Knowledge, and fundamental information can be imparted using piecemeal instruction with frequent feedback to help the learner acquire a basic understanding before progressing. However, students who may wish to review this basic information later, or who know it but want a refresher, should also have an opportunity to get in and out quickly once they find the piece they need. Do not limit tutorial access to a single linear progression from beginning to end, but keep a menu available at every screen for users to enter and leave at any point.

Is there a context in which the information can be placed?

All information, even at a basic level, needs a context such as an example that the student can recognize in order to help with comprehension. In addition, if the student can use his/her own example or select from several examples, all the better.

Is there an activity the student can be asked to perform in relation to the information?

If the instruction asks the student to use the information to perform some activity, this raises the level of learning to Application, and applying what they have learned will help students retain the knowledge better than simply reading or hearing it. The sooner the application follows the instruction and the more opportunities for practical application, the better retention will be.

Is the information more advanced or more conceptual?

Using cognitive techniques, try to build on learners' prior understanding with metaphors, analogies, and concept maps to help them visualize the information and how it fits with what they already know. Advance organizers, such as a pre-exercise for learners to try, or an overview of the concept about to be learned, set up the learning at the beginning of each section of a tutorial. Outlines, in the form of a clickable menu at the side, help students see the hierarchy of the information and where the instruction is headed and, as mentioned above, allow free movement as needed among the sections.

Does the learning involve reasoning or problem solving, applying facts or rules to new situations?

Once again, cognitive techniques will help to prepare the learner. In addition, opportunities to practice reasoning and problem solving can be created with scenarios, simulations, or case studies. Reflection gives students the time and ability to do their reasoning or problem solving. Herrington and Standen state that "In order to provide opportunities for students to reflect on their learning, the program need[s] to provide both an authentic context and non-linear navigation to enable them to return to any element of the program." (2000)

Would students benefit from discussing the information with each other or helping each other?

In a full online course, this can be structured into the course assignments, using conferencing software or e-mail. Discussions should be given some structure by the instructor to encourage those online learners who favor independent work, and to provide the personal connectedness that concrete learners need.

In a stand-alone tutorial, directions may be given at the start to do the tutorial with a partner, or an outside instructor may assign the tutorial to be done in pairs. This is especially helpful where problem-solving experiences in the tutorial can benefit from shared thinking.

Do you want to consider various learning styles in the online learning experience?

See the earlier discussion under Learning Styles for specific suggestions. Basically, as in face-to-face learning, try to include a variety of methods and experiences to appeal to different styles of learners.

What level of control do you (as instructor) want in the learning environment? What level of control do your students want or expect?

Because most students have experience as passive acceptors of teacher-controlled education, instructors must often bring students, even older students returning to school, into active involvement with their learning gradually. Mixed classes of students who have varying levels of experience with learner-managed learning can be especially challenging. In the online environment, options for control can be built in to allow for differences between those who wish to be led and those who wish to select their own path. In a tutorial this can be accomplished with a structured yet flexible environment, including flexible navigation and multiple choices for exercises or activities (while specifying "at least one" must be completed). In a full course, broadly defined assignments, and for advanced students even mutually defined assignments, within certain parameters will allow students who wish to take control of their learning to do so, and more guidance can be given to those who desire it.

Are multiple learning outcomes acceptable? Or does the learning situation involve high levels of problem solving?

Where more than one approach to a problem is possible, a learning environment can be created in which the learner chooses how to approach the problem. This could apply, for example, to a large research scenario in which the student could seek information from many sources, and within the larger scenario a number of options can be explored. This is a constructivist environment, within which can be placed shorter tutorials, selected resources, and access to the instructor and other students online. If the student *must* use all aspects of the learning environment, it is not a truly constructivist situation; one may wish to reserve this technique for more advanced students. Alternative possibilities in a full course include: after completing their individual or paired projects, students could share their experiences with each other; they could be required to do more than one information project; or students could be tested on various scenarios to see what they learned. Using these techniques, even if students "should" use all the available resources, the environment is approaching constructivism in that students are managing how and when they use the resources and what they do with them. This is andragogy in action.

Should I use pedagogical or andragogical methods?

Probably both. Learning must involve some "lecturing" so that foundational information is available. But learners will quickly lose interest and retain little if they are not engaged in the process, and wherever possible online instructional designers should add elements that encourage interactivity and student management of learning. Even when one is not planning a full-scale constructivist online course, andragogical elements of applicability, flexibility, and interactivity are all possible even in a stand-alone tutorial. One should keep Bloom's *Taxonomy* in mind so that online learning challenges the highest level of thinking possible in students. Likewise the *Seven Principles for Good Practice in Undergraduate Education* and the research on learning styles also are excellent guides for all education, including online learning. Programmed instruction has been around for over half a century, but the scholarship of teaching and learning has progressed beyond the linear drill-and-practice days, and online learning should reflect that.

CONCLUSION

Computerized instruction has been shaped by several learning theories. Behaviorism focused on external behaviors of the learner, and one outcome of this focus was self-paced programmed instruction. Bloom and others analyzed cognitive behaviors and sought to measure learning outcomes, creating the *Taxonomy of Educational Objectives*. Cognitivism focused on internal cognitive processes, where the learner is viewed as a more active participant in the learning process, assimilating new information into his/her existing understanding or accommodating his/her understanding to the new information. In considering how learners perceive and process information, learning style theories were developed. Constructivism took cognitivism one step further in focusing on the learner's mental processes, to see the learner as constructing his/her own new knowledge rather than simply acquiring existing knowledge.

Each of these theories enriched pedagogical philosophy and brought useful elements to online instruction. The andragogy movement brought to pedagogy an understanding that once learners have been provided with a basic level of knowledge in a discipline, they can become increasingly more active learners. When the higher levels of understanding are sought (such as in Bloom's higher taxonomic levels), constructivist learning situations can be used to maximize the learner's potential.

Undergraduate education has aimed to employ principles of active, learner-centered learning. The *Seven Principles for Good Practice in Undergraduate Education* has guided higher education since 1987, and they were recently applied to educational technology. Principles of instructor-student communication, cooperation among students, active learning, prompt feedback, time on task, high expectations, and respect for different ways of learning bring the best of educational theories to bear on computer-based instruction. Understanding and applying instructional theories to the online setting will create a high quality learning environment.

REFERENCES

Bloom, Benjamin, et al. 1956. *Taxonomy of Educational Objectives*. New York: David McKay.

Carlson, Robert. 1989. "Malcolm Knowles: Apostle of Andragogy." *Vitae Scholasticae* 8, no.1 (Spring). Chicago: National-Louis University. Available: www.nl.edu/ace/Resources/Knowles.html.

Chickering, Arthur W., and Stephen C. Ehrmann. 2002. "Implementing the Seven Principles: Technology as Lever." Washington, DC: TLT Group. Available: www.tltgroup.org/programs/seven.html.

Chickering, Arthur W., and Zelda F. Gamson. 1987. "Seven Principles for Good Practice in Undergraduate Education." Washington, DC: American Association for Higher Education. Available: www.aahebulletin.com/public/Archive/sevenprinciples1987.asp.

Coomey, Marion, and John Stephenson. 2001. "Online Learning: It Is All About Dialogue, Involvement, Support and Control—According to the Research." In *Teaching and Learning Online: Pedagogies for New Technologies* edited by J. Stephenson: 37–52. London: Kogan Page.

Diaz, David P., and Ryan B. Cartnal. 1999. "Students' Learning Styles in Two Classes: Online Distance Learning and Equivalent On-Campus." *College Teaching* 47, no.4 (Fall): 130–135.

Dille, Brian, and Michael Mezack. 1991. "Identifying Predictors of High Risk Among Community College Telecourse Students." *The American Journal of Distance Education* 5, no.1: 24–35.

Ehrmann, Stephen C. 1995. "Asking the Right Question: What Does Research Tell Us about Technology and Higher Learning?" Washington, DC: Annenberg/CPB. Available: www.learner.org/edtech/rscheval/rightquestion.html.

Ertmer, Peggy A., and Timothy J. Newby. 1993. "Behaviorism, Cognitivism, Constructivism: Comparing Critical Features from an Instructional Design Perspective." *Performance Improvement Quarterly* 6, no.4: 50–72.

Feuer, Dale, and Beverly Geber. 1988. "Uh-oh . . . Second Thoughts about Adult Learning Theory." *Training* 25, no.12 (December): 31–39.

Furth, Hans G. 1970. *Piaget for Teachers*. Englewood Cliffs, NJ: Prentice-Hall.

Grasha, Anthony F. 1996. *Teaching with Style*. Pittsburgh: Alliance Publishers.

Herrington, Jan, and Peter Standen. 2000. "Moving from an Instructivist to a Constructivist Multimedia Learning Environment." *Journal of Educational Multimedia and Hypermedia* 9, no.3: 195–205. Retrieved from Education Full Text database.

Imel, Susan. 1989. "Teaching Adults: Is It Different?" Columbus, OH: ERIC Clearinghouse on Adult Career and Vocational Education. (ERIC Identifier ED305495). Available: www.ed.gov/databases/ERIC_Digests/ed305495.html.

Ip, Albert, and Som Naidu. 2001. "Experience-based Pedagogical Designs for E-Learning." *Educational Technology* 41, no.5 (September–October): 53–58.

Jonassen, David H. 1991. "Objectivism versus Constructivism: Do We Need a New Philosophical Paradigm?" *Educational Technology, Research & Development* 39, no.3: 5–14.

Knowles, Malcolm S. 1995. *Designs for Adult Learning*. Alexandria, VA: American Society for Training and Development.

Kolb, David A. 1981. "Learning Styles and Disciplinary Differences." In *The Modern American College*, edited by A. W. Chickering and Associates: 232–255. San Francisco: Jossey-Bass.

Lee, Virginia S. 1999. "Creating a Blueprint for the Constructivist Classroom." *The National Teaching and Learning Forum Newsletter* 8, no.4 (June). Reprinted in *"NTLF's Frequently Asked Questions on College and University Teaching & Learning."* Westport, CT: Greenwood. Available: www.ntlf.com/html/lib/faq/bl-ntlf.htm.

McNeil, Sara. 2000a. "A Hypertext History of Instructional Design: Behaviorism." Houston: College of Education. Available: www.coe.uh.edu/courses/cuin6373/idhistory/behaviorism.html.

McNeil, Sara. 2000b. "A Hypertext History of Instructional Design: The 1950s."

Houston: College of Education. Available: www.coe.uh.edu/courses/
cuin6373/idhistory/1950.html.
Ross, Jonathan L., and Robert A. Schulz. 1999. "Using the World Wide Web
to Accommodate Diverse Learning Styles." *College Teaching*, 47, no.4 (Fall):
123–129.
Rourke, Liam, and Linda Lysynchuk. 2000. "The Influence of Learning Style
on Achievement in Hypertext." Paper presented at the Annual Meeting
of the American Educational Research Association (New Orleans, LA,
April 24–28, 2000). (ERIC Identifier ED446102).

Chapter 5

Educational Technology

Scott Macklin

Science and industry are exponentially improving the methods by which information can be collected, assembled, edited, upgraded, archived, displayed, distributed, and accessed interactively. Now is the time to ask, "In what ways can the progressive innovations in information technology enhance the outcome of our educational efforts across the full spectrum of our institutions' missions?" Educational technology has the potential to contribute enormously to meeting challenges facing us today, significantly enhancing both teaching and learning. In order to achieve this promise, there must be an intimate coupling between the evolution of educational technology and the evolution of educational practice and educational science: each must inform the other, in a continuous cycle.

We have moved through and beyond the hype of technology. Proclamations, such as Edison's "Books will soon be obsolete in the schools," have abounded since the turn of the century. Similarly, Larry Cuban tells the story of how enthusiasm for film, radio, television, and desktop computers has not had the systemic impact on teaching practice as had been hyped (1996). His point is that teachers did not and do not have adequate voice and sway in technology implementation. Paralleling the post high-tech industry bubble burst (Kelly, 2000; Marlatt, 2000), there is now a more sober discussion concerning teaching and learning with technology among practitioners in education.

Of the many publications and studies dealing with this topic, the recent report by the Web-based Education Commission to the President and Congress pulls into focus the need to:

> . . . establish a pedagogical base for the effective use of Internet learning. We need a vastly expanded, revitalized, and reconfigured educational research, development, and innovation program, one built on a deeper understanding of how people learn, and how new tools support and assess learning gains. (Kerrey et al., 2001: 71)

This chapter will provide perspectives on innovative and effective ways that technology can be integrated into instruction that enhances learning. One upshot of technological innovation has been a shift from a teacher-centered to student-centered model of learning, as instructors use technology for inquiry-based, problem-based, or collaborative exercises and assignments. This movement is helping to accelerate new knowledge and create new educational opportunities in terms of learners, learning domains, instructional approaches, assessment techniques, structures of learning environments, and characteristics of learning technologies.

The claim here is not that technology is the shining knight charging in to fix what ails us in education, but rather the use of technology in teaching and learning opens up a space to critically examine one's educational goals. Further, significant changes in educational technology have introduced new perspectives on instruction, leading many instructors and programs to reconsider how and what they teach.

Vital to this effort are the research-informed design, development, and dissemination of appropriate technologies that meet the needs of learners and teachers using them as effective instruments for a task.

To provide some context, it is necessary to note some important shifts taking place:

- Technology both drives and enables the transformation of the educational experience.
- Mass customization is one important goal in educational transformation, in that it adapts education to the learner

in numerous venues from learning styles to navigation through a complex and varied curriculum.

- Technology accelerates decompartmentalization among areas of scientific inquiry and among different groups of people, blurring the boundaries between teacher and learner.
- Instructional technology offers an unequalled opportunity to make good on the traditional mission of transmitting knowledge to society, through a different and expanded concept of whom we serve and how we serve them.
- Experimentation is the critical methodology in this arena: identify a question or an opportunity at the intersection of teaching, learning, and technology; design an initiative and carry it out; evaluate the results, and insist that future investments be disciplined by the results of that evaluation.
- Technology expands partnerships among educational, business, and civic organizations, and allows the walls of institutions to be permeable.

UNDERSTANDING AND RESPONDING TO THE NEEDS OF LEARNERS

During a presentation given to a group of thirty orthopedic surgeons—where I was demonstrating how one could use a digital video camera and a laptop to capture, edit, and import footage of diagnostic procedures into PowerPoint—one of the physicians stood up and adamantly pronounced, "I would have an easier time teaching you how to do pelvic surgery than you would have teaching me PowerPoint." I thought to myself, "He has a point."

Indeed, reducing the barrier points of entry for making use of educational technologies is a crucial driver, but underscoring the above story is the notion that even though technology may show us what is possible, the instructional goals and needs should drive applications of that technology. It is interesting to note that once the pronouncement was made, other physicians started to add to the conversation about how technologies can respond to learner/patient expectations and information needs. They provided examples to each other of how technology can pragmatically integrate into the service of their activities. From that standpoint, one lesson learned is that instructor input is critical to the success, and iterative improvement, of instructor support. Once the need was established, I was able to finish the presentation by having the physicians do some hands-on work, and although the above physician may not be a PowerPoint expert, his challenge was met and I will be going in for my first scalpel lesson soon.

One of the biggest challenges facing educational institutions in terms of deployment and support of effective uses of technology for teaching and learning is choosing between buying off-the-shelf products, or building or developing your own suite of educational technologies. There are arguments supporting both approaches and much depends on a particular institution's computing infrastructure and technology support strategies. This chapter is less concerned with the specific choice between types of third party courseware (Maricopa Center for Learning and Instruction, 2002), HTML editors (Educational Technology Development Group, 2002), or multimedia codec (KeyLabs, 1999) de jour, than with the process of assessing needs and making decisions regarding categories of technologies that can afford the best learning opportunities. (Donovan and Macklin, 1999) The categories include:

- Educational technologies and strategies for collaboration and simulation.
- Educational technologies and strategies for reflective learning.
- Educational technologies and strategies for making learning visible.

Moore's Law states that "the number of transistors per square inch on integrated circuits doubles every year since the integrated circuit was invented." (Webopedia, 1998) That is, the computing power of a chip doubles every 12 to 18 months. What has not kept pace is a social equivalent to Moore's Law—specifically, our understanding of the impact of technology on teaching and learning. Although a work in progress, at the University of Washington (UW) we are developing Educational Impact Assessments (EIA) as a tool that can be used as part of instruction to support and enhance learning. Assessment and evaluation techniques need to be synchronized with and inform contemporary educational practice in the development of learning environments where inquiry is the norm, and a focus on problem solving and thinking critically is part of the process.

Systemic in character, EIAs do not gauge a sequence of discrete events but rather the whole dynamic learning ecology under investigation. Recent exponential growth in the development of educational technologies has not been matched with equal growth in a quality research base of informing effective practice.

EIA's characterizations serve as a backdrop for recommendations for enhancing the learning experience and thus are best used as a planning activity. The model focuses on opportunities for changes to the environment, resources, and overall instructional approach (factors 3–6 in Figure 5–1) that might better serve to help learners acquire specific learning objectives.

**Figure 5–1. Factors Associated with Describing
a Learning Experience**

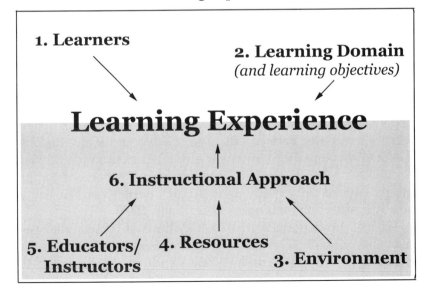

Figure 5–2. Student Responses to Survey

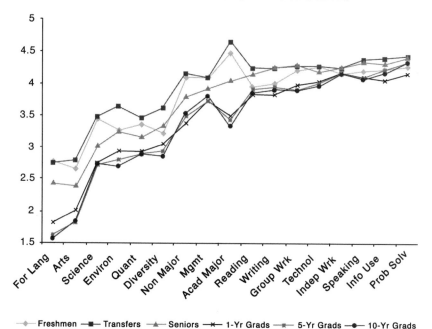

Before describing and providing a list of questions regarding EIAs, I would like to offer some context as to what learners say they want in terms of learning technologies.

What Students Say

Recent studies have found that college students have increasing expectations of technology use in their academic experience. Nearly 20 percent of today's college students began using a computer between the ages of five and eight, and by the time they are 16 to 18 years old, all current students had begun using the computer. Furthermore, 79 percent of the sample agreed or strongly agreed that Internet use has had a positive impact on their education. (Jones, 2002)

In a survey conducted by UW's Office of Educational Assessment, students (Freshman, Transfers, Seniors, 1-Year Graduates, 5-Year Graduates, and 10-Year Graduates) were asked to rate their competence on seventeen abilities (Gillmore, 1999).

The top five abilities that students said were most important were:

1. Defining and solving problems.
2. Locating information.
3. Speaking effectively.
4. Learning independently.
5. Working with technology.

Learning has become a continual process rather than a distinct event and students are expecting enhanced motivation, performance, collaboration, and innovation as we evolve into a knowledge-based economy, putting a premium on intellectual capital whereby lifelong learning is an imperative.

RESEARCH-INFORMED DESIGN AND DEVELOPMENT

Last fall we put a fishpond in our backyard and it was my four-year-old son's job to feed the fish everyday. Two days ago the raccoons got the last of the fish and my son asked, "Papa, what happened to all the fish." I told him that in the fall the fish hibernate in the house. "Where in the house are they?" he asked. "Well, the fish move very fast so you have to be very quiet . . . there they are in the living room," I respond. He runs in. "Where are they Papa?" "They swam away, you made too much noise. They are now in my briefcase," I say. Again, he cannot find them and I reiterate, "You have to be very quiet if you want to see them." The next day I get up to go to work and find my briefcase . . . full of fish food. The lesson from this story is be careful *what* you teach your children, and *how* you teach them.

Our complex learning environments require us to approach our research from a variety of perspectives, which include the science of learning, design methodology, human-computer interaction, technology adoption by educators and learners, and technology-mediated assessment practices.

An emerging perspective in the learning sciences involves an iterative process of research on learning with the design of integrated pedagogical practices and technological tools (Brown,

1992). As we conceive of applying this in the proposed work, there are four basic phases:

1. Perform studies in real settings to investigate what is learned, who learns, and how it happens,
2. which in turn inform the design of appropriate tools.
3. These new tools are integrated into educational settings,
4. in which new studies are conducted to understand how these new tools have affected learners and learning.

EDUCATIONAL TECHNOLOGIES AND EDUCATIONAL PRACTICE

One of the exciting transformations happening at many educational institutions is a move to a more active learning approach—whether that is the implementation of problem-based learning curriculum in the Health Sciences, service learning in Engineering, or portfolio-based assignments in Arts and Sciences. What has not kept pace is how "we" assess and evaluate the outcomes, efficacies, and impact of these approaches.

Effective implementation and deployment of educational technologies and practices fosters collaboration in learner-to-instructor and learner-to-learner models; allows instructor and learners the opportunity to actively reflect on assignments and learning; and helps make connections between classroom activities and course objectives—connections between classroom learning and what happens outside of the classroom. It will help make the process of learning visible. In order to move toward this vision, take to heart the words of Gavriel Salomon, "If nothing significant changes in the classroom save the introduction of the tool, few if any important effects can be expected." (1993: 189)

EDUCATIONAL IMPACT
ASSESSMENT (EIA) QUESTIONS

During the 2002 Super Bowl, I witnessed an interesting educational phenomenon. I was watching the game at a house of a friend who happens to be a die-hard Patriot fan—I watch the big game mostly for the commercials. Pepsi teamed up with Britney Spears to develop an ad campaign whereby they would film and screen Britney in different time modes—50s, 60s, 70s—and some future setting. The network aired the different time modes in the first half of the game commercials, so viewers could vote online during halftime festivities as to which extended version would be played in the fourth quarter. During the game, I observed my friend's nine-year-old daughter log on to instant messaging and then engage in fairly sophisticated reflection, discussion, and assessment with her cohorts (approximately 200 people) about each commercial. They argued the merits of each version, came to a conclusion, and then each voted as to which mode they wanted to watch. I thought to myself, if only they could muster as much energy for what goes on in school.

Researchers from UW's Program for Educational Transformation through Technology (PETTT) and the Center for Instructional Design and Research met with teachers and learners to design and redesign thoughtful, appropriate, and transformative uses of educational technology. The questions below are modified from their worksheet, designed to help you develop and redesign instruction incorporating educational technology by reflecting on your instructional objectives, learning approaches in your discipline, and how technologies may help your audience learn.

Context for Your Instruction

Teaching and learning in a discipline

- How is instruction typically taught in this discipline?
- What does a person need to learn in order to work well in this discipline?
- What do you think are the best ways to learn these things?

Teaching and learning in a department

- How is instruction typically taught in this department?
- What prior knowledge and experience do learners bring to the topic?
- What are learners' goals for taking this instruction?

Designing and Revising Instruction

Reflecting on your background with this topic

- What is your previous experience teaching this material? What other courses and topics do you teach?
- How do your research interests and other professional interests relate to this instruction?
- How does your way of thinking about this material reflect your teaching philosophy?

Defining learning objectives for the topic

- What do you hope your students will learn from this instruction?
- What do students typically find challenging about this material or topic?
- What helps learners when they encounter these challenges?
- How do you expect your uses of technology to support student learning in this instruction?

Characterizing the learning environment

- How is the instruction or class time usually structured?
- Will using technology change what you do during the instruction?
- What are the assignments you give to learners? How might the introduction of educational technology affect these assignments?
- In what ways do you think technology might support achieving your learning objectives?

Assessing student learning

- How do you know if students have learned what you wanted them to learn?

- In what ways do you share with students the criteria you're using to evaluate their work?
- How do you evaluate students' participation?
- Do you think that using technology will change the way you think about and assess student learning in this course?

Reflecting on your teaching

- What teaching strategies are most effective for helping students learn this material?
- What would you say is the greatest challenge in teaching this material?
- What strategies help you respond to these challenges?
- How are your ways of teaching this material affected by your uses of technology?

Incorporating Educational Technology

Reflecting on your experience with educational technology

- What is your overall experience with using educational technology so far?
- Are there things you found to be problematic with using technology?
- What feedback, if any, do you get from learners when you require them to use technology?
- Have you attempted to evaluate your instructional uses of technology beyond the standard course evaluation forms?

Current plans for using educational technology

- How will the technology help support your learning goals for the instruction?
- How will you ask learners to use the technology?
- How will learners assess technology in this instruction?

Assessing previous uses of educational technology

- Are you convinced that the technology you implemented improved the quality of the instruction?

- If you use the same technology again, what will you do differently?
- What do you think was most helpful about using technology in the instruction? Is there anything that you wanted to do with the technology but have so far been unable to do?

Effects of educational technology

- How do you think this technology will affect your learners' work or thinking? What will you look for to help you determine that?
- Using technology, do you think you might learn anything about your students' thinking that you wouldn't have learned otherwise?
- What do you hear about how others are using educational technology?

You can use the above set of questions, selectively, as you work with the project team and your target audience to understand their specific educational needs.

CASE STUDIES

In a previous section, three categories of educational technologies were discussed including:

- Educational technologies and strategies for collaboration and simulation.
- Educational technologies and strategies for reflective learning.
- Educational technologies and strategies for making learning visible.

The following brief sketches highlight projects in each of these categories; detailed accounts are available from http://depts.washington.edu/pettt/projects/.

Educational Technologies and Strategies
for Collaboration and Simulation

How can you foster creative learning? Some of the best instruction takes place beyond the classroom. With this in mind, UW Political Science associate professor John Wilkerson built LegSim, an online congressional simulation tool to enable students to better understand the legislative process by actively participating in it. In short, students spend the quarter serving as representatives of a virtual U.S. Congress, drafting and voting on bills, filing committee reports and, of course, crafting compromises with other virtual legislators. The project has been a great success—it has been acknowledged by the American Political Science Association as the 2002 Information Technology and Politics Award winner—but its impact may be better evidenced by the percentage of students (88 percent) that found the tool preferable to classroom lectures.

Professor Wilkerson's project is a bold example of how technology in the classroom can be successful when instructors embrace it. With PETTT's assistance, it has also become an example of how it can be improved. PETTT researchers have consulted with Professor Wilkerson to help design a rubric for grading student participation, establishing, as PETTT researcher Gina Cherry says, "explicit connections between theory and practice." The result has been an increased means by which Professor Wilkerson can assess student performance through the use of the tool—effectively eliminating exams from the classroom.

Educational Technologies and Strategies
for Reflective Learning

How can you promote learning among students? To discover the world is not enough—students at the UW are expected to discover themselves. MyPortfolio, developed by Catalyst and PETTT, is a unique means by which students can keep a digital record of their work—papers, artwork, research data, projects—and have them archived on the Web, a curricula vitae so to speak of a young student's collegiate career.

MyPortfolio is a tool that is designed to teach students about themselves by encouraging reflective thought. The mere process of building a Portfolio is introspective in nature—in essence, asking *what does your Portfolio say about who you are?* To foster such thinking, PETTT researchers helped Catalyst establish a series of "reflective prompts" within the tool, designed to foster creative thinking *as well as* critical thinking—issues such as criteria, audience, purpose, and relevance. Such guidance can be self-directed or facilitated by faculty, who can use "mentored portfolios" to further advance the learning process by tailoring MyPortfolio's reflective prompts to address specific classroom issues.

During the 2002 autumn quarter, more than 4,000 first-year students and 162 leaders were introduced to Portfolio as part of the Freshman Interest Group (FIG) program. FIG students were taught how to use the tool, and then asked to use it to address a social issue—such as the death penalty—discussed in the seminar. Following the series of prompts crafted by PETTT researchers, each student built a Portfolio to address such issues. Portfolio will be used in other capacities as well—both the career counseling center and academic advising unit have inquired about tailoring the tool for their use.

Educational Technologies and Strategies for Making Learning Visible

How can you help assess student and teacher performance? Created by Dr. Reed Stevens, Associate Professor of Education at UW, Video Traces is an invention that PETTT researcher Janice Fournier calls "a tool that makes learning visible." Such evidence could not be clearer than what happened in Maria Simpson's dance composition classes in spring quarter of 2001.

Video Traces is a tool where media-rich video is captured digitally, downloaded into a laptop computer, and then viewed on a computer monitor. The unique component of Video Traces is the ability to annotate that video, layering both audio and visual annotations on top of the original recording. The tool takes advantage of a mode of learning Dr. Stevens calls "temporal coordination" or "real-time annotation"—the notion that, everyday, in nearly all personal interactions, people gesture and point *as well as* speak to help convey information. Video Traces helps utilize this relatively untapped method of instruction.

In the case of Professor Simpson's dance composition class, she was able to record each student's performance, view it at a later time, recording her comments as the visual image is being played. That Video Traces is a valuable tool for a student of dance is clear—a student can see a recording of his or her own performance, an assessment technique used in professional dance. The ability for a dance student to watch that performance, annotated with a simultaneous recording of the instructor commenting on and pointing to aspects of that very work, is also clear.

An additional benefit of the Video Traces research was the ability for Professor Simpson to evaluate her own assessment methods. "I hear this from students in different ways every year: 'I've never known what the teacher wanted,' " she says. "This year they told me that they've never received feedback like this before. I've always given them feedback after every project, but it's been less clear, less specific."

The result was a paradigm shift for Professor Simpson—as well as for her students. With the help of Video Traces and PETTT researchers, she was able to reflect on her assessment methods. In effect, Professor Simpson discovered that she did not use the assessment criteria handed out at the beginning of the quarter; she found that she tended to assess student skills "intuitively." Meeting with PETTT researchers, Professor Simpson was able to develop a rubric by which she could measure the learning of her students.

CONCLUSION

There has been a lot of hype about how technology can transform education. In order to avoid the snake oil and technological cul-de-sacs, there must be a coupling of innovative methods of learning technology use to innovative teaching practices. We can't just bolt new technology onto existing educational systems. It's also important to understand that no new technology can replace a teacher. The primacy of importance in education is still the relationship between the learner and the instructor. Successful learning experiences are dependent upon a range of factors—an educational ecology made up of instructors receiving appropriate training and continued assistance as they begin to work with educational technologies, upon the appropriate use and implementation of technology that leads to authentic learning, and upon an understanding and application of content and process design that emphasizes interaction and engagement. Most important is that instructor's uses of educational technologies be based on their experiences and needs. These critical success factors help support instructors in the search and practice of knowledge, skills, attitudes, and techniques that help foster successful online learning communities and experiences for the learner.

REFERENCES

Brown, Ann. 1992. "Design Experiments: Theoretical and Methodological Challenges in Creating Complex Interventions in Classroom Settings" *The Journal of the Learning Sciences* 2, no.2: 141–178. Available: http://depts.washington.edu/edtech/brown.pdf.

Cuban, Larry. 1996. "Techno-Reformers and Classroom Teachers." Bethesda, MD: Editorial Projects in Education. Available: www.edweek.com/ew/1996/06cuban.h16.

Donovan, Mark, and Scott Macklin. 1999. "The Catalyst Project: Supporting Faculty Uses of the Web . . . with the Web." *CAUSE/EFFECT Journal* 22, no.3: 18–25. Available: www.educause.edu/ir/library/html/cem9934.html.

Educational Technology Development Group. 2002. "Catalyst Planning Considerations: Desktop Web Editor Comparison." Seattle, WA: University of Washington. Available: http://catalyst.washington.edu/catalyst/planning/desktools.html.

Gillmore, Gerald M. 1999. "Ratings of Competence: From New Freshmen to Ten-Year Alumni." Seattle: WA: Office of Educational Assessment. Available: www.washington.edu/oea/9912.htm

Jones, Steve. 2002. "The Internet Goes to College: How Students are Living in the Future with Today's Technology." Washington, DC: Pew Internet and American Life Project. Available: www.pewinternet.org/reports/toc.asp?Report=71.

Kelly, Kate. 2000. "Is This The End.com?" *Time* 156, no.1 (July 3): 42+.

Kerrey, Bob, et al. 2001. "The Power of the Internet for Learning: Moving from Promise to Practice. Report of the Web-based Education Commission to the President and Congress of the United States." Washington, DC: Web-Based Education Commission. Available: www.ed.gov/offices/AC/WBEC/FinalReport/WBECReport.pdf.

KeyLabs. 1999. "RealNetworks Codec Comparison." Lindon, UT: KeyLabs. Available: www.keylabs.com/results/realnetworks/realnetworks.htm.

Maricopa Center for Learning and Instruction. 2002. "Web Courseware Comparisons and Studies." Tempe, AZ: Maricopa Center for Learning and Instruction. Available: www.mcli.dist.maricopa.edu/ocotillo/courseware/compare.html.

Marlatt, Andrew. 2000. "Business-To-Unemployment (B2U) Dubbed Next Big Thing." Branford, CT: SatireWire. Available: www.satirewire.com/briefs/b2u.shtml.

Salomon, Gavriel. 1993. "On the Nature of Pedagogic Computer Tools: The Case of the Writing Partner." In *Computers as Cognitive Tools,* edited by Susanne Lajoie and Sharon J. Derry. Hillsdale, NJ: Lawrence Erlbaum Associates.

Webopedia. 1998. "Moore's Law." Darien, CT: Jupitermedia. Available: www.webopedia.com/TERM/M/Moores_Law.html.

Part II

Evaluation and Assessment

It is unusual to discuss evaluation before development, but the actual practice of designing an instructional site suggests you to do just that. Design is an iterative process of developing an idea, testing that idea, and making improvements. In the case of Web-based instruction, it is likely that your first round of research and evaluation will begin once you have a general idea of the product you are planning to create, and other rounds will continue as an integrated part of your design and ongoing review processes. To put this into practice, adequate time must be allotted throughout the timeline to allow for not only testing, but also any changes that will need to be made in light of your findings. Evaluation and assessment methods can assist you in determining project success, as well as the efficacy of the site you design and the effectiveness of your instructional design for student learning. To draw these conclusions, you will likely dabble in measurement theory, educational theory, learning outcomes, social dynamics, human-computer interaction, and performance analysis.

Evaluation and assessment should be an integral part of your process for a number of reasons. Through research with your target audience and stakeholders you can learn more about the actual educational needs and expectations of these groups. By testing prototypes of your instructional site, you can determine if you are on the right track before development progresses too far and resources are wasted. Review and analysis of the site with the project team and external participants, you can uncover errors in scripting, content, and site design. Perhaps above all, evaluation allows you to improve your product, address learners' needs, and prevent false starts in development.

Many aspects of your project can be analyzed, such as usability of the site, learner satisfaction with the product, resource utilization, competencies of participants, and effectiveness of the instructional approach. Lest it sound as if evaluation and assessment should become your primary focus, remember to keep this aspect in balance with the other goals and priorities of the project. Determine what data and feedback will be useful to the project team and for analyzing the project for a few years in the future. To make the most of your limited time, it is important you design research methods and devise statistical analyses that will specifically address those issues, rather than simply collecting all data possible.

The following chapters discuss a number of evaluation and assessment methods that will aid you in gathering qualitative and quantitative data. Quantitative data generally appears as or can be converted to numerical values and, as such, lend themselves to statistical analysis. For example, server statistics can be relatively easily gathered and are useful for creating benchmarks to judge past use and project future use of your site. If statistically correct and displayed clearly, quantitative data can be a valuable resource. Qualitative data, though less easily analyzed and generalized, can be an equally revealing method of gauging opinions, attitudes, and beliefs. For example, a group of members of your target audience can be asked about their experiences with and attitudes related to your project prototype. Although qualitative is not as easily extrapolated to a larger group, personal contact with people can be useful for uncovering deeper, less concrete issues than may be revealed in statistics. Besides directly assisting you in improving the product, quotations and "stories" from participants may be useful narrative additions to highlight points in your project status reports to stakeholders.

One reason to consider evaluation early in the process is that you can design formative as well as summative assessment measures. Formative assessment occurs through the span of your project, or throughout the process of learning. It provides feedback to assist you in refining your design or instructional strategy. Common types of formative evaluation and assessment might include comments from focus groups during development, initial usability tests, and measures of student learning through student journals or draft assignments. Alternately, summative assessment assists you in drawing conclusions at the end of development or the term of instruction. From summative analysis you can make generalizations about whether you have met your goals for the project and for student achievement. When conducted over time, the series of data from summative evaluation will assist you in determining the impact your Web-based instruction has had since its inception. For example, a post-instruction test is a form of summative assessment.

These types of evaluation and assessment are useful for varied purposes, with various groups, and at various stages of the planning, design, and redesign processes. Chapters in this section will discuss statistics and metrics, focus groups, usability testing, and assessment of learning. A myriad of other techniques such as surveys, short answer questions, and cognitive walkthroughs are also useful, and can easily be modeled from other sources. Rather than choosing just one method, it is useful to use a medley of different methods to gather feedback. Consider using the various methods to elicit input from the project team, colleagues, target audience, stakeholders, as well as from the servers themselves. From each, you are likely to receive slightly different perspectives that—when brought together—will show you a richer picture of the overall product.

Before you begin collecting data, it is wise to consider exactly what elements you need to analyze and what information you wish to archive. Unless you are pursuing a long-term research study relating to your Web-based instructional project, after a certain period of time, you may choose to primarily keep aggregate data about learners, rather than specific names. If storing or archiving this data electronically, consider issues of computer security and learner's privacy.

Accurate evaluations and assessments require familiarity with statistical methods, sound methodology, and strong interpersonal skills. If you are not fortunate to have this expertise within the project team, you may be able to find a suitable project partner who works with a measurement center at a local campus or within the community. It is wise to also collaborate with the other instructors who will be sharing or contributing to the instruction being designed. By contacting these groups early, you can gather data needed to compare student learning before and after the Web-based instruction was used to later extrapolate the impact of your product on your programs and organization.

Another important group to contact is the staff who manages the servers on which your site will be hosted. Early discussions with system administrators will set the foundation for better long-term communication about what information you need to gather and how they can best provide that data. Depending on the size of that staff and the frequency of your collection of data, you might request that the system allow the project manager to check on the statistics at regular intervals, perhaps even clearing out older data at the end of the training session, semester, or calendar year.

After the project planning has begun, it is likely that the team will have developed deep attachments to the philosophy, goals, and intent of the final product. This is a healthy outcome of a strong project team and a worthwhile project—though it may create some aversion to evaluation and assessment. One might hesitate, wondering "what if our evaluation suggests the product fails?" In the most extreme cases, people may shun feedback or select only the data that justifies their previous decisions, believing that since they have spent the greatest amount of time working with the project they ultimately know what is needed. The project team must be committed to creating the best product, and understand that the information they gain from a range of sources will assist them in that endeavor. Developers should accept all input with an open mind, whether in the form of positive comments or constructive criticism. All comments and data collected need to be discussed by the project team. It is likely that after analysis some feedback will be deemed trifling or irrelevant, though there will also be emerging trends or patterns that lead to important revisions. By conducting evaluations and assessments throughout the process, you are able to make improvements sooner and are more likely to have a suitable, effective final product. The skill is determining at what point you have evaluated and revised enough, and are ready to release the final product.

Evaluation and assessment can provide important insights into the effectiveness of the instructional approach, technological choices, site design, and content. The following chapters discuss ways to gather statistics, set benchmarks, conduct and analyze focus group discussions and usability tests, and assess student learning.

Chapter 6

Statistics and Metrics

Trudi Bellardo Hahn

Electronic data from a range of sources can be analyzed for evaluation purposes, monitoring server performance, quantity of use, and learner choices. However, in spite of the fact that these data can be collected and summarized relatively easily, or perhaps *because* they can so easily be obtained and manipulated, pitfalls await the unwary.

Metrics are tools and techniques that help determine standards of use and track against them. Metrics can be qualitative ("intangible, non-calibrated measures that are subjective, such as measures of satisfaction") or quantitative ("tangible, calibrated measures that are objective"). (Kliem and Ludin, 1998: 214) Most of the metrics discussed in this chapter are quantitative, and often they need to be combined with qualitative measures that have been collected through other means such as focus groups, usability studies, or questionnaires.

Statistics are tools and techniques for collecting, analyzing, and interpreting data. This chapter will not cover details of statistical analysis; Kliem and Ludin (1998) provide an introduction to data analysis and statistical summarization, covering topics such as definitions of key concepts; statistical calculations such as mean, media, mode, and standard deviation; and options for presentation and communication of results.

To develop metrics and collect statistics, it may be necessary to partner with staff familiar with scripting and information systems. You probably will need to work with the system administrator responsible for your Web site to extract the data you wish to analyze. You may need also to consult with a programmer to set up files for storing and analyzing the data. Rather than waiting until your project is already in development, start discussions with staff that have the technical skills as soon as you know what type of data would be useful for your project.

USEFULNESS OF WEB METRICS AND STATISTICS

Web metrics and statistics may be used for a variety of evaluation purposes. Some of these are:

- Justify the cost of developing and sustaining Web-based instruction.
- Analyze the demographics of, and access methods used by, your audience.
- Investigate how and when the Web-based instruction is being used.
- Detect broken links or other technical problems.
- Create reports for the project team and stakeholders.

Although the most important goals of evaluation—assessing and improving the instruction—will not be achieved directly by collecting and analyzing electronic data, they are a good starting point for detecting some basic usage patterns. Furthermore, much of the electronic data can be collected automatically and nonintrusively.

WHAT DATA TO COLLECT

Deferring for a moment the issue of whether these data *should* be collected or analyzed, the data that *can* be collected fall into two groups. In the first group are data from log files either generated automatically by the server activity or from user actions within the site. The data types are summarized in Figure 6–1, along with details about what you can learn from that data. As we will see in the next section, these automatic data can be fairly easily summarized and analyzed through log analysis.

In the second group are data that you could collect from users who are required to register at the point of login, usually

Figure 6–1. Data That Can Be Collected Automatically

Type of Data	What Data Tell You
Referring URL	Which other Web pages users visit to get to your site, such as another library page, another page at your institution, or a search engine.
IP (Internet Protocol) address	Where users' computers are located, based on the domain names (such as .com, .edu, .gov, and city, state, or country codes) to determine if access is primarily from computers within the library, within your institution, or more remote.
Browser	Which browsers and versions are most often used to access your site.
Login time and session end time	How much time from beginning to end of the visit (may approximate time required to complete tutorial, but not reliably) and times of the day and week when the site is used the most and the least.
Number of hits or accesses to the tutorial	How many times a site has been visited.
Server load or responsiveness	How quickly a user is able to access pages during peak periods of demand.
Time at the beginning of page viewing, time when next page is accessed	How long users view particular pages (or, how long a page is on the screen).
Sequence of pages accessed	Which paths users choose through the site.
Choices in interactions	What responses users give to interactions within the site.
Test results	How well users perform on tests.

Figure 6–1. *(Continued)*

Type of Data	What Data Tell You
Number of retakes on test	How many times a user retakes a quiz or test (presumably to improve their score).
HTTP status of a browser's request • 200: page found and sent normally • 403: page with restricted viewing • 404: page was not found	How many times, and under what circumstances, users encounter errors or restrictions on access.
Number of logins for each registered user	How many times an individual accessed the site.
Length of user's session or sessions	How long each individual spent within the site or how many repeat visits they made.

via Web forms. These types of data and what they tell you are summarized in Figure 6–2.

Given that so much data can be collected, it is important to focus energy on collecting and analyzing only what you will use to measure the goals you are trying to achieve. For example, if you are concerned about whether users will be able to utilize all the "bells and whistles" of the site, you will want to examine which browsers they are using, and test your site using those browsers. The data about users' choice of paths through the site, answers to quiz questions, and other performance data will be worth analyzing only if you intend to make modifications to the site architecture or content of the instruction based on your findings.

It is important to collect usage or performance data *before* implementing your Web-based instruction if you will want to compare it with data collected *after* the site is launched, in order to measure students' performance or other issues related to instruction in various modes.

Figure 6–2. Data That Can Be Solicited from Registered Users

Type of Data	What Data Tell You
Name	The name of the individual, unless they supply a false identity.
E-mail address	A method for future communication.
User's status and affiliation	Verification of the individual's identity, affiliation, and demographics such as with ID number or barcode, course enrollment, grade or year in school, and department or major.
Other data from surveys or questionnaires	Opinions or comments.

TOOLS FOR COLLECTING AND ANALYZING DATA

Web Servers

By default, the software running a Web server will produce some basic statistics related to usage or "traffic." These typically include "hits" (any request for a particular URL including the text, graphics, and other page elements), the IP address or domain name of the user's computer, the user's browser and version, date and time of request, whether or not the request was successful, and the URL of the page the user was viewing before requesting the current page.

Log Analyzers

Log analyzers for Web servers, available in a range of prices from free to several thousand dollars, help you manipulate and display the server log data, which will be thousands of lines of text and impossible to summarize manually. The more expensive products are likely to produce more complete and detailed statistics, with enhanced graphical displays. However, the best log analyzer for any particular application is the one that is appropriate for the local needs, and this decision can be made only after it is clear what you need to know. It is important to choose log analysis software that allows you to exclude staff or Intranet IP addresses, which would not represent your target audience. Popular products for log analysis at the time of this writing are WebTrends, NetTracker, Webalizer, Wusage, wwwstat, Analog, and SiteServer. Besides compiling various types of data, they display results summarized in colorful graphs and tables. For more information about currently available log analysis tools, use a Web search engine and keywords such as *log analysis* and *server*, or specific names of log analysis software. As an alternative to specialized log analyzer software, general-purpose software such as Microsoft Excel or Microsoft Access can also be used to organize data for further analysis or manipulation. You may wish to consult with a programmer about using these tools appropriately and effectively.

Transaction log analysis (TLA) is a purposeful summary and examination of the data collected by the server or log analyzer software. Unlike focus groups, usability studies, questionnaires, or other methods of data collection and analysis, TLA does not measure student learning, attitudes, or opinions. Instead, TLA is a way to observe actual human-computer interaction in uncontrolled, nonlaboratory environments. Because it is unobtrusive, it is unlikely to affect or distort students' behaviors or perceptions. More details about reading and interpreting Web server log files are discussed in Bertot, McClure, and Moen (1997) and Ramey (2000).

Cookies

Tracking students through the site and specific interactions can be accomplished using cookies. A cookie is a simple text file that allows a Web server to store information on an individual's hard disk and retrieve it later during the same visit or the next time the individual visits your site. A cookie may contain details of each student's choices within the site, such as pages visited or scores on tests. The contents of cookies can be collected and stored on the server for later analysis. A cookie is not a program and therefore cannot carry viruses or interfere with any other files on a user's computer. It cannot retrieve information from other cookie files and cannot access any other information on the student's computer. For tracking purposes, cookies are necessary through a stateless environment like the Web. However, not all Web users choose to accept cookies on their machines.

Scripts

Web scripts—such as those written in PHP, perl, or ASP—can be used to record registration information, write quiz or test scores into a database, write comments or answers into a log file, or capture similar data as a user interacts with your site.

Pop-up Surveys

Triggered by visits to a particular portion of your site, a pop-up survey or questionnaire can be created to collect data about user satisfaction with or impressions of the instruction. Use these mechanisms sparingly so they do not annoy your users or detract from your primary content.

Benchmarking

A complex, but powerful tool for assessing certain aspects of your project, benchmarking involves identifying other Web-based instruction sites that are used in environments similar to yours, and that have similar goals. The next challenge is to identify metrics that you can collect about those other sites and compare with your own. For example, you could simply measure and compare how fast pages load. With more effort, you could check to see whether special plug-ins are required to use interactions within the site, or whether the site provides for text-based navigation for users with slower Internet connections. A much more time-consuming benchmarking exercise would be to check what special features or content the other sites provide. Misic and Johnson (1999) describe a thorough benchmarking study of a business school's Web site. Their study may offer some useful ideas for benchmarking a Web-based instruction site.

CAUTIONS IN ANALYSIS AND MEASUREMENT

The fact that computer-generated data can be so easily gathered and summarized for analysis is generally thought of as a major benefit of the method, but actually may be a *threat* to drawing accurate or meaningful conclusions. Data accuracy and validity are two specific areas to consider.

Data Accuracy

Because you are not present at the point of use and cannot attest to the veracity of the data, it is important to consider what elements may contribute to the data you see. A number of conditions can lead to inaccurate conclusions. For example, if a student logs into your site and then takes a coffee break or makes a telephone call, the connection time will be greatly extended. Or if a second student takes over mid-tutorial, several important data points will be skewed.

Accuracy in counting visits or sessions may be compromised by Web practices over which you have no control. For example, when a user visits a Web page, the browser may store that page in memory. This temporary storage of Web pages on the local hard drive, called "caching," allows a user to visit the same page again and get much faster retrieval because the browser pulls the page from its memory. The user gets faster access to the page, but the server cannot detect that the user is accessing the page more than once. Hence the server log will underreport the actual number of hits and accesses.

Another source of undercounting is a caching proxy server, which is a shared memory for a group of users. A request to a Web server from the browser of a member of the group is first routed to the caching proxy server. The server checks to see if it already has the requested page in memory. If it does, it distributes that page directly to that user. Thus the original server will have no record of the visit to the page. All visits to your tutorial from members of that server group will be recorded by a single IP address.

Search engine robots are a source of overcounting visits to your site. The search engines will send "robots" or "spiders" to visit your site periodically in order to update their index to your pages, and each of these visits will be counted as hits and accesses.

Unfortunately not all of the users you hope to track will be easy to identify either. Many Internet Service Providers (ISPs) assign IPs dynamically for their customers; thus it will be impossible to discern if a user is a return visitor.

Because of the miscounting that can result from caching, proxy servers, dynamic IPs, and robots, the data from log analysis will not represent accurate usage figures. Instead, that data should be used primarily for administrative purposes to determine loads on the server and to track general usage trends over time.

Data Validity

In addition to questioning the accuracy of the data, one needs to be cautious about interpreting what the data really mean. This is the issue of *validity*—do the data actually represent the phenomena you are trying to measure?

For example, as a measure of tutorial use, it is important to distinguish between hits, accesses, and user sessions. Sheets defines these terms as follows: "A hit on a Web server is a single request for content, or a graphic, or any other single element of a Web page . . . Grouping of all the hits on a particular page is known as one access . . . Accesses can be grouped into single sessions or visits." (1998: 18) Thus, if a user visits a site and looks at six separate pages, each with four single elements, that one session can also be described as twenty-four hits and six accesses. If you redesign a page by adding five graphic images, each visit to that page will be recorded as five extra hits. The number you want to collect and compare is either number of accesses for individual pages, or number of sessions at the site. Even if you have fairly good data about which pages are used the most or for the longest periods of time, you have to be careful not to jump to the conclusion that you know which pages are read thoroughly or whether the content is understood.

HOW TO USE THE DATA

The most important thing is to keep an open mind about what the data will reveal before you examine them—to avoid making prejudgments and avoid using the metrics simply to justify previously made decisions. The main goal should be to look for ways the data collected could be used to improve the instruction.

Because of the limitations and the problems in using Web data, it is wise to use more than one set of data and more than one data collection method to measure usage and other performance measures you seek. For example, data collected automatically, such as how long a user takes to complete a portion of the instruction, could be connected to data collected at a focus group where users are asked about their perceptions of the length of the instruction.

Scores on quizzes can be compared with other learner performance metrics—for example, scores on paper-and-pencil tests, grades on similar assignments, or even data from surveys of students' self-report of skills. Not all such comparisons will yield interesting results, however; one such study (McNulty et al., 2000) found virtually no relationship between students' self-reported "computer literacy" and the extent of their later use of a medical tutorial. However, they did find a correlation between the number of times students logged onto the medical tutorials and their overall grade in the course.

If many learners get a quiz question wrong, you might consider changing the question. Alternatively, you might change, add, or delete content of certain pages, add emphasis to important points, add new pages, or supplement this Web-based instruction with other types of online and face-to-face instruction.

If many students retake a quiz or test, this might reflect that students are breezing through or skipping tutorial content altogether. You might consider changing how quiz scores are calculated. O'Hanlon described how she made changes to the manner in which quizzes were graded. At first:

> Users were allowed unlimited attempts to answer quiz questions correctly and once a correct answer was selected, were awarded full points for their answers. Beginning in spring quarter 1998, users taking quizzes were limited to one attempt at each multiple choice quiz question. Although users are still allowed unlimited attempts to choose the correct answer, points are now deducted for any incorrect answers selected prior to choosing the correct one. The user's quiz score reflects the sum of all answers chosen. (1999: 222)

The result of this change was that students were more likely to read lessons carefully before taking quizzes so that the quiz scores reported to their instructors would be in the acceptable range.

You might detect differences in patterns of use of the site related to the type of user. O'Hanlon discovered significant differences between students enrolled in a course at Ohio State University and the "general users" who came from outside the university. For example, "General users were more likely to view only the lesson portions of the tutorials, skipping quizzes . . . General users also spent almost twice as much time as [university] students on tutorials." (1999: 217) She also reported, "Of the course-affiliated users . . . almost 37 skipped the lesson and went straight to the quiz." (1999: 221) She concluded, "This behavior may result when students are required by instructors to complete tutorials that are too elementary for their skill level." (1999: 227)

Evidence of 404 error codes will suggest which pages and which links need to be updated or fixed. The presence of 403 access-restricted codes could be a problem if certain categories of students cannot get access to pages, such as databases, that are linked to your tutorial.

Information about nonregistered visitors (discovered by the referring URL or visitor's IP address) may reveal that visitors are coming from unexpected quarters, and may suggest needed changes to the site to accommodate those users.

When you know the browsers (and versions of browsers) that people are using, you will want to check your pages to see how they look in those versions of browsers. Do all users have browsers that support all the features in the tutorial? "From the use of Cascading Style Sheets to PNG format images to specific JavaScript functions, the percentage of users who will benefit from these features is tied to the percentage who have upgraded to browsers that support them." (Dowling, 2001: 35)

Registration or login data that you have collected could be used in various ways:

- **ID numbers**
  Student, patron, or employee ID numbers can be matched to the person's name and provide an easy way to match test scores with individual students, or provide evidence of completion of the instruction.
- **Status**
  Student's grade, year in school, or identification with a particular age group could help you determine if you are attracting the audience you expected. If your data collection indicates a different audience than you intended, you might use some of the other data or evaluation method to determine why.
- **Interest**
  Classes, majors, and departments all indicate a subject or disciplinary focus that could help determine the topics and examples that might be emphasized within the instruction.

The data on total length of time for users to complete the instruction, compared to total length of time users spend in a comparable face-to-face instructional environment could be compared. How does the time spent in either activity affect scores on tests of skills or grades on similar assignments? The findings of such a study might suggest which type of learning environment—Web-based instruction or a live class—is most effective.

Also, you could use transaction log data about peak usage

periods to decide when it would be minimally disruptive to take the site down for revision, and systems staff could use the same data to decide when to bring the server down for maintenance or upgrading.

Note that in all of the examples above, the points of analysis are merely suggestions of what you might consider—the final decision about what is most appropriate for your project is absolutely dependent on your particular learning goals.

ETHICAL AND LEGAL ISSUES

The ease of automatic data collection opens doors for violations of privacy and confidentiality, especially since most data can be gathered without the students' awareness. If you are collecting any data other than anonymous traffic information of user patterns in coming to and navigating around the site, you should let the students know what you are collecting and how you will make use of their personal data. For example, if you collect names, e-mail addresses, or demographic data about individuals, along with test scores or other performance measures, you should tell them who will see these data and for what purpose. Inform students by putting a privacy and confidentiality statement on the homepage of your site.

If you restrict your data collection to server log files, confidentiality is much less of a problem. "The good news about log file limitations is that they represent at least some protection of user privacy." (Bauer, 2000: 4) Nonetheless, any data that could potentially identify an individual (such as an IP address) must be treated carefully. If you display log file data publicly, even on a staff Web site or Intranet, you should mask or remove individual IP addresses.

CONCLUSION

Web-based instruction presents opportunities for collecting a wide array of data about use, users, and operations of the server. Much of this data can be generated by the Web server and analyzed through transaction log analysis, though other methods and mechanisms such as cookies, pop-up surveys, and benchmarking can be equally beneficial. The ease of data collection, however, presents temptations for misuse and misinterpretation. Nonetheless, if the data for analysis are chosen carefully, and handled carefully, they can yield useful insights, which will aid you in improving your site.

REFERENCES

Bauer, Kathleen. 2000. "Who Goes There? Measuring Library Web Site Usage." *Online* 24, no.1 (January/February): 25–26, 28, 30–31.

Bertot, John C., Charles R. McClure, and William E. Moen. 1997. "Web Usage Statistics: Measurement Issues and Analytical Techniques." *Government Information Quarterly* 14, no.4: 373–395.

Dowling, Thomas. 2001. "Lies, Damned Lies, and Web Logs." *Library Journal* (Spring): 34–35.

Kliem, Ralph L., and Irwin S. Ludin. 1998. *Project Management Practitioner's Handbook.* New York: AMACOM.

McNulty, John A., James Halama, Michael F. Dauzvardis, and Baltazar Espiritu. 2000. "Evaluation of Web-Based Computer-Aided Instruction in a Basic Science Course." *Academic Medicine* 75, no.1 (January): 59–65.

Misic, Mark M., and Kelsey L. Johnson. 1999. "Benchmarking: A Tool for Web Site Evaluation and Improvement." *Internet Research* 9, no.5: 383–392.

O'Hanlon, Nancy. 1999. "Web-Based Tutorials: Does Course Use Differ from General Use?" *Journal of Interactive Learning Research* 10, no.2: 217–228.

Ramey, Judith. 2000. "Guidelines for Web Data Collection: Understanding and Interacting with Your Users." *Technical Communication* 47, no.3: 397–410.

Sheets, Scott. 1998. "Understanding WWW Statistics." *Managing Office Technology* 43: 18–19.

Chapter 7

Focus Groups

Pat Davitt Maughan

The popularity of focus groups is attested to by the number of books and articles written about them, and by the range of settings in which they are applied. Focus groups have been used to study consumer reactions to products ranging from food packaging to soap operas, to assist trial attorneys in jury selection, and to help politicians strategize their campaigns and publicity. They are now also used in higher education, health care, public policy and wildlife conservation settings, and libraries. And yet, their purpose is all too often misunderstood.

Frequently, the term "focus group" is incorrectly applied to group discussions held with the aim of making decisions, "selling" ideas, building consensus, or resolving disagreements. In contrast to these goals, focus groups have a very specific purpose. Their purpose is to *collect data* which, in turn, is analyzed and interpreted by a trained moderator and reported back to a project team or customer group. The data can be used at a later time by the project team to evaluate programs, design products or services, develop models, or assist in decision making. Focus groups are a form of qualitative research whose origins can be traced back more than 50 years to Columbia University's Bureau of Applied Social Research. There, a group of social scientists set about developing a standardized set of protocols for interviewing groups of people and describing the subjective reactions of group members. Since that time, focus groups have enjoyed a growing popularity in the business and public sectors.

CHARACTERISTICS OF FOCUS GROUPS

Focus groups are a form of research that involves listening, guided discussion, and observation as ways of collecting data. They record participants' comments, experiences, and feelings in the participants' *own words*. Their focus is on documenting personal experience, rather than requiring participants to record their experiences or opinions in prescribed response categories as is more commonly done in surveys and questionnaires. Participants are not selected through statistical means such as sampling, and the information collected through focus groups, though potentially very rich, cannot be said to be representative of any larger population. Being a form of qualitative research, focus groups are not intended to provide definitive answers to questions.

Focus groups typically consist of eight to twelve participants who have some knowledge or experience with the topic being discussed and who share certain characteristics. They are composed of homogeneous groups, which have been selected based on specific criteria and the needs of the project. In a university setting, appropriate groupings might be undergraduate students, graduate students, and faculty. For a public library, they may be library users within specified age groups such as children, teenagers, or adults, who have Internet access in their homes and who use the Web to search the library's catalog remotely. Why is homogeneity so important? An important quality of focus groups is they encourage lively interaction and the free flow of ideas among group members. If members sense a difference in status among their fellow group members, this free exchange is unlikely to occur. The interaction among participants frequently leads to the expression of opinions that might not be brought out through other means of qualitative research, such as individual, in-depth interviews or dyads, or through quantitative research, such as surveys or questionnaires. This is the beauty of focus groups!

Unlike an interviewer, the focus group moderator does not work from a list of specific questions. Instead, he or she develops a moderator or discussion guide based on the customer's input and consisting of a sequenced series of approximately ten to twelve, open-ended questions and probes. During the actual focus group, often lasting ninety minutes to two hours, the moderator introduces topics to guide the discussion, actively encourages interaction among the group participants, stimulates group discussion as necessary, and tries wherever possible, to steer clear of participating in the discussion itself. The discussion is always audiotaped to preserve a permanent record. Depending upon the resources and facilities available, it may also be videotaped or observed by the customer from behind a two-way mirror. Lastly, focus group participants are typically compensated in some way for their time.

While quantitative research is more systematic—employing standardized methods which allow libraries to gather data from large numbers of respondents that can be more easily compared, aggregated, and occasionally projected to larger populations—focus groups make a unique contribution to the project development plan. They can add value to the design of Web-based instruction because they allow libraries to experience reality in the same way as the participants—members of their target audience—do. This can prove invaluable when designing learning models that more readily map to library users' ideas, perceptions, feelings, and behaviors. To the extent that libraries believe users are the ultimate arbiters of how good their products and services are, focus groups can help the project team learn valuable lessons from their audience—provided they are willing to listen. Focus groups can also assist in identifying pitfalls, contribute to a framework for the design of the product, and aid in decision making.

STRENGTHS OF FOCUS GROUPS

Mary M. Wagner and Suzanne H. Mahmoodi, in their focus group interview manual for librarians, provide an excellent description of situations where the use of focus group methodology makes sense to employ. These include instances where you want to collect information from people concerning:

- Directions they are moving.
- Needs they feel are unmet.

- Changes they are recognizing in the world around them.
- Insights they have into current situations.
- Trends they see.
- Problems they are encountering or anticipate. (Wagner and Mahmoodi, 1994: 2)

Still other appropriate uses of focus groups include soliciting participants' reactions to product prototypes, identifying strengths and weaknesses of the product, discovering the best ways to describe a particular product or service, and gaining information about the participants' use or avoidance of the product. Focus groups can also be employed to solicit suggestions for improvements to a product, to gain reactions to a product presentation, or to solicit reactions to promotional and advertising materials under development. The use of focus groups to test a product concept can be both a cost-effective and time-saving strategy, allowing researchers to perceive participants' attitudes, needs, and reactions to a concept before investing heavily in product development.

It is always useful to employ focus groups in situations where exploring the participants' attitudes and perceptions is a significant component of the research goal. Conversely, it is inadvisable to employ this method in situations requiring the participants to have a command of the budgetary implications of a product or service decision or in instances that require participants to understand and evaluate competing elements, such as choosing between services. As implied earlier in this chapter, focus groups are inappropriate in situations that require statistical data and are completely unreliable in determining how the target audience *as a whole* might feel about a particular issue under discussion. If this is an important consideration, the choice of a quantitative research method is required.

With this in mind, at what points in your Web-based instruction planning process might it make sense to employ focus groups? Before designing Web-based instruction, it might be advisable to use focus groups to explore what the intended audience feels it needs to know, what the members' unmet needs are, trends they like or dislike in other forms of online instruction, and problems they might anticipate with the general concept of Web-based instruction. A second time in the planning process where focus groups might make sense would be the point at which you want to test audience reactions to a pilot or prototype. A third place where focus groups would make sense is when you have developed a strategy and materials for advertising and promoting the new Web-based instruction product.

PREPARATION FOR DISCUSSIONS

Once you have decided that focus groups will provide valuable and needed data for your research purposes, you will need to accommodate them in your timeline. The success of a focus group relies largely on the quality of the preparation, including sufficient consultation between the project team and moderator, agreement on the goals of the research, development of an adequate discussion guide by the moderator, proper screening of focus group participants, selection of a skilled moderator, arranging for adequate facilities, and advance testing of equipment.

Recruiting Participants

The activities that need to be accommodated within your timeline begin with identifying the characteristics of individuals who are likely to produce the most valuable input for your project. Revisit the analysis of your audience you created in the planning stages. Once you have determined the profile, you will need to prepare a recruitment script or announcement, arrange staff to recruit your participants, and begin your screening and enrollment process. This can be done by telephone, at staffed desks, by e-mail, or by postal mail. One particularly effective method for recruiting participants, either in-person or by telephone, is to employ recruiters who closely resemble the profile of the participants you wish to attract. Many feel it is preferable to actively solicit participants rather than posting flyers and announcements and relying on self-selected volunteers. These volunteers will sometimes possess strongly held opinions about a topic that they wish to communicate and this may interfere with effective group dynamics during the actual focus group.

Questions to consider when screening for participants might include: do participants need to be familiar with the service or product under discussion in order to provide meaningful input? Conversely, would limiting participants to those who actually currently use the product or service on a regular basis eliminate a stream of valuable data—one that could be provided by those who've tried and abandoned it or who presently have no interest in using it? It would be wrong to assume that current users of the service possess the same attitudes, values, and opinions as those who do not. In the case of Web-based library instructional services, it may well be important to hear from those who don't use the service, to identify obstacles and prejudices which have dissuaded them from using it. More random methods of identifying participants, as opposed to issuing a call for volunteers, may ensure a better mix of discussants. As mentioned earlier, the more homogeneous the participant groups, the better. Separating participants into distinct groups by sex, age, education level, or status will likely increase your chances for a lively and successful discussion and ensure the free flow of communication among group members.

Organizing Facilities and Supplies

The room you select should comfortably accommodate from ten to fourteen people (eight to twelve participants plus the moderator and the observer). If possible, the facility where the focus group occurs should be on "neutral" ground. In the case of a Web-based library instruction project, for example, it would be advisable to hold the discussion outside of the library. The chairs need to be arranged around a table in such a way that the participants can easily see one another and the moderator. The audio recording equipment requires central positioning to produce the highest quality recording of participants' comments regardless of where they are seated.

To accurately capture the focus group discussion the finest audiotaping equipment possible must be secured and tested in advance. Allowing more than one speaker to speak at a time, differences in voice volumes, shuffling of papers, the sound of glasses and dishware if refreshments are served, even pencil tapping and ventilation sounds can seriously impair the official record of discussion. Every effort should be made to limit these potential sources of distortion and obfuscation to gain the best possible recorded content. If they are provided, refreshments should be placed on a table off to the side and care should be taken to select foods that are unlikely to create extraneous noise when consumed.

A list of needed supplies will include:

- Tape recorder.
- Microphone.
- Extension cords (both power and microphone).
- Duct tape to secure the cords.
- Blank cassette tapes.
- Backup batteries.
- Pens and notepads.
- Participant name tents.
- Laptop and projector if you intend to demonstrate the online prototype.
- Copies of any printed materials you want the participants to examine.
- Refreshments.
- Compensation for the participants.

At the beginning of each focus group, the observer should audio record the date, time, location, and topic of the focus group, in addition to his or her own name and that of the moderator. This will allow for the testing of the recording equipment and at the same time identify the tape for future listeners.

Also in the interest of completely documenting the process, all field notes, transcripts (if generated), audiotapes, prediscussion questionnaires, and any other materials produced in conjunction with the focus group requires careful labeling and organization for future retrieval.

Developing Discussion Questions

Some moderators opt to work from a general discussion guide, organized around broad topics. This allows them the freedom to compose questions on the spot that are best suited to the individual circumstances of the group. Other moderators are more comfortable working out a set of more defined questions in advance, thus relieving themselves of the burden of having to formulate questions "on the fly" during the focus group discussion. If you are undertaking a focus group for the first time, this latter strategy is recommended. Above all, the development of individual questions for the discussion guide must be determined by your project goals. When the moderator meets with a customer to discuss the project goals, what the customer hopes to learn from or about the participants will naturally lead to the development of questions that can then be adapted for use in the discussion guide.

Normally, more than ten to twelve questions are considered too many for a two-hour focus group. If specificity of response is needed, even fewer questions should be posed. Immediate follow-up with requests for amplification or expansion of ideas and illustrative examples is sometimes needed. There is also the temptation to ask participants for solutions when what is needed is a more detailed examination and better articulation of the problems. When formulating questions, moderators do well to steer clear of the philosophical and abstract, and focus instead on specific, concrete, and open-ended questions.

Focus group questions should always be designed in such a way that they maximize group discussion. There is always the temptation to seek specific answers to questions: Do you like the look and feel of the prototype instruction site? Does it look easy or hard to use? Would you be likely to use this? Posing closed-ended and limiting questions like these will foil your attempts at collecting needed information. Questions that force participants to respond to specific aspects of a topic in a directed or closed-ended manner will result in the loss of spontaneity on the part of participants. You will undoubtedly lose data that may have been uncovered serendipitously had you taken a more open-ended line of questioning.

Examples of Focus Group Questions

Closed-ended: Is this product easy to use?

Open-ended: What features of online instruction do you find easiest to use? Which ones are most frustrating?

Closed-ended: Do you go to the library when you want to learn how to find information?

Open-ended: Think of a situation where you needed to learn how to find information. Where did you go for answers? What attracted you there?

Closed-ended: What are the least important features of this site?

Open-ended: What are some important features of the instructional methods you prefer?

Closed-ended: How often do you use Web-based instruction tools? How easy is it to use them?

Open-ended: Think of a time when you learned something quickly or easily. What were conditions that facilitated your learning?

Nondirective questions, which allow participants latitude in responding, are the preferred approach to take with focus groups. Rather than asking a question that can be answered with a single word, consider beginning your questions with the words *when, where, what* or *how*. Stage your questions in parts, avoiding compound questions in which you ask more than one thing in a single sentence.

After developing your questions, ask yourself:

- Are the questions too long?
- Am I using jargon?
- Am I being too vague?
- Are any questions too theoretical?
- Have I included any compound questions?

Sequencing of Focus Group Questions

It is advisable to order your questions in such a way that you move from the more general questions to the more focused questions as the discussion develops. It's good to begin with a question that everyone in the group will likely be able to answer. Starting with a simpler question—one which doesn't require a great deal of thought to respond to—serves to put the group as ease, especially when it follows on the warm-up introductions described later. Building a knowledge base about the participants from their earlier responses also helps the moderator better understand and interpret the participants' responses to more detailed aspects of the subject later on. An alternate strategy for sequencing questions recommended by Mary Wagner and Susanne Mahmoodi involves ordering questions in a chronology, from present day to future tense (1994). This requires participants to first reflect on their current experiences and only later to project their experiences into the future. At that point, they will be more able to evaluate possible strategies for addressing what they think might happen.

As with surveys or other forms of interviewing and data collection, it is always a good idea to pre-test your questions to see how they work and whether or not they are successful at securing the data you seek.

Organizing the Discussion Guide

The discussion guide can be thought of as consisting of three parts: the introduction, the central questioning, and the wrap-up. Before introducing the first question, the moderator must first set the stage for the discussion, welcoming the group members, handling introductions, giving them an overview of the topic, and orienting them to the ground rules. The first question is typically an "ice breaker," calling for a "round robin" where group members introduce themselves and give a brief reply to a question designed to emphasize what they all have in common. An outline for the welcoming script will include the following elements:

- Introduction of the moderator and observer.
- A statement of why the participants were selected.
- An overview of what will be discussed: The moderator might say, "We'll start with a few things you've encountered in the past with programmed instruction, then we'll ask about your experience with Web-based instruction in particular, finally we'll discuss the obstacles or incentives you see to using Web-based instruction."
- A description of how the data that is being collected will be used.
- Reassurance that there are no right or wrong answers, that a full airing of opinions is what is being sought.
- The ground rules for the discussion: The moderator might say, "Please speak one at a time, since we're recording the discussion," or "Some of you might be quieter than others and I may call on you to make sure your opinions are heard," or "Some participants enjoy talking at length and I may have to ask you to hold back so that we can cover all of the topics being explored," or "We are going to be on a 'first-name basis' today."
- An indication of how long the session will last.
- A statement that participants' identities will remain confidential in any subsequent reports.
- The introduction of the "ice breaker" question.

The next part will consist of the actual questions, discussed earlier. The third part will consist of a wrap-up or summary section. Thomas L. Greenbaum, a leader in the field of focus group methodology, suggests concluding each focus group with a section entitled "Advice to . . . " (2000). The moderator would ask participants to imagine that the project team has requested a minute of their advice about the discussion topic that could direct the team's efforts in the next few days. Advice could include anything, even abandoning the project. The moderator might also invite each participant to offer suggestions to the project team that might make the idea or the project viable in the eyes of the participant. The purpose of this exercise is to elicit from each participant a summary thought about the topic under discussion which represents his or her individual perspective and which he or she thinks might prove to be the most useful to the project team. Greenbaum urges that each discussant be required to write down his or her advice in advance of sharing it. This allows the moderator to solicit the participant's true feelings, unadulterated by what others in the group might say. Each person is then asked to read aloud his or her one minute of advice. The "Advice to . . . " section can also serve as good way to draw the discussion to a close.

ROLES OF THE MODERATOR AND OBSERVER

Many feel a skilled moderator is the linchpin of a successful focus group. It is the moderator who sets the tone for the project and directs all of the planning elements in such a way that the research goals of the project are met. These elements include:

- Working with the customer to determine the desired characteristics of the participants.
- Grouping them into homogeneous sets for the focus groups.
- Arranging for the facility.
- Preparing a written discussion guide.
- Briefing the observer on the discussion guide and how he or she will be interacting with the moderator and with the participants during the focus group.
- Welcoming the participants and making them feel at ease.
- Evaluating the participants, in advance of the session, to determine their placement around the table.
- Introducing the discussion topics and keeping the discussion flowing.
- Noting comments requiring further probing and follow-up.
- Keeping the group on target and moving it from topic to topic.
- Finishing the discussion on time.
- Analyzing the data and preparing the post-session focus group report.

The role of the observer is to assist the moderator wherever needed. The observer has primary responsibility for taking comprehensive notes, setting up the room, testing and operating the tape recorder, securing and laying out the refreshments and supplies, handling any problems with the environment (such as heating, cooling, or outside noise), dealing with unexpected interruptions, and distributing any compensation being offered to the participants. The observer's note taking should be comprehensive in the event the tape recorder malfunctions or the tape is unintelligible for any reason. It is critical that the highest quality microphone and recording equipment be used during the focus group in order to preserve a reliable and easily interpretable record of the discussion.

Typically, the observer does not sit at the discussion table, but instead is positioned somewhere to the side. The observer may be called upon by the moderator to sum up the group's comments at various stages during the discussion or at its conclusion, so that participants have the opportunity to verify that their ideas, behaviors, and feelings have been accurately registered. Along with the moderator, the observer is an active participant in the post-discussion debriefing and analysis.

QUALITIES OF A SUCCESSFUL MODERATOR

Being an effective moderator involves both skill and training, a combination of careful preparation, good group interaction skills, and mental and emotional discipline. Novice moderators often go astray by talking too much, offering their opinions, or feeling they have to defend the product under discussion or the organization itself. Some of these problems can be avoided by selecting moderators who have little or no investment in the product or service under discussion.

An accomplished moderator is someone who can resist the overwhelming temptation to actively join into the discussion; someone who is a careful listener, who can listen to people with incomplete or inaccurate knowledge of the topic and resist the urge to correct them. Effective moderators possess a strong short-term memory; they can easily paraphrase what they have heard, and link earlier comments to those made later on in the discussion. Beyond that, successful moderators are well organized and able to move the discussion along from the general to the specific. They are personable and energetic, and capable of injecting verve and energy into the group. With experience, effective moderators learn to tread a thin line between overly directing the discussion and allowing it to run out of control unchecked. They are people who can "think on their feet," and who—through experience—have learned to recognize the optimal moment in the discussion to introduce those questions which will generate the most relevant data. Successful moderators must be experienced in group dynamics and able to deal with a range of possible challenges, including reticent groups, domineering individuals, participant nervousness, and discussion tangents. Thomas L. Greenbaum provides good tips for dealing with all of these occasional situations and more. (2000)

SETTING THE STAGE FOR DISCUSSION

The moderator's work begins before the discussion ever gets started. As the participants arrive, the moderator and observer greet them individually, engaging them in small talk and creating a warm and welcoming atmosphere. As the small talk continues, and as new participants arrive on the scene, the moderator should be observing the discussants and attempting to determine who among them is likely to be reticent, and who might be more dominant during the focus group discussion. Later on, this will determine the placement of the participants around the table.

In advance of the focus group, the observer should have prepared name "tents" for the moderator and each of the discussants, indicating their first names. Shortly before the focus group is to begin, the moderator will drop the name tents in a seemingly casual arrangement around the table. If well prepared, the moderator will have positioned the name tents of the more reticent participants directly across from the moderator's seat. During the discussion, this will allow the moderator to more easily maintain eye contact with the quieter participants and invoke nonverbal cues to encourage them to speak. Conversely, the more outgoing and potentially dominant group members should be placed to the moderator's side. This will allow the moderator to turn slightly away from them if necessary during the discussion, thereby giving a nonverbal cue to hold back from excessive commentary.

TECHNIQUES FOR MODERATING

A primary responsibility of the moderator is to insure that all of the participants contribute to the discussion. Favored tools in the moderator's toolkit to encourage full participation are the pause, the probe, and the prompt.

The pause is used in several ways. When a moderator allows for a pause after introducing each new question, this creates time for participants to reflect and organize their thoughts before speaking. It takes some getting used to on the part of the moderator and the participants to accustom themselves to this brief period of silence known as "the pause." Once one person has responded, a pause by the moderator will more often than not draw out additional comments and ideas. A consequence, over time, is that the participants will begin to interact with one another, rather than addressing their remarks to the moderator. A pause on the part of the moderator can also signal that she is not yet ready to move on to the next topic, and serve as a means for collecting additional reactions from the group. Moderators must also develop a sense about when best to end the silence. In situations where not all participants have shared on the topic, the moderator might accomplish this by inquiring of the non-participants whether they agree with what has been said or what additional thoughts they might have to add.

Probes are another favorite tool among the moderator's toolkit. The probe is used to encourage more in-depth contributions from participants. Examples of probes include: "Can you give an example of what you mean?" or "Tell me more" or "I'm not sure I fully understand, can you explain that a little further?" Another useful probe involving others in the group might be something like, "Tim, I noticed you raised your eyebrows (. . . or, you were nodding your head, or you shook your head) when Diane was speaking. What was going through your mind?"

Prompts can also be helpful in drawing out additional commentary. For example, by raising his or her eyebrows at the end of a participant's comments, the moderator can offer nonverbal encouragement to that person to amplify what he or she has just said. Another popular prompting technique among moderators is to repeat a significant phrase that the discussant has shared earlier, for example, "You said, 'I don't like to read a lot of text. . . .'" This will usually draw out further amplification on the topic from the participant.

By nonverbal and verbal cues, the moderator may also unwittingly discourage participants from fully expressing their ideas or opinions or encourage them to focus too much on one aspect of the topic. Nonverbal cues, such as eye contact, an open facial expression, smiling or head nodding, should be extended to all participants, each and every time they contribute to the discussion. When used by the moderator, verbal cues like "good" or "great" present threats to focus group effectiveness. Neutral responses such as "um hum" or "thank you" imply neither agreement nor approval.

Occasionally, the presence of dominant members in the group might compromise the goal of a well-balanced discussion in which all participants contribute. Should this happen, the moderator needs to be prepared to intervene in order to maintain the integrity of the process. This can be done nonverbally by turning away from the dominant member while he or she is talking, or by avoiding eye contact with that person when they speak. Another technique involves the moderator inquiring more directly of the rest of the group, or of an individual, "What do you think?"

ANALYZING AND REPORTING RESULTS

At the conclusion of the focus group discussion(s) you will be left with an extensive amount of data. What you decide to do with it will vary, depending upon individual circumstances. At this point, the data resides in several different places: in the moderator's and observer's notes, in notes from the debriefing session(s), in the tape recordings of the discussion, and in any transcriptions of these recordings.

Debriefing

It is standard practice for the moderator and the observer(s) to meet immediately after each focus group to compare thoughts and impressions about the major themes that emerged during the discussion, including any surprises that may have occurred. If the focus group is but one in a series, the moderator and observer might explore how experiences with this particular group were either like, or dissimilar from, the other groups. Their conversation may also reveal areas requiring additional probing later on or new findings that should be explored with subsequent groups if they are scheduled. The debriefing session is also the time to test the quality of the tape recordings and, if necessary, to reconstruct from memory any missing parts of the discussion.

Another area to compare notes on now is the observations made by the moderator or observer about nonverbal communication occurring during the session or any unusual interactions taking place among the members of the group. These sorts of observations, which will be reflected neither in the tape recording nor the transcripts, could prove useful later on when the data is analyzed. Most definitely, the debriefing session is not the place to begin analyzing the data itself. The appropriate time to conduct your analysis is only after all of the groups have ended, and a thorough review of the moderator's and observer's notes, debriefing notes, tape recordings, and transcripts (if they exist) has taken place.

Transcripts

Many practitioners recommend that transcriptions of the tape recordings be prepared if you can afford to do so. Others urge that interpretation of these transcripts be left in the hands of the moderator and thus avoid the temptation on the part of customers to scan the transcripts for quotations that support their previously held beliefs or to jump to conclusions from reading a single transcript. The moderator is in the best position to balance the data reflected in the transcripts with the nonverbal communication which took place during the group as well as with the reactions of other groups to the same topic.

Depending on how formal a report you need to prepare—
and for whom—transcripts may or may not be necessary. If transcripts are prepared, the moderator is responsible for annotat-
ing them with any needed corrections (based on having been
in the room when the comments were made) and for amplify-
ing the text with notes regarding nonverbal communication taking place at the time when the comments were made. This sort
of editing is necessary in order to leave the most complete
record of the focus group discussion as possible and to compensate for any deficiencies arising from audiotaping the discussion.

Data Analysis

The main areas of inquiry and the objectives of the focus group
research will largely determine the organization of your major
findings. Often, these will already be reflected in the focus group
discussion guide, which can serve as a structure for your analysis. As you refer to the moderator's and observer's notes, listen to the tape recordings, and read through the transcriptions,
you will need to carefully note discrete and significant statements as they occur in the tape recordings and in the written
records. Your analysis should be done quickly and as close to
the conclusion of the focus group as possible, when your
memory is still fresh.

Because the discussion is often fast and free-flowing, important and discrete statements may occur anywhere in the transcript and often where you least expect them to be, given the
topic under discussion. For example, a comment about how frequently a participant uses the Internet might occur at the point
in the discussion where participants are talking about their preferred conditions for learning. In these cases, care needs be taken
by the moderator to capture both discrete reactions and place
them under the appropriate "theme" or "finding" within the
analysis document. If not, you will in effect be creating a chro-
nological record of comments as they were made, without applying any form of analysis to what was said. The moderator's
analysis of the focus group data allows comments to be brought
together and grouped by major theme regardless of when they

occurred during the discussion. During this phase of the project, the moderator is looking for recurring patterns and trends and exploring the connections between them. This is not always easy. In some groups, the findings are more or less consistent. In others, serious disagreements can arise among the participants and a single, consistent pattern or trend does not readily emerge. In dealing with this type of situation, whatever conclusions are drawn must be supported by the data. It is advisable to enlist the support of an independent colleague or colleagues to examine the notes and check your interpretation against their own. Another useful device is to check your analysis against the findings of the wrap-up section of the focus groups, where "one minute of advice" was proffered by each of the participants at the conclusion of their groups. Objectivity and balance are key concepts in focus group analysis.

Report

The project team, stakeholders, and research goals of the project will determine whether or not a formal report and presentation of focus group results is warranted or if a verbal report will suffice. They will also dictate the level of detail required in the analysis. A collection of statements following a restatement of each of the questions provides little in the way of analysis. When a written report is required, it will typically include the following elements:

- A description of the research objectives for the project.
- Information about the research methodology employed (such as the number and characteristics of the participants, how they were recruited, the number of groups held, and the location of the groups).
- A summary of the research findings, perhaps including some direct quotations.
- Detailed findings, including more quotations.
- Conclusions.

Depending on the circumstances, some moderators will stop with the summary of research findings. Your findings might legitimately include a description of the extent to which participants agreed or disagreed on a particular topic. It is best, however, to avoid quantification of any of the results. Focus groups are qualitative—not quantitative—research. It may also prove worthwhile to identify those thoughts and perceptions that emerged spontaneously in the discussion versus those which arose only after some prompting from the moderator. Providing relevant quotations to support your findings is also useful to those reading the report.

Finally, a well-organized and clearly labeled archive of focus group research materials should be assembled. The archive would consist of the discussion guide, the moderator and observer notes, debriefing notes, audiotapes, transcripts, final report, and any cost information you have assembled associated with the project such as salaries, room rental fees, equipment, materials, and compensations. This will form the official record of the focus groups, which you or the project team can refer to in the future should additional questions arise about the research.

CONCLUSION

Before you enlist the services of a moderator, recruit participants, arrange for a facility, or develop your question areas, you must first develop a clear understanding of the project team's goals and enumerate the research objectives you hope to achieve. This will permit you to verify that focus groups are in fact the best method of collecting the data you need.

The moderator and project team must agree in advance as to the format of the focus group findings. The moderator's task in preparing his or her analysis is data consolidation, reduction, and interpretation. There is always a temptation for the moderator or project team to selectively consider only those comments that confirm a particular point of view. During the focus group, moderators can avoid overemphasizing the importance of a single point of view by seeking summative advice from each participant. After the focus group, the moderator and observer can schedule a meeting to compare impressions, discuss the most significant participant quotations to be captured, and highpoints of the discussion, as well as comparing the results of the particular focus group with earlier discussions in the series.

Focus groups provide a unique window to understand the target audience: their perceptions, their ideas, their behaviors, and their attitudes. If we are willing to listen, and to listen carefully, focus groups allow librarians to experience the end-user learning process and the world of information they face in the same way that the group participants do. At times, this will serve to confirm what librarians have thought all along about learning and libraries. At other times focus groups can lead to some unexpected outcomes. The ability to listen to audience members expressing themselves, their desires, their likes and dislikes *in their own words* is a valuable result of the focus group process—one that can lead to better planning, better services, and better learning products, given the open nature of this research methodology.

REFERENCES

Greenbaum, Thomas L. 2000. *Moderating Focus Groups: A Practical Guide for Group Facilitation*. Thousand Oaks, CA: Sage Publications.

Wagner, Mary M., and Susanne H. Mahmoodi. 1994. "A Focus Group Interview Manual." New York: American Library Association, Continuing Library Education Network and Exchange Round Table.

Chapter 8

Usability Tests

Jerilyn R. Veldof

A good interface should get out of the way of the learner. In fact, it should be nearly invisible, allowing the learner's complete focus to be directed on the content. If we fail this challenge—if the Web navigation is confusing, labels obscure, framework incomprehensible, and screens dense—we may lose our audience before they begin to learn. Interface usability is, therefore, essential to the development of effective Web-based instruction products.

"Know thy user, for they are not you" is an oft-cited maxim repeated by many usability experts. (Dodge, 2000, Mandel, 2000) You probably know a great deal about your audience either from personal interaction or your research in the planning stages of the project. Despite this, there can still be a wide chasm separating the way librarians think about both research and Web-based instruction and the way students think about those things. In a study conducted during the development of the online tutorial at the University of Minnesota (U of M) we labeled this distinction the "clash of the mental models" (see Figure 8–1).

When we at the U of M designed our Web-based tutorial to fit librarians' mental models, we were unwittingly setting our target audience (lower-division undergraduates) up for failure. One of the keys to designing a usable Web site, then, is gathering information about the target audience and the way that they interact with the site or product.

Figure 8–1. Clash of the Mental Models

LIBRARIANS	STUDENTS
Research is an end.	Research is a means to an end.
Good research is valued.	Good grade is valued.
Research is complicated.	Research is fast and easy.
Research is something to learn how to do.	Research is simply something you do.
Learning is preferred through books and pathfinders.	Learning is preferred through games and interactive simulations.

(Veldof and Beavers, 2001)

USER-CENTERED DESIGN

The degree to which a Web site is usable is in direct proportion to the degree that it is user centered. User-centered design challenges us to create a design that fits the user—not to make the user fit the design. With this approach, we shift from designer-centered questions such as "Does it work for me? Do I like it? Do I find it easy to use?" to user-centered questions such as "Does it work for the learners I'm designing this for? Do they like it? Do they find it easy to use?"

This is a significant shift. Many library Web sites have been developed "behind closed doors" with input only from librarians and technical staff. The results are often text-heavy, jargon-filled sites that require users have prior experience with libraries and online research. Ultimately, these Web sites create barriers between the audience and the content, increasing users' frustration and failure rates.

User-centered design, on the other hand, provides the project team with evidence that their design works before it ever gets released to the public. The best way to ensure a functional design is to involve members of the target audience in the process from the beginning. Users should help define what should be on the site and offer the project team feedback on the effectiveness of the site. Usability methods assist project teams in obtaining this valuable input. The Usability Methods Toolbox (http://jthom.best.vwh.net/usability/) includes the range of usability methods including heuristic evaluations, cognitive walk-throughs, mix-and-match tests, and card sorting. Dickstein and Mills illustrate use of these techniques in a library setting (2000). All of these methods can be useful in a user-centered design process but, ultimately, the usability test is the most telling.

In the simplest terms, a test for usability involves observing a user as he or she navigates through a Web site and taking note of where they run into trouble. These observations allow you to fix problems before the site is released to the public.

Many products that we buy have been usability tested with customers. Large companies, such as Target Corporation and Microsoft, have in-house usability labs while smaller sized companies may hire outside usability experts to conduct testing for them in their own facilities. Computer usability labs have rooms with one-way mirrors and cameras inconspicuously placed to capture keystrokes, screens, and facial reactions. The room behind the one-way mirror might have a video capture board and several monitors so the project team and usability experts can observe. When users are brought in to test a product, no reaction, no move, no comment, goes unrecorded. The result is well-documented analysis and feedback for the project team.

Most likely, however, your library or institution is not blessed with access to such a facility or with the experts to conduct your testing. Because most project teams have limited budgets and restricted timelines, the usability process explained here is stripped down to the most basic, effective elements.

ITERATIVE DESIGN PROCESS

Your Web-based instruction site should be tested with users throughout the entire process—from planning through evaluation. Project teams will often test with users, build parts of the site, test with more users, and rebuild, many times during development.

In the planning stage, the project team might choose to test products similar to the one they are designing. Usability testing of these sites provides the team with an opportunity to learn from the best and avoid the worst. Questions that the project team has about the site architecture, metaphors, interactivity, labels, language, and tone can be addressed during this initial round of testing. At U of M, for example, we initially tested up to nine other Web sites in fifteen-minute rotations. Three tests at a time were held simultaneously in a reserved computer lab. In this way within hours we were able to quickly test how well elements of other Web sites performed before borrowing or adapting these elements in the first draft of our design.

In user-centered design, the initial design is often created and tested through basic paper prototypes, a technique where the project team sketches out designs on paper to test with users. The team may create several versions of paper prototypes that are tested and improved until they reach a level of usability that justifies the time and expense to move the design online. The computer prototype may not be fully functioning initially— perhaps just a graphical design without the programming behind it. During early usability tests, the test moderator may move between the computer interface and a paper prototype for different layers of the site. These tests are usually brief since the team will have few layers of the site developed at this early stage.

Once the team is satisfied that they have a usable prototype and that the basic functionality of the site appears to be effective, they may invest in some programming and interface design. These iterations are again tested with members of the target audience until the team has enough evidence that learners are able to successfully use the site.

ROLES AND RESPONSIBILITIES

There are generally three to four people present at each usability test: a test monitor, a recorder, an observer, and a test participant.

Test Monitor

The test monitor is the person who administers the usability test and may also be the person who writes down the path, or series of clicks, the user takes throughout the test. Usability experts warn that the people creating the product should not do the testing. It is extremely hard to remain objective if one is extricably connected to the product. Test monitors may say rather innocuous things like, "Wasn't that difficult?" and "That looked easy. Was it?" that are in fact leading questions and reflect their own personal biases about the interface. Bias will discredit the test results, potentially turning the entire testing process into wasted time. Recruiting someone not involved in the design to be your test monitor may be the easiest low-cost option to reduce test bias. If that person is also developing a site, you might be able to trade test monitor responsibilities for each other's projects.

If you work in an institution where others are unfamiliar with usability testing, the project team may need to lead the effort themselves. Choose a test monitor on your team who can be most objective and least defensive about the product. Including time at the end of each test for the recorder and the observer to give the test monitor feedback may help reduce obvious testing bias. Jeffrey Rubin's *Handbook of Usability Testing: How to Plan, Design, and Conduct Effective Tests* has an excellent chapter on conducting usability tests. (1994: 213–242)

Recorder

The recorder documents everything the user is saying—verbatim if possible. The verbatim record of the test helps the project team to separate out what they think they heard with what was actually said. Do not rely on memory alone. It is easy to remember only the things that you want to hear, that you expect to hear, or that support your beliefs about the design. After the test, return to the notes to make sure your biases did not overpower the test participant.

Another benefit of the verbatim record is that it provides the project team with the specific language of the test participants. This language may be exactly what you need to improve usability in the next iteration's labels, descriptions, text, and help pages.

Observer

The observer pays close attention to the reactions of the test participant. While the test monitor and the recorder are often busy with their responsibilities, the observer has no other task than listening and watching the participant. Before the test is over, they may notice certain nuances and perhaps even develop possible solutions. At some point, each of the project team members should play this testing role.

One of the greatest benefits for allowing observers into testing is that they often become strong advocates for the usability of the product. Even the most obstinate person is likely to have their assumptions jarred when they witness students struggling and failing with the site design. There is no better way to build support for iterative user-centered design.

Test Participant

Test participants should be people who reflect the demographics and characteristics of the target audience. If your target audience includes freshmen in introductory composition courses, then ensure your test participants are freshmen who haven't yet used the library. If your target audience includes retired senior citizens learning to use the Internet for the first time, find individuals who fit that profile.

Typically, it can take anywhere from five to ten test participants per design iteration to uncover the majority of a site's problems. Jakob Nielsen points out that "As you add more and more users, you learn less and less because you will keep seeing the same things again and again. There is no real need to keep observing the same thing multiple times . . . " (Nielsen, 2000)

Do not "reuse" test participants from iteration to iteration. They will become too familiar with the intent of the product, the navigation, the labeling, and will build expectations for what they are able to do at the site. Recruitment of participants will be discussed below.

PREPARING FOR AND
CONDUCTING USABILITY TESTS

Now that you know who will be involved in testing, let's talk about how to prepare for and conduct the test.

Step 1: Identify tasks to test.
A usability test is made up of tasks that the participant is asked to complete. What is tested is often what gets improved, so it is important to choose tasks wisely. Focus groups and a review of the goals and learning objectives for the site are essential for task identification.

Focus groups should be designed to identify 1) reasons the learner might use the product and 2) goals they might want to accomplish with it. Focus groups might be conducted with several stakeholder groups. For example, an online tutorial might be designed to augment faculty's own instruction on library research, so a focus group of these faculty and their expectations for the product would be very helpful. A focus group with the end user of the tutorial would round out the information gathered from the faculty focus group. Responses and discussion in the focus groups should be recorded verbatim. Often the exact wording for tasks can come from these transcripts.

The project team should also examine the site's goals and learning objectives developed in the planning stages. Why are you designing the site? What do you want your learners to learn? Do the learners' needs and expectations dovetail with the designers' expectations? Based on these responses and focus group data, begin to make a list of the key tasks.

Note that with Web-based learning, tasks change in relation to the way the learner will be using the learning product. For example, the designers of the U of M's information literacy tutorial learned through focus groups that most undergraduates would not take a tutorial voluntarily. The primary audience for the tutorial became, therefore, students who are required by their instructor to complete the tutorial. A relevant task for this audience might be: "You have been assigned to complete Module 3 of the library tutorial, take the quiz at the completion of the module, and send the results to your instructor. How would you go about doing that using this Web site?" This is a "real" user task as opposed to a task that might say, "You're trying to find articles in the library. How might you do that using this site?" since that is not a task that the target learner would be completing in the actual product.

Task questions should be piloted with members of your target audience for clarity. It is easy to write a question that tests something unintended, or to confuse a test participant with an unclear question. Piloting questions also allows the project team to determine approximately how long an actual test will take and to adjust incentives accordingly.

Step 2: Build a post-test questionnaire.
A questionnaire given after the test is completed is sometimes a good way for introverted participants to provide thoughtful feedback in a relaxed manner. It gives the participant time alone without the monitor, recorder, and observers hanging onto every word. The downside to including a post-test questionnaire is that someone has to compile the data and analyze it. Depending on how quickly the iterative design process is going, this could needlessly slow down the group. One way to address this is to add open-ended debriefing type questions to the end of the verbal part of the test such as:

- What did you think about the site?
- What were the best features of this site?
- What would make it easier to use this site?

These kinds of questions may elicit some of the most insightful comments from participants and lead to dramatic design improvements.

Step 3: Choose and train the test monitors.
There are a number of ways that a monitor can ensure that the test goes smoothly, just as there are a number of ways a monitor can sabotage a test. Monitors should be trained in the practice of administering the test and have a chance

to conduct pilot tests. Other team members can provide feedback and guidance to the trainee. Rubin (1994) wrote an excellent guide useful for training test monitors, in which he lists and elaborates on the key characteristics of a good test monitor. Although it is true a monitor can be trained, identifying individuals who may be predisposed to being a successful monitor may help speed the process along.

Characteristics of a good test monitor include:

- Grounding in the basics of usability engineering.
- Quick learner.
- Instant rapport with participants.
- Excellent memory.
- Good listener.
- Comfortable with ambiguity.
- Flexibility.
- Long attention span.
- Empathic "people person."
- "Big picture" thinker.
- Good communicator.
- Good organizer and coordinator. (Rubin, 1994: 67–71)

Step 4: Recruit test participants.
Unless you have administrative staff who can schedule test participants, you might leave recruitment until you are ready to administer the test. Try recruiting participants from areas where they congregate, such as dining halls and study areas in the case of students, or shopping areas and food courts in the case of the public. Setting up a laptop or using the corner of a nearby computer lab may be sufficient. Only recruit users from within the library if current library users are your target learners. Otherwise, push yourself to go where your target audience is—outside the library.

For tests over 10 or 15 minutes, you will most likely need to offer incentives for participation. Students may be motivated to participate with as little as $5 for a 15-minute test, or $10 or $15 for a full hour. A free-lunch voucher, gift certificate, free copy cards, or private one-to-one instruction session after the test might motivate some people (such as faculty). Experiment with incentives and recruiting locations until you find a good formula that matches your audience's interests and needs.

Some institutions will require that the group responsible for testing complete a report outlining the usability test and testing procedures in order to comply with human-subject testing guidelines. You may also be required to have your test participants sign a special waiver developed by an attorney. These requirements will vary by institution.

Step 5: Administer the test.
The test monitor will be the main contact with the participant during the test. He or she should be sitting in such a way that they can easily make eye contact with the participant but also see the computer screen. The recorder should be sitting out of the sight of the participant but still in easy view of the screen. Observers should sit as far away as hearing and viewing permits. All observers and the recorder need to refrain from any comments, sighs, laughs, or gasps during the test (and honestly, this is very difficult to do!).

The monitor should introduce himself or herself, the recorder, and the observers to the participant and work to put that person at ease. Emphasize that this is not a test of the participant's skills or knowledge, rather a way to find out what is working or not working with a Web site that the library is designing. Notice that you do not want to put the participant in the position of criticizing you as a designer, so try to distance yourself a bit from the product.

Participants are then asked to think aloud while completing the test. The think-aloud protocol sounds almost like a stream of consciousness from the participant: "Oh wow, there's a lot to read on this page. I have no idea where to go. Oh, maybe I'll try clicking on this link here or, no, no, I'm going to try this one—I think this is the right one . . . " The monitor might gently interject with, "Why do you think that's the right one?" And the thinking aloud would continue. Whenever the participant lapses into silence the test monitor's job is to draw the person back out. The monitor might ask questions like, "What are you thinking right now? Where are you looking? What are you looking for? What did you think should have been here on this page? Where were you expecting that link to go?" Questions need to be extremely neutral and non-leading.

Step 6: Administer the post-test questionnaire.
Some participants are harder than others to coax into the think-aloud process. Introverts may appreciate some time to mull over questions and provide some feedback without the stress of the actual test. Let participants take the post-test questionnaire in a quiet area where the group is not debriefing.

Step 7: Debrief with the group.
At the end of each test, schedule time for a short debriefing while your thoughts are still fresh. Capture the key observations that you have consensus on and the key changes that you think address the problems. You might review the transcripts from the recorder to address any conflicting recollections. At this point there may be a few obvious problems that you already agree need to be fixed. After all testing in a particular round has been completed, meet again to compare across tests. Are there recurring themes? Are most test participants getting confused in the same places? Does the entire site organization need to be rethought or would it be enough to improve the language and relabel the links? What kinds of pointers can you place around the site in case learners get lost?

Step 8: Make changes.
Depending on how far into the iterative design process you are at this point, you might now be able to sketch out a new design, or if further in the process, you might create a list of specific changes for the Web interface designer or programmer.

Step 9: Start again.
The design team should decide before even starting how they will define success for the site. Initial testing with

other products can help the team define reasonable benchmarks. For example, if testing shows that 60 percent of participants are successful completing a particular task in a similar product, the team might decide to set their target at 80 percent. During each iteration, the team would capture whether or not the participant was able to complete the task on his or her own before giving up. As soon as the target of 80 percent is reached, the team could then focus on other problematic aspects of the site. Alternatively, success is sometimes defined by the time it takes to complete a task. You might set a goal that a task should only take a certain amount of time to complete. If a participant takes that amount of time or less, the site would be deemed successful for that particular task.

Regardless of how you define success, taking the time to define your success measures may pay off in the end. I have yet to see a Web site without usability problems. Even if you undergo a dozen iterations of design and testing, your site will still cause confusion for some learners. But at some point you are going to have to stop testing and redesigning. Having set success measures will allow you to report to the library that you have good indication that "x" percentage of your users will be successful, that this was your goal, and that the product is therefore ready to be released. Case closed . . . until the next redesign.

What drives a whole new redesign cycle? There might be a number of factors that point to a need for a redesign:

- Availability of new technology that would improve the effectiveness of the site.
- Wider use of newer technologies by users, allowing you to upgrade your site.
- Shift in the goals of the project, use of the site, or nature of the target audience.
- Higher expectations from your target audience over time.
- Outdated or old-fashioned design compared to other sites your target audience visits.

CASE STUDY

In the fall of 1998, the U of M conducted usability tests focusing on the online tutorial "QuickStudy: A Library Research Guide." Twelve undergraduates completed a test consisting of eight tasks and four follow-up questions. After the first round of testing it became apparent, particularly from student comments, that the team had designed task questions unrealistic for the target audience. The project team reworked all test questions, redesigning them to reflect how students would use the site. The new task questions were reduced in number, although the time spent on each task was more substantial.

Some questions focused on specific tasks such as:

You're taking a Biology course on environmental management and your final project is to write a ten-page paper. Your professor has asked each of you to come up with a great topic. Practically the whole class is made up of freshmen and you're all unsure about how to create a good paper topic. Your professor tells you to use something called QuickStudy and includes these directions in your syllabus [student is shown the following]:

   a) Go to QuickStudy: Library Research Guide at: http://tutorial.lib.umn.edu.
   b) Choose and complete "Starting your Research"

Now, let's say you're sitting in a computer lab ready to start this assignment. What do you do?

Other questions asked participants to consider the site more generally after they had completed the task questions:

- What are your general thoughts about this tool?
- What did you think about how the site is arranged?
- What are your thoughts on navigating the site?
- Specifics (anything the test monitor wants to follow up on from the test).
- What were the best things about this site?
- What things you would like changed on this site?

- Would you ever use this again? Why or why not?
- Questions from observers.

Undergraduate students completing a project in a usability class conducted a third round of testing of the QuickStudy tutorial. The class first met with the project team in the library to discuss the goals for testing and then devised a test script, arranged and administered testing, and provided a report to the project team. The ability to observe the tests and ask follow-up questions of the participants helped make this experience useful to the project team. Veldof and Beavers offer a more complete discussion of a range of the testing methods used throughout the process. (2001)

User insight and feedback shook up many assumptions about the learners and their use of the site. Comments helped inform nitty-gritty decisions about navigation, labels, tone, content density, page length, and instructional approaches. Examples below reflect some changes made to early design iterations:

- Removed elements of the book metaphor, such as "table of contents."
- Removed a search button that implied the product was a search engine.
- Added formatting such as spacing, bolding, and bullets in recognition that users skim content.
- Repositioned links at the bottom of pages with warnings that they would lead out of the tutorial.
- Added guided exercises for more hands-on learning.
- Added as much interaction and application as programming and time permitted.

Over time the team got closer to a product that students proved was relatively usable. Figure 8–2 shows the homepage of the older version of the tutorial and Figure 8–3 shows the homepage of the redesigned site. Although the project team was aware that other changes could be made to design a more effective learning environment and to improve usability, the team was confident that the redesigned product was reasonably effective and would ensure the site had a shelf life for another two to three years.

Figure 8–2. Initial Version of QuickStudy Tutorial (1997). URL: http://research.lib.umn.edu/tutorialold/

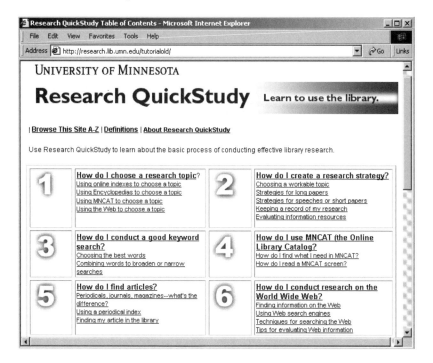

CONCLUSION

Usability testing will uncover just how challenging it is for our users to effectively navigate through our Web sites, including those developed for online education. During testing, you will see users struggle with the most basic tasks, look right over the links they need to choose, and click on other links at inappropriate times. They will express frustration—some will get angry, others teary-eyed.

You, as a designer, now have the tools to reduce that frustration and anger by making your Web-based instruction site as usable as possible. Sometimes just changing the names of some links, moving buttons to a different part of the screen, and removing clutter from your pages, can make a substantial dif-

Figure 8–3. Revised Version of QuickStudy Tutorial (1999). URL: http://tutorial.lib.umn.edu/

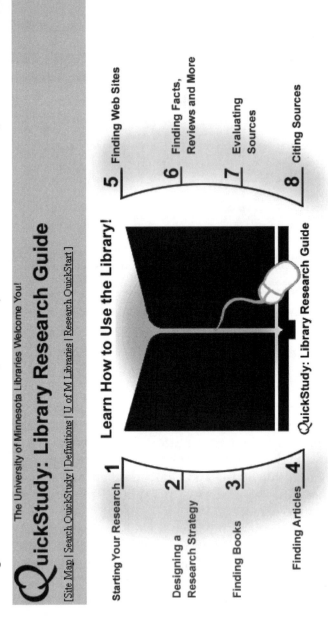

The University of Minnesota Libraries Welcome You!

QuickStudy: Library Research Guide

[Site Map | Search QuickStudy | Definitions | U of M Libraries | Research QuickStart]

Learn How to Use the Library!

1 Starting Your Research

2 Designing a Research Strategy

3 Finding Books

4 Finding Articles

5 Finding Web Sites

6 Finding Facts, Reviews and More

7 Evaluating Sources

8 Citing Sources

QuickStudy: Library Research Guide

[Ask Us! | Contact Us | For Instructors | About QuickStudy] ference. There is so much that can be done to help make the user successful. Even if you can't figure out how to remove a barrier, or how to redirect users to the "right" place on the page, create safety nets where your users tend to stray so that, as far as they know, everything's going smoothly.

If you're still looking for the silver bullet and asking "What is one thing that I should do if I want to make sure my site is easy to use," heed usability consultant Steve Krug's advice. "The answer is simple," he says. It's not, "Nothing important should ever be more than two clicks away," or "Speak the user's language," or even "Be consistent." It's . . . "Don't make me think!" (2000: 11)

Your Web-based instruction product should be so easy to use that your test participants think it's been a waste of their time to be part of testing it. So easy to use that they say to you, "Well, obviously I'd click here." So easy to use that they look at you funny when you ask them at the end of the test what they'd suggest you do differently. You want them to say things like, "Well, maybe you could make this part of the page a lighter color," and not, "It's really confusing. I just don't think I'd use this at all." Users should not have to think about using the interface—they should be thinking about the content. Conducting even just two or three rounds of usability testing could make the difference between a confusing site and an easy-to-use one.

REFERENCES

Dickstein, Ruth, and Victoria A. Mills. 2000. "Usability Testing at the University of Arizona Library: How to Let the Users in on the Design." *Information Technology and Libraries* 19, no.2: 144–151.
Dodge, John. 2000. "Testing, Testing: Firms Look to Science to Design Web Sites." *WSJ.com: The Wall Street Journal* (September 19) Available: http://cob.jmu.edu/williakc/mktg470/dailyupdate/Websites.htm.
Krug, Steve. 2000. *Don't Make Me Think! A Common Sense Approach to Web Usability*. Indianapolis, IN: New Riders Publishing.
Mandel, Theo. 2000. "Usability Myths and Maxims." Available: www.theomandel.com/tm-resources/myths.html.
Nielsen, Jakob. 2000. "Why You Only Need to Test with 5 Users." *useit.com: Jakob Nielsen's Alertbox*. Available: www.useit.com/alertbox/20000319.html.

Rubin, Jeffrey. 1994. *Handbook of Usability Testing: How to Plan, Design, and Conduct Effective Tests.* New York: Wiley.
Veldof, Jerilyn R., and Karen Beavers. 2001. "Going Mental: Tackling Mental Models for the Online Library Tutorial." *Research Strategies* 18, no.1: 3–20.

Chapter 9

Assessment of Learning

Trudi E. Jacobson

The term "assessment" is often used interchangeably with the term "evaluation." However, they do not mean the same thing. "Assessment is defined as the activity of measuring student learning and other human characteristics such as aptitude and motivation whereas evaluation is focused on judging the effectiveness and worth of educational programs and products. In short, we assess people and evaluate things." (Reeves, 2000: 102) Assessment of student learning provides feedback to students about their mastery of course or lesson material, but it is also vital in providing feedback to instructors about the material and the way it is being taught.

Assessment of student learning is critical in Web-based instruction, just as it is in a more traditional teaching and learning environment. Consideration of assessment should not be relegated to the end of the process of designing Web-based library instruction. Choices about student-learning assessment should be considered and decided throughout the planning and development of the instruction.

It is extremely important that assessment measures are aligned with other aspects of the instruction. "Alignment is evident when the articulation among learning objectives, content, instructional design (especially the tasks in which students will be engaged), instructor expertise, technological affordances, and assessment strategies is as clear as possible." (Reeves, 2000: 106) Effective assessment:

- Is integrated into the design of the instruction.
- Is ongoing.
- Uses diverse methods.

As you develop your instruction plan and the assessment mechanism, you will be closely connecting the assessment to your stated goals and objectives. Three questions to keep in mind are, "'What are the essential skills and knowledge I am trying to teach?' 'How can I find out whether students are learning them?' 'How can I help students learn better?'" (Angelo and Cross, 1993: 5) "Assessment, rather than being something added, is an integral, ongoing aspect of teaching and learning." (Rovai, 2000: 142) You may want to develop draft assessment tools as soon as you have identified your goals and objectives, or the essential skills and knowledge you would like students to take away with them. You can fine-tune the tools once the instruction is taking place, but this initial attention to assessment will ensure alignment.

Assessment should not be planned to occur at just one or two fixed points. Assessment, of various types, should be designed to occur throughout the instruction. Informal methods of assessment, used in conjunction with more formal methods, make this feasible. For course-related instruction, ongoing assessment would continue after your instructional session, and would involve students' mastery and use of the material in meeting course goals and objectives.

Ongoing assessment is closely linked to diverse assessment mechanisms. "Sound assessment strategy is not limited to a single measurement, such as a traditional selected-response test, but consists of a system of multiple measurements that include diverse assessment tasks." (Rovai, 2000: 142) The length and nature of the instruction will determine whether you will be developing all the assessment tools, or if you will be doing it through cooperative efforts with others, such as with course instructors.

This chapter will consider assessment concepts and types, compare assessment in online versus traditional environments, address the use of assessment in a variety of library instruction settings, and examine a number of assessment methods that are appropriate for Web-based instruction. It will also highlight the advantages of developing assessment in partnership with others.

ASSESSMENT CONCEPTS AND TYPES

There are gaps, sometimes considerable ones, between what was taught and what has been learned. By the time faculty notice these gaps in knowledge or understanding, it is frequently too late to remedy the problems. To avoid such unhappy surprises, faculty and students need better ways to monitor learning throughout the semester. Specifically, teachers need a continuous flow of accurate information on student learning. (Angelo and Cross, 1993: 3)

Insufficient assessment, or assessment using only one method, will not provide the type and flow of data on student learning recommended by Angelo and Cross. The following types of assessment may be combined to provide a multifaceted picture of student learning. More specific information about the techniques mentioned within the categories below will be found in the Assessment Options section at the end of the chapter.

Formative and Summative Assessment

Assessment can take two forms: formative and summative. Formative assessment "is an ongoing process that can occur at any point throughout the course; it can surface gaps in course material or in learners' ability to grasp that material. Formative evaluation gives instructors a way to shift focus if the course is not proceeding according to plan." (Palloff and Pratt, 1999: 144) Summative assessment is a final, overall assessment. If you are teaching a course, summative assessment provides data for determining a student's grade. "Good summative assessments— tests and other graded evaluations—must be demonstrably reliable, valid, and free of bias. They must take into account student anxiety, cheating, and issues of fairness." (Angelo and Cross, 1993: 5) Frequently, the same technique can be used for either formative or summative assessment, or both. Your objectives for the assessment will be the determining factor. For example, a first submission might receive feedback but no grade, while a second, revised effort might be graded.

Informal Assessment

Informal assessment methods generally take less time than other methods, and allow you to analyze the results more quickly. They allow you to get a snapshot of how your instruction is or is not addressing student needs. Informal assessment in online settings may involve reviews of discussions, responses to instructor's questions, and draft materials.

Cognitive Assessment

Cognitive assessment, along with performance assessment and portfolio assessment, are "three major directions for integrating alternative assessment approaches into online learning environments. . . . 'Cognitive assessment' is focused on measuring students' higher order thinking abilities, attitudes, and communication skills." (Reeves, 2000: 107) Cognitive assessment may take the form of open-ended questions, problem solving, and concept mapping.

Performance Assessment

Performance assessment is a particularly rich method for Web-based instruction. "Unlike traditional tests, performance assessments require that students create an answer or product that demonstrates their knowledge and skills . . . These assessments are frequently authentic and help instructors pay heed to the close alignment that should exist between the intended, taught, and tested outcomes." (Rovai, 2000: 143) The use of rubrics is important in performance assessment. Developing the rubric will also help you to fine-tune your objectives for the assignment and your directions for completing the assignment.

Examples of performance assessments include:

- After teaching students concepts and skills related to database searching, students would select an appropriate database, conduct a search, and select the best items from the results. The search strategy, results, and perhaps even an analysis of the process might be e-mailed to the instructor.
- After teaching students how to evaluate Web sites, assign students the evaluation of one or more Web pages, either of their or your choosing. The Web page (or URL) should be submitted electronically along with the evaluation.

Authentic Assessment

Cognitive and performance assessment, along with some varieties of informal assessment, may be labeled as authentic assessment. "Authentic assessment is geared toward assessment methods which correspond as closely as possible to real world experience. . . . The instructor observes the student in the process of working on something real, provides feedback, monitors the student's use of the feedback and adjusts instruction and evaluation accordingly." (Pickett and Dodge, 2001)

Use of Rubrics

A number of authentic assessment methods diverge significantly from traditional quizzes and exams in regard to grading. Quiz and exam questions generally have correct or incorrect answers, and students' responses will generally be either right or wrong (for selected response questions) or will fall somewhere in between (for essay questions). However, students and instructor will generally have the same expectations that the goal is to answer questions correctly. Assessing students' work using authentic tools may be less clear cut. Consider online discussions. It is important that your expectations be conveyed clearly to students: is it important to contribute frequently? Does the content of a message matter? Should new messages comment on earlier ones? Without clear guidelines, students are uncertain about what is expected, and you may find it difficult to grade or provide feedback on discussion participation.

Rubrics, a formative type of assessment, provide needed guidelines. Rubrics "focus on measuring a stated objective (performance, behavior, or quality), use a range to rate performance, [and] contain specific performance characteristics arranged in levels indicating the degree to which a standard has been met." (Pickett and Dodge, 2001)

Advantages of using rubrics in assessment are that they:

- Allow assessment to be more objective and consistent.
- Focus the teacher to clarify his/her criteria in specific terms.
- Clearly show the student how their work will be evaluated and what is expected.
- Promote student awareness . . . about the criteria to use in assessing peer performance.
- Provide useful feedback regarding the effectiveness of the instruction.
- Provide benchmarks against which to measure and document progress. (Pickett and Dodge, 2001)

Develop rubrics in close conjunction with your goals and objectives for the instruction. Work closely with course instructors, where applicable. It may be helpful to have another librarian read a draft version of your rubric with a copy of your goals and objectives in hand. Examining existing rubrics can be very useful when you are just getting started writing them. (Pickett and Dodge, 2001; Fourie and van Niekerk, 1999; Schrock, 2002)

ASSESSMENT IN ONLINE ENVIRONMENTS

There are elements of assessment that remain stable regardless of the teaching environment. Concepts such as formative and summative assessment apply equally to both settings, though the form they take may differ, or may be surprisingly similar. Call upon your existing knowledge of assessment as you plan for assessment in the online environment, but keep in mind the differences, advantages, and disadvantages inherent in online instruction.

Differences

Web-based instruction offers some inherent challenges, such as not necessarily seeing your students, setting the introductory tone, clarifying each other's expectations, determining students' prior knowledge and skills, and communicating more frequently and at any hour. Other differences include the need for all students to participate (unlike in a traditional classroom, where some may remain mute during some formative assessment activities), and, potentially, the use of more assignments and different methods of submission in online courses than in traditional ones. Some of these differences will have an effect on assessment.

As an example of a difference and its effect on assessment, online instruction often involves the submission of student materials electronically. Particularly when the instruction involves a course that is taught completely or predominantly online, students will expect a quick response to the materials that they submit. However, this expectation also arises when students ask questions via e-mail, whether the questions are about assignments, content of the instruction, or responses to online tutorials.

Web-based instruction may also make use of online learning management systems such as WebCT or Blackboard. These tools provide a variety of features that can be used for assessment purposes, including quiz features, and online discussion and chat mechanisms.

Advantages

The advantages of assessment in the Web-based environment will depend upon the form of instruction in which you are engaged. In general, the advantages center around the ability to conduct numerous, more frequent, small assessments; the absence of fixed-time limits, allowing for increased reflection and reduction of student stress; a quicker return of assignments or other feedback about student-learning; and the ability to log or analyze feedback more easily. Whether your Web-based instruction entails an entire course online, a module or two of course-related instruction, or online tutorials, you will be able to embed assessment. Feedback might come as a result of assignments submitted directly to you, or may be a function of a tutorial or other program students are using. "A major advantage of online learning environments is that assessment activities can be embedded unobtrusively into the interactive structure of the program via interactive multimedia simulations." (Reeves, 2000: 108) You can build in features so students get immediate responses to their answers; timely feedback enhances students' learning of the material.

Another advantage is provided by online discussions. During in-class discussions, not all students participate. Online discussions have the advantage in that all students are generally required to take part, particularly for courses taught entirely online. Even in classes where student participation in online discussions is not mandatory, the contributions that are received help assess student learning and will affect the content and format of subsequent instruction.

Disadvantages

Some disadvantages in online courses include an overwhelming focus on the written word, and an inability to easily adapt to each individual learner's needs. A number of disadvantages of online assessment are connected to summative assessment in online courses, issues connected to proctored testing, identity security, and academic honesty (Rovai, 2000). Quizzes and exams will need to take into account identity issues: is the correct person actually taking the exam? Another potential disadvantage in online courses relates to the difficulty for students to engage in small-group work. (Dereshiwsky, 2001: 18) Meeting in person might not be possible, but e-mail and other electronic venues may be used to advantage in such situations.

Some instructors rely heavily upon observation for the formative assessment of student learning. Observing students' expressions, reactions to material presented in class, and their actual hands-on work in the classroom are informal but effective means of determining how students are doing. If instruction is entirely online, it will require a period of adjustment to become comfortable assessing student learning without the use of these visual clues and through the use of other tools.

Adapting Existing Assessment Tools

When planning assessment of Web-based instruction, you may think that you need to start from scratch, and that little connected to assessment in the more traditional teaching environment can be used. But Housego and Freeman emphasize that "the learning activity, and not the technology or medium in which it is used, is the key to improved outcomes." (2000)

One study of faculty members teaching courses via the Web found that "many if not most of the traditional live classroom assessment procedures can be adapted for use online." (Dereshiwsky, 2001: 24) This finding can be extremely liberating when designing assessment for Web-based instruction. As you begin the process, you should not feel the need to design a new specialized assessment method (and thus have a perfect excuse for procrastinating); instead, you can adapt the methods you have used in the past. For example, in-class discussions can migrate to the electronic setting, and informal "minute papers," in which you ask students to jot down their thoughts on a particular question, can easily be asked electronically. As you continue to gain experience with an assessment method, you can make changes based on what you find works best.

But it is important to be cognizant of the differences that exist between Web-based and traditional instruction, and to be willing to make use of the advantages that Web-based instruction presents. You also need to be aware of the problems that may occur. In addition assessment both in and of Web-based instruction is a nascent field of research, hence there are many unanswered questions. You should evaluate your assessment methods as you proceed with the instruction. Do not hesitate to adapt how you assess, as well as how you teach, based on feedback that you receive.

A later section of this chapter will examine a variety of assessment tools appropriate for Web-based instruction. As you read over the list, you may notice other types of assessment you currently use in a traditional setting that are equally appropriate in an online environment.

SETTINGS FOR WEB-BASED INSTRUCTION

Web-based instruction can take a number of different forms, in which duration and location of instruction may vary widely. Let us examine assessment in various library instruction settings in the context of duration and location.

Online Credit Course

Librarians teaching their own online credit course have the most potential for assessment. They will be able to use a variety of types of measures throughout the course, and will need to plan for both formative and summative assessment. This form of Web-based library instruction is the most dramatically different from more traditional library instruction, and requires the most planning for alignment of assessment with the rest of the course.

Course-related Instruction

Course-related instruction has a variety of permutations. It may occur in the classroom with accompanying Web-based tutorials or assignments, or may be completely Web-based. In general, however, course-related instruction provides less scope for assessment than librarian-taught credit courses. Some course instructors are willing to involve a librarian beyond the library-related instruction itself and any attendant assessment. Aim to work with other instructors to develop assignments that will function as cognitive- or performance-assessment tools.

Web-based Tutorials

In some cases, library instruction will be provided entirely through the use of tutorials. Assessment contained within tutorials may be formative or summative, or a combination of both. Tutorials may be designed so that students need to answer questions correctly before they continue with the tutorial, or may contain a quiz that students can take more than once to improve their scores, learning from responses provided to incorrect answers, a feature of the TILT tutorial (http://tilt.lib.utsystem.edu/).

ASSESSMENT OPTIONS

A number of assessment possibilities work for various types of Web-based instruction. Their appropriateness will naturally depend upon the type of instruction in which you are engaged, but this list may suggest a number of complementary methods for your setting. Remember that effective assessment is integrated into the design of the instruction, is conducted on an ongoing basis, and should employ diverse methods. Many of the options that follow can be used either for formative or summative purposes. A resource list at the end of this chapter provides a number of sources with actual examples of many of the methods listed below.

Selected Response

Selected response assessment tools include those that involve multiple choice, true/false, and matching questions. They are frequently used in quizzes and exams, but may be found in other types of assessment as well. Online tutorials may utilize them to provide immediate feedback to students about their grasp of the material. They are often used in pre- and post-tests, to provide instructors with feedback to gauge student learning and the effectiveness of their teaching. Pre- and post-tests can be used at the beginning and end of a credit course or course-related library instruction; post-tests are often most valuable after the conclusion of a course once students have had the opportunity to apply the material and reflect on what they have learned. Pre- and post-tests have also been used to compare student learning in Web-based and classroom-based formats of the same instruction. (Germain, Jacobson, and Kaczor, 2000; Holman, 2000)

Short Answer/Narrative

Short response assessment tools allow students more leeway in their answers than selected response tools, and can, depending upon the design of the questions, provide you with more evidence of a student's thought processes. Rather than simply measuring Knowledge, as with selected response assessment, you may also be able to measure Comprehension ("distinguish between a database and a search engine"), Application ("relate how the use of the Boolean operator AND would affect the following search"), and Analysis ("differentiate between exact and keyword searches"). (Cross and Steadman, 1996: 137)

Discussion/Reflection

Rovai comments tellingly on the benefits of online discussion as a form of informal assessment: "Its ability to promote text-based communication for the purpose of discourse can support the construction of knowledge, as learners formulate their ideas into words and build on these ideas through responses from others. The opportunity for reflective interaction can be encouraged and supported, which is a feature not often demanded in traditional classroom settings where discussion is often spontaneous and lacks the reflection that is a characteristic of asynchronous online interactions." (2000: 146) He encourages the use of online interactions for both formative and summative purposes, and suggests the use of discussion rubrics. (2000: 147–148)

Questions posed to students electronically outside of class can be an excellent way to follow up on and expand points covered in the instructional session. These questions should encourage reflection and critical thinking, and can be used to check the depth of students' understanding of a topic, and their ability to relate it to other issues or situations to contextualize it.

In instances where tutorials are used in conjunction with other instruction provided either by a librarian or a professor, it is possible to build in reflective questions that students respond to in writing, and which are then discussed in class or electronically.

Review of Students' Work

Too frequently with written assignments, students do not have the opportunity to learn from their instructor's feedback. Review of students' work is a powerful form of formative assessment, and an excellent way to gauge student learning. It is possible to structure written assignments so that there are opportunities for students to submit drafts of their work prior to submitting the finished product. For example, if students need to complete an annotated bibliography, ask that they turn in several citations each week for review. Alternatively, for a traditional paper, set due dates for each component: topic, thesis statement, selected sources, paper draft, and final paper. This will serve as an ongoing method to gauge how students are doing, and will provide critical feedback to students.

Concept Mapping

Concept mapping "is the process of constructing concept maps—of identifying important concepts, arranging these concepts spatially, identifying relationships between those concepts, and labeling the nature of the semantic relationship between those concepts." (Jonassen et al., 1997: 290) Concept mapping can be used before instruction occurs to assess student understanding in order to know how to focus the ensuing instruction. It can also be used after instruction, to learn how students have integrated new with existing knowledge. As an example, you might ask students to draw a concept map of the Internet. Done before instruction about the topic, it would reveal students' mental constructs and help you to determine how to focus your instruction. If you use it after instruction about the Internet, it will help you to gauge the effectiveness of the instruction.

In-class concept mapping can be done with paper and pen after an introduction to the method, but might also use software especially designed for the purpose. Web-based concept-mapping tools also exist. (Reeves, 2000: 107) If you are teaching a full course, it is very illuminating to ask students midway through the course to connect all course topics studied to date using a concept map. This exercise can help you to understand how they see (or do not see) the connections between course topics.

Problems and Cases

Problems and cases that need to be solved encourage students to use higher-order thinking skills, such as Analysis, Synthesis, and Evaluation. "The case method is appropriate whenever the teacher wishes to place emphasis on stimulating new ideas, promoting creativity and independence of thought, encouraging new people to assume leadership roles, and fostering willingness to take risks." (Lynn, 1999: 38) Cases and other problems allow you to assess aspects of student learning and growth that might otherwise be difficult to track. Problems and cases can be assigned either following or as a part of the actual instruction. These methods are extremely adaptable to a variety of topics and types of instruction. Students' responses can help you to determine their ability to use and adapt what has been taught in class to a hypothetical or real-life situation. As an example, Angelynn King has developed a scenario called "City Council Lab," in which students assume the role of town councilors who must "formulate a policy for Internet filtering of the public terminals in the city library." (2001: 267)

Portfolio Assessment

A portfolio is a purposeful collection of student work that exhibits the student's efforts, progress, and achievements in one or more areas. The collection must include student participation in selecting contents, the criteria for selection, the criteria for judging merit, and evidence of student self-reflection. (Paulson, Paulson, and Meyer, 1991: 60)

A portfolio . . . provides a complex and comprehensive view of student performance in context. It is a portfolio when the student is a participant in, rather than the object of, assessment. . . . [I]t provides a forum that encourages students to develop the abilities needed to become independent, self-directed learners. (Paulson, Paulson, and Meyer, 1991: 63)

Portfolios that are used with Web-based instruction may be electronic portfolios, mounted in a learning management system such as WebCT or Blackboard, or paper-based.

Portfolios build upon performance-related assignments, and are similarly useful for library instruction. Full credit courses allow the most scope for the use of portfolios, but other courses using portfolios that include a segment of library instruction would also provide an appropriate venue.

Fourie and van Niekerk provide an in-depth examination of the use of portfolio assessment in a module in Research Information Skills taught at the University of South Africa, a distance education institution. Concepts they found particularly valuable were systematic observation, record of student performance, multiple methods, different contexts, and over time. (Fourie and van Niekerk, 1999:336) These concepts were manifested in features of the portfolio assignment including:

- A selection of sources (from the library catalog, two databases and the Internet).
- A search strategy (including main terms, search terms, etc.).
- An explanation of how the search results were evaluated and how the search strategy was adapted accordingly.
- A personal database with fields that will help the student compile a bibliography and keep track of their sources.
- Twenty-five to fifty records in the database (five of which are also indexed).
- Proof that they have evaluated the database according to set guidelines.
- A bibliography which meets the requirement for their discipline. (Fourie and van Niekerk, 1999: 343)

Fourie and van Niekerk's article provides information not only on use of portfolios in the design of their module, but also examines the value of portfolios and portfolio assessment, uses of criteria (rubrics) for assessment, issues of validity and reliability, student reactions, weaknesses of the method, and advice on the use of performance assessment.

COLLABORATIONS

Assessment is an area in which collaborations are natural and extremely helpful. When you are just beginning to design assessment for Web-based instruction, consider asking for advice from those who are more experienced with assessment of traditional or online instruction, perhaps even partners or stakeholders you have already identified. With time, these initial contacts may grow into collaboration in the true sense of the word.

Possible partners include:

- **Librarians.** For ideas related specifically to library Web-based instruction, poll other librarians on campus, in the region, or even on a wider scope. The ILI-L listserv is an excellent way to reach librarians focused on instruction. Besides looking for advice from other librarians, you might want to pair up with another librarian as you develop assessment tools.
- **Faculty Members and Teachers.** Let other instructors you work with know of your interest in assessing student learning from the library component in the larger context of the entire course. Volunteer to help develop appropriate assessment tools.
- **Centers for Teaching Excellence.** Staff and faculty connected to these centers are a rich source of advice and ideas about many pedagogical issues. They will be able to provide local examples and refer you to someone who might serve as an assessment mentor.
- **Schools of Education.** Like teaching centers, members of a school or department of education on campus or at a nearby institution may be excellent resources for, and possible collaborators in, assessment projects.
- **Students.** In longer-term instructional settings, you can ask students to help design rubrics for authentic assessment projects. Students also may provide essential feedback on assessment tools and advice on revising them.

CONCLUSION

As with assessment of other forms of student learning, the assessment of Web-based instruction needs to be considered in the initial stages of the instructional design process, so that it can be fully integrated into the instruction. It should also be conducted on an ongoing basis, and use a variety of different methods. You may well be able to adapt assessment that you use in more traditional settings to Web-based instruction, keeping in mind the particular characteristics of the precise form of instruction you plan to use. Collaborations with instructors, educational and technology experts and colleagues will smooth the process, and may be invaluable for developing and evaluating initial efforts.

REFERENCES

Angelo, Thomas A., and K. Patricia Cross. 1993. *Classroom Assessment Techniques: A Handbook for College Teachers*. 2nd Edition. San Francisco: Jossey-Bass.

Cross, K. Patricia, and Mimi Harris Steadman. 1996. *Classroom Research: Implementing the Scholarship of Teaching*. San Francisco: Jossey-Bass.

Dereshiwsky, Mary I. 2001. "A is for Assessment: Identifying Online Assessment Practices and Perceptions." *Ed at a Distance* 15, no.1 (January): 16–25. Available: www.usdla.org/html/journal/JAN01_Issue/ED_JAN01.PDF.

Fourie, Ina, and Daleen van Niekerk. 1999. "Using Portfolio Assessment in a Module in Research Information Skills." *Education for Information* 17: 333–352.

Germain, Carol Anne, Trudi E. Jacobson, and Sue A. Kaczor. 2000. "A Comparison of the Effectiveness of Presentation Formats for Instruction: Teaching First-Year Students." *College & Research Libraries* 61, no.1 (January): 65–72.

Holman, Lucy. 2000. "A Comparison of Computer-Assisted Instruction and Classroom Bibliographic Instruction." *Reference & User Services Quarterly* 40, no.1 (Fall): 53–60.

Housego, Simon, and Mark Freeman. 2000. "Case Studies: Integrating the Use of Web Based Learning Systems into Student Learning." *Australian Journal of Educational Technology* 16, no.3: 258–282. Available: www.ascilite.org.au/ajet/ajet16/housego.html.

Jonassen, David. H., et al. 1997. "Concept Mapping as Cognitive Learning and Assessment Tools." *Journal of Interactive Learning Research* 8, no.3/4: 289–308.

King, Angelynn. 2001. "City Council Lab." In *Teaching Information Literacy Concepts: Activities and Frameworks from the Field*, edited by Trudi E. Jacobson and Timothy H. Gatti. Pittsburgh: Library Instruction Publications, 267–268.

Lynn, Laurence E., Jr. 1999. *Teaching & Learning with Cases: A Guidebook.* New York: Chatham House.

Palloff, Rena M., and Keith Pratt. 1999. *Building Learning Communities in Cyberspace: Effective Strategies for the Online Community.* San Francisco: Jossey-Bass.

Paulson, F. Leon, Pearl R. Paulson, and Carol A. Meyer. 1991. "What Makes a Portfolio a Portfolio?" *Educational Leadership* 48, no.5 (February): 60–63.

Pickett, Nancy, and Bernie Dodge. 2001. "Rubrics for Web Lessons." San Diego, CA: Educational Technology Department, San Diego State University. Available: http://webquest.sdsu.edu/rubrics/weblessons.htm.

Reeves, Thomas C. 2000. "Alternative Assessment Approaches for Online Learning Environments in Higher Education." *Journal of Educational Computing Research* 23, no.1: 101–111.

Rovai, Alfred P. 2000. "Online and Traditional Assessments: What Is the Difference?" *The Internet and Higher Education* 3, no.3: 141–151.

Schrock, Kathy. 2002. "Kathy Schrock's Guide for Educators: Assessment & Rubric Information." Discovery.com. Available: http://school.discovery.com/schrockguide/Assess.html.

Part III

Design and Development

Your work in the planning and initial evaluation stages will have prepared you for the design and development of your instruction. Creating a quality Web-based instruction product is not the same as simply placing instructional materials online or creating an informational Web site. Instead, it is more akin to designing a virtual classroom, an environment in which people can learn and develop their skills on a topic. Your final product should weave together elements of graphic design, instructional design, and site design in a seamless package with content that resonates with your target audience and meets your project goals.

There are many ways to approach the project you have outlined, whether by developing a site from scratch, modeling a similar instructional project, or using an off-the-shelf learning management system. Creating a site of your own design allows for much greater flexibility and creativity, but will require you to allot more time to programming and usability testing. As another option, you might seek similar instructional and open source sites on which you might model your own project, though these too will require additional time for adaptation to your needs. Alternately, an off-the-shelf product offers built-in elements such as registration and quizzing, but may be too confining for the project you have in mind or may be of too great an expense. Each possibility has benefits and drawbacks, and your choice will depend on the resources available in your organization and your project goals.

Regardless of the technological approach you choose, it is

difficult to overstate the importance of designing your project for your chosen target audience—understanding their motivation for learning the content, their familiarity with aspects of the topics, their experience with online educational environments and technologies, and their willingness to take an active role in their learning. This knowledge combined with an awareness of the instructional strategies embraced by the teachers and trainers who will be using the instruction, and the objectives of the instruction, will be the defining elements for your final product.

Familiarity with your audience will help you determine how to present your material. Many sites employ an overarching theme or metaphor relevant to their learners. Your choice of theme, terminology, colors, as well as instructional approach must be meaningful to your audience. All learners—regardless of age—benefit from authentic, useful, clear instruction, spurning sites that seem contrived, condescending, and confusing.

A successful learning environment is a supportive learning environment, one that is appropriate for, and in some cases adaptive to, the needs of an individual learner. Ideally, your content would begin at a point identical to where the learner lacks knowledge, include examples relating to their prior experiences and educational interests, be written in language appropriate for their comprehension level, complement a variety of learning styles, and offer additional assistance at the times the learner needs it. While all of these issues may be difficult to address based on your constraints of time and budget, you may find creative ways to offer even basic levels of each. For example, your instruction might offer different paths through the materials— a linear or recommended path for novices, and a flexible path for more advanced learners. You might develop a paper or online pre-test that maps to segments of the instruction, allowing learners to "place" into different sections of the Web-based instruction. To address various interests, you might devise different problems, cases, or examples from which a student can select those most interesting to them. To compensate for the absence of the traditional classroom instructor, you might offer online consulting hours, use a discussion list or chat for students to talk with the instructor or peers, or even learn from focus group discussions where additional descriptions would be helpful.

A number of pedagogical approaches were explored in the planning section and are more fully discussed and applied to the concepts in the opening chapters of this section. This book places a strong emphasis on constructivist approaches to instruction, and learner engagement. To this end, discussions of interactivity and media are not perceived merely as "games" and "entertainment," but as methods for addressing various learning styles and allowing students to actively participate in learning.

Similarly, people expect customization within online educational sites, and this personalization may indeed be the key to designing instruction best suited to an individual learner's cognitive abilities. But the complexity of designing such elements is exponential; not only will the programming require more advanced skills, but the instructional design will require a deeper focus as you design multiple levels of content for the various permutations of learner competencies. These caveats are not meant as a deterrent, just a caution to allocate enough time for development.

Design, development, and evaluation are iterative processes. Chapters in this section cover discrete topics, but in practice you will be drawing pieces from various chapters throughout your development as suits your project goals and plans. Consider initial steps such as:

- Articulate goals and objectives.
- Select the instructional approach.
- Select the general site architecture.
- Organize the content by each component, module, or subsections.
- Create a site flowchart and determine global navigation.
- Test (perhaps with paper prototyping and focus groups).
- Review and revise with project team and partners.

Once the foundation of the instruction is determined, you can focus on creating a prototype or pilot of your full project. Possible steps might include:

- Outline and roughly draft content.
- Develop relevant interactions.
- Write core content and create graphics.
- Review and revise with project team and partners.
- Put all content online.
- Review and revise with project team and partners.
- Test (perhaps with focus groups and/or usability testing).

After the prototype has been developed and tested, you could repeat the steps to develop the remaining components or subsections of your instruction. Though a general development outline is proposed, many elements of the process can be handled concurrently, utilizing team members' time to the fullest. The key will be creating strong communication mechanisms so the final project, developed by a number of people, will stand together as a coordinated and coherent product. As mentioned earlier, it is most useful when the project team consists of members with various perspectives and backgrounds such as subject specialists, instructional designers, Web designers, programmers, artists and graphic designers, and assessment specialists. The act of creating Web-based instruction is highly creative. Your content may be based on materials used in more traditional classes or may be developed uniquely for this project. With so much personal energy and thought contributed to this project, you may wish to investigate ways for the creators to retain some of the intellectual property rights to the materials designed.

With a group of people working on a shared project, it is good practice to develop systems that prevent irrevocable mistakes and document important aspects of the project. Back up all segments of your work regularly and systematically including drafts, initial scans of graphics, original site designs, and program scripts. Doing so will create a safety net in case of a system or human error. Another good practice is to create documentation for standard elements, processes, and decisions. For example, you might create a list of all pages within your site that include scripting, the steps for clearing statistics from the server, or a list of the common fonts and colors you use in various parts of the site. This information will be useful for development and for ongoing maintenance of the site, especially once new staff inherit and continue to sustain the project.

Chapters in this section discuss goals and objectives, interactivity, content organization and development, site design, and putting content online. Each chapter offers a variety of theories and practical insights from which you can determine the best approaches for your project. After successful development of the site, you are ready to go into production, publicize and promote your site within your organization, and, of course, celebrate.

Chapter 10

Goals and Objectives

Craig Gibson

Setting goals and objectives is one of the key steps—indeed, one of the commonplaces—of the instructional design process. Goals and objectives are often referred to as the "blueprint" for any instructional delivery whether through a class, a course, printed materials, or any other media format—as the guideposts, the benchmarks, the intellectual markers, and the indicators of student learning. Without goals and objectives, there can be no instructional plan; without an instructional plan, there can be no instruction and therefore no learning. Such is the classic view of the role of goals and objectives.

The chain of reasoning exhibited here in this classic rationale for goals and objectives is not in itself flawed; but in terms of newer environments for learning, such as Web-based instruction, some implications and modifications of the role of goals and objectives need to be teased out. Pedagogical and andragogical theories, discussed in Chapter 4, offer the framework for designing appropriate goals and objectives for Web-based instruction. Traditional behaviorist training models emphasize the practice of isolated skills, often determined solely by the instructor. Newer constructivist models embrace the use of problem-solving and critical thinking abilities through personalization and active learning, often developed by the instructor in conjunction with the learner. The contrast between Web-based instruction based on constructivist and active learning principles, and older models of programmed instruction, is significant and has implications for the instructional designer preparing goals and objectives for any Web-based learning or training experience.

THE TRADITIONAL VIEW

The classic and almost canonical explanation of educational goals and objectives can be found in the works of Mager (1962, 1988), Gagne (1977), and Bloom (1956).

Behaviorist Approach (Mager)

Mager's almost prescriptive approach for writing objectives is well-known—task analysis for isolating the components of a learning activity, and goal analysis for identifying concrete, visible steps necessary for learners to demonstrate "hidden" mental states, thinking processes, or affective dimensions. His approach still influences instructional design in lesson planning, course design, and even employee performance plans in workplaces. (Mager, 1988)

Mager's use of three terms in writing goals and objectives is crucial to understanding his approach and its impact on teaching and learning practices at all levels of American education:

- "Behavior" "refers to any visible activity displayed by a learner."
- "Terminal behavior" refers to "the behavior you would like your learner to be able to demonstrate at the time your influence over him ends."
- "Criterion" is "a standard or test by which terminal behavior is evaluated."

The behaviorist approach is obvious in the very words Mager uses. From "terminal behavior" we get the concept of "terminal objective" which is a statement identifying the visible behavior the student is expected to show as a result of instruction. From "criterion" we get "criterion-referenced tests" which are still much in vogue in educational circles today. Mager also clearly differentiates between goals (taken to be general, global statements of educational purpose or intent) and objectives (taken to be concrete, measurable statements of student behavior).

Cognitivist Approach (Gagne, Bloom)

Robert Gagne's approach to goals and objectives reveals another educational school of thought at work: that of the information-processing school, which is one of the myriad cognitivist learning theories which became prevalent in the 1960s. Gagne speaks of the "events of learning" and divides all learning into five types of "capability": intellectual skills, cognitive strategies, verbal information, motor skills, and attitudes. (1977) Gagne observes that these five types of capabilities cross disciplinary or subject matter categories and differ in the conditions favorable to their success: these categories can be either *internal* or *external* to the learner. Internal performance may arise from within the learner as a result of prior learning, whereas external performance requires explicit, direct instruction. (1977) Gagne's views on cognitive strategies and attitudes are an expansion of what can be considered "learning" and therefore move beyond the classic behaviorist view of "visible performance"; however, like Mager, Gagne insists that the instructional designer complete a "task description" that details the requirements for planning a learning activity; and like Mager as well, he proceduralizes learning into small, discrete steps, as in a "job task."

Another well-known paradigm for instructional objectives is Bloom's *Taxonomy of Educational Objectives*, which categorizes cognitive behavior into five domains: Knowledge, Comprehension, Application, Synthesis, and Evaluation. (1956) From its initial publication, Bloom's *Taxonomy* has occasioned much discussion and debate among educational theorists and teachers, with general agreement that the *Taxonomy* represents a progression from simplicity to complexity in mental abilities, with the higher levels of the taxonomy building upon and subsuming the more basic ones. Some members of the critical thinking movement, however, argue that Bloom's *Taxonomy* should be thought of as almost recursive, with an interleaving and embedding of mutually reinforcing abilities and skills. Instead of a strictly sequential development from Knowledge to Comprehension and onto the higher levels, they believe that these mental abilities grow in concert with each other through various levels of complexity—and to separate them too artificially into "stages" of development misrepresents the reality of learning. For the instructional designer, the most crucial dimension of the *Taxonomy* may be its overall schema or road map for thinking about mental development and learning—and for designing learning experiences that intermingle the various levels of the taxonomy in a general movement toward higher-order thinking skills.

Behaviorist and Cognitivist Learning Objectives

Both Mager and Gagne identified a crucial element for the instructional designer in writing objectives: the use of *standard, specific, unambiguous verbs* in place of abstract states of knowing. Hence we have Mager's classic list of unacceptable verbs he identifies as vague and open to too many possible interpretations, such as: to know, to understand, to learn. Mager suggests more specific verbs should be used when writing objectives, such as: to write, to recite, to identify. (1962: 11) Like Mager, Gagne supports the use of specific action verbs in writing objectives in order to identify how the student "knows," but adds a behavior that illustrates performance. Mager's insistence on three elements of acceptable objectives—*statement of terminal behavior, definition of conditions under which behavior should occur, and specification of criteria for acceptable performance*—would require that a benchmark of acceptable performance be added.

For example, an imprecise objective might be stated as:

> The student will know the general locations of capitals of European countries.

A more precise objective might be stated as:

> The student identifies the locations of all major European capitals by using a standard world atlas.

With performance conditions, an objective might be stated as:

The student identifies the locations of all major European capitals by using a standard world atlas in less than 15 minutes with no errors.

What is notable about the Mager-Gagne approach to writing goals and objectives is the conflation of classic behaviorist assumptions about learning with some elements of the cognitivist approach to learning. According to Mager, a meaningful statement "is one that succeeds in communicating [the teacher's] intent; the best statement is one that excludes the greatest number of possible alternatives to [that] goal." (1962: 10) Mager and Gagne agree that learning objectives must be *precise*, with learning conditions clearly stated; with *action verbs* that indicate visible or demonstrable activity; and with *student performance specified as an end product*, rather than with any focus on the learning process. Gagne differs from Mager in adding the need for an "executive routine" that controls the entire set of specific skills that students might be expected to learn in any complex activity. An executive control process guides the student to learn concepts in a specified sequence to be successful. (Gagne, 1977: 263) This focus by Gagne on an executive control process is an important harbinger of contemporary concerns about students' abilities to monitor their own activity and their own thinking.

Implications for Web-based Instruction

The classic approach to writing goals and objectives is so well known and widely used that it is not surprising that it has heavily influenced computer-based and Web-based training and instruction in libraries and other educational arenas. After all, a computer-based module is an ideal vehicle through which behaviorist, skill-and-drill approaches to learning or training can be offered. Carefully prepared sequences of learning activities can be planned in linear progressions so that students achieve "mastery" of discrete, specific steps or bits of knowledge before advancing to other parts of the overall activity. So-called programmed instruction, traditionally offered through workbooks and practice sets of questions and answers, can be offered using a variety of software programs. A classic work on programmed instruction in the early 1960s points out the potential for stimulus-response approaches, operant conditioning, and other behaviorist techniques in developing programmed materials, and laments the lack of "devices" to offer such instruction at that time. (Green, 1962: 40–65, 194) Such devices were called "teaching machines" and much time and thought were given to developing the ideal device, one that would save teachers time and administrative costs to cover material—for example, in grading papers and training large numbers of students with limited numbers of teachers. (Fry, 1963: viii)

Changes in learning theory and technology since the early 1960s have presented greater opportunities (and complications) for instructional designers. The shift toward cognitive learning theories beginning in the 1960s, the personal computer revolution of the 1980s and 1990s, and the development of customizable software programs such as HyperCard™ in the 1980s, all provided opportunities for making a more student-centered, student-controlled approach to learning available through these new technologies. Computer-assisted instruction (CAI) was valuable in that it offered the potential to teach large numbers of students the basics of library resources and search strategy, as well as orient students to library policies, procedures, and facilities. Such instructional programming included learning objectives based on the classic Mager model and tests of students' factual recall of information. Less certain was the capability of such an approach to teach critical thinking, problem solving, and self-monitoring or self-regulatory behavior.

Educators and librarians have continued to use the classic behaviorist approach when writing goals and objectives because it has merit in measuring some aspects of learning. Even with the shift toward more flexible software programs and the potential for more variable, customized approaches to learning, the endurance of measurable objectives as a way of identifying carefully sequenced "visible" learning is obvious. This persistence of classic behavioral objectives reflects tradition, in part, but also the staying power of behaviorism itself. Even with the shift to concept-based approaches in library instruction in the 1980s, behaviorist teaching methods continued, and the computer-assisted instruction allied with them focused to a great deal on training in the use of tools and skills and the imparting of facts. Hence computer-assisted instruction of this pre-Web generation marked a *technological advance* in delivery of instruction, but not necessarily *pedagogical innovation* based on evolving conceptions of learning.

The advent of the graphical World Wide Web in the mid 1990s engaged librarians and other educators rapidly with its enormous instructional potential. Not only could the Web be a publishing medium, but it seemed to offer unlimited possibilities because of its distributed nature through global networks, its interactivity, its multimedia capabilities, its linking with diverse information resources, its ease of use, its learner-controlled nature, its option for collaborative learning, and the creation of "virtual cultures." (Khan, 1997: 11–18)

From the practical viewpoint of instructional designers and teaching librarians, what is not clearly understood is how to write goals and objectives that truly capitalize on the possibilities presented in an online environment. Web-based instruction can limit itself to behaviorist training approaches as well as more cognitive approaches if the content or subject matter taught is seen as additive—small pieces of data, information to be memorized and recalled, or skills associated with specific tools to be practiced. The potential of Web-based instruction to develop understanding of underlying concepts as well as problem solving and critical thinking abilities will be missed if the traditional, behaviorist, goal-and-objective setting is the *only* approach to developing educational Web sites or tutorials.

In preparing goals and objectives for Web-based instruction, three considerations must be paramount:

1. **The type of technological "teaching approach" to deliver the instruction**

   How can the instruction promote a "conversational framework" between the content, pedagogical strategies and learner, moving from surface-level "Web page turning" to a more engaging interaction?

2. **The conception of content embodied in the instruction**

   Is the content conceived as a set of skills, resources, and tools? Or is the content developed with a problem-solv-

ing approach focused on information literacy abilities?
3. **The overall instructional design and assessment embed-ded in the instruction**
How can the assessment of the instruction and the learn-ing be integrated into the planning stages of the design of the Web-based instruction?

THE CONSTRUCTIVIST VIEW

Because of the easy alignment of behaviorist training models with classic goals-and-objectives writing, earlier generations of programmed instruction may have shaped and limited our view of what is possible with Web-based library instruction. In some cases we make decisions about instructional design without con-sidering fundamental questions about educational technologies themselves. Enriching Web-based instruction by moving beyond rote skill development into critical thinking abilities and prob-lem-solving scenarios is possible through development of goals and objectives based on a more integrated, holistic approach to instruction through technology in general.

Diana Laurillard's theory moves us toward a more constructivist approach to goals and objectives. She offers librar-ians wishing to look deeper at the possibilities of Web-based in-struction some "first principles." Laurillard says that all learn-ing must occur within a "conversational framework," involv-ing a "dialogue between teacher and student" in order to culti-vate more fundamental levels of understanding in students. (1993: 94, 104) She believes learning objectives must be *precise*, with agreement that students can readily achieve the objective; *necessary*, to ensure the teaching goal can be realized; and *com-plete*, addressing the entire content defined in the teaching goal. (1993: 184)

While these characteristics look similar to those of classic be-havioral objectives, Laurillard links the process of setting goals and objectives to a design template for teaching that involves a more interactive and iterative process between teacher and stu-dent:

1. Describe teacher's conception
Detail the concepts, facts, skills, and processes that students are to learn.

2. Elicit students' conceptions
Conduct needs analysis of student knowledge, accomplished through pre-tests, interviews, and examinations.

3. Preempt teacher's redescription of conception
Select alternative ways of describing topics for students, based on feedback about misconceptions gathered from the previous step.

4. Elicit students' redescription
Have students compare their conceptions of the topics with those of the teacher, and reflect on those comparisons.

5. Define form of interaction: task goal, student actions, and feedback
Identify instructional experiences, options for remediating misunderstandings, and possibilities for using continued dialogue with the instructor to assist students in modifying their actions to achieve the task goals. (Laurillard, 1993: 195–196)

Thus Laurillard's "conversational framework" is embedded into the entire instructional design process, particularly in the preliminary dialogue between teachers and students about understandings and misunderstandings of new content. Learning objectives, for Laurillard, retain the qualities of the behaviorists—precision, exhibition of visible behavior, and completeness—but they are not static, they evolve. There is a constant process of adaptation of goals and objectives for any learning experience, and the teacher must guide this process of adaptation and modification. There is also, for Laurillard, a striving for integrated student understandings—her critique of Gagne's emphasis of analyzing learning tasks into myriad component elements shows that a shortcoming of traditional behavioral objectives has been their isolated, context-free nature. In Laurillard's constructivist approach, setting goals and objectives is a dynamic process, arising from a unique interaction between a specific teacher and a specific group of students, in a unique place. This is very removed from programmed learning envisioned with the use of "teaching machines" and much traditional computer-based instruction.

Laurillard offers us a blueprint for constructivist instructional design, with a goals-and-objectives process embedded in a conversational framework among teachers and students. Selection of an appropriate educational technology will therefore depend on our overall teaching goals for Web-based instruction, and we will be required to think about how we can select instructional experiences—simulations, microworlds, tutorial exercises, Web-based conferencing, paper-and-pencil reflections, or student journals—to facilitate student understandings. Objectives will still be written to be measurable, but they will be subject to revision and modification as part of the ongoing dialogue between teacher and students, and among students. The most obvious example of the use of goals and objectives in this manner for Web-based instruction is usability testing, but usability testing adapted to the fundamental concepts of a prototype and not focusing just on more superficial "interactive" features of the Web tutorial.

Constructivist Learning Objectives

In keeping with Laurillard's first step in her teaching design template, we as instruction librarians and instructional designers must reflect on what it is we're teaching. What are the concepts, principles, facts, skills, and strategies students will be expected to know and do? How will these elements be combined into a coherent Web-based instructional package?

One of the most crucial contemporary challenges for instruction librarians is focusing on information literacy as the "content" for instruction, as opposed to more traditional types of library instruction. The latter—all too often—has focused only or primarily on specific tools and resources, institution-specific information, and orientation; some conceptual information may be included but it is not presented in such a way to create flexible reasoning, sound problem-solving, self-reflective or self-assessment opportunities for students to negotiate the very complex, information-intense environment in which they live. Information literacy, on the other hand, is a dynamic, evolving set of abilities students must acquire to move across multiple databases, information resources, information providers, experts, interest groups, think tanks, community organizations, and political groups. This set of abilities—the ability to be fluent and highly adaptable in the midst of uncertainty and rapid change in the information environment—also calls for an ability, like Gagne's "executive control" process, to arrange and sequence the steps in a process. However, this ability goes beyond sequencing in that, to become information literate, students must reflect on their own understandings and misunderstandings, and self-correct.

Continual adaptability and self-correction are the guiding abilities that oversee or govern all the other information literacy abilities enumerated in the *Information Literacy Competency Standards for Higher Education* written by an ACRL Task Force (2000). These *Standards* reflect contemporary thinking about curriculum development by using such terminology as "standards," "performance indicators," and "learning outcomes." This hierarchy of these *Standards* is very different from the carefully structured hierarchies of learning tasks envisioned by Mager and other behaviorists; instead of a carefully ordered, prescribed series of steps, the *Standards* are a curricular template, a planning document from which learning objectives or "outcomes" can be derived. In the taxonomy of this document:

- Each "standard" sets a programmatic goal.
- Each "performance indicator" specifies a specific piece of content that students should learn.
- Each "outcome" gives a specific method by which students can demonstrate the knowledge or skill.

Thus we have this hierarchy:

Standard Two. The information literate student accesses needed information effectively and efficiently.

Performance Indicator Two. The information literate student constructs and implements effectively designed search strategies.

Outcome Five. Implements the search strategy in various information retrieval systems using different user interfaces and search engines, with different command languages, protocols, and search parameters.

(Information Literacy Competency Standards for Higher Education, 2000)

These standards and learning outcomes can be used to write measurable learning objectives, just as with the classic Magerian pattern, if the instructional designer specifies "conditions" under which the learning will occur and arranges them in a carefully ordered sequence for a "one-shot" class, a course unit, or a Web tutorial.

However, the *Standards* also lend themselves to a very different approach for developing instruction because the "content" they describe is information literacy abilities and understandings, rather than discrete skills to be taught in isolation from other kinds of content and unconnected with a specific discipline, course, campus environment, or other contextual surrounding. The *Standards* also speak to "executive control" abilities that students should develop—a set of abilities that cause them to question, self-assess, and self-correct during the entirety of their research process. For example, each standard has a number of performance indicators, and each performance indicator has a number of learning outcomes. A complete list of learning outcomes for the performance indicator mentioned above includes the following:

Learning Outcomes:

1. Develops a research plan appropriate to the investigative method.
2. Identifies keywords, synonyms, and related terms for the information needed.
3. Selects controlled vocabulary specific to the discipline or information retrieval source.
4. Constructs a search strategy using appropriate commands for the information retrieval system selected (e.g., Boolean operators, truncation, and proximity for search engines; internal organizers such as indexes for books).

5. Implements the search strategy in various information-retrieval systems using different user interfaces and search engines, with different command languages, protocols, and search parameters.
6. Implements the search using investigative protocols appropriate to the discipline.
   (*Information Literacy Competency Standards for Higher Education*, 2000)

The self-correcting or metacognitive strategies explicit in these outcomes, and implicit in many of the other learning outcomes listed in the *Standards*, call for a different approach to writing learning objectives—one that focuses on a dynamic, adaptive goals-and-objectives process, as suggested by Laurillard. Learning objectives, recast in the language of "learning outcomes," become an opportunity for both teacher and student to learn together through modification of assignments and student self-assessments. Thus Learning Outcome 5 above can undergo iterations as the situation warrants—as the instructional designer and instruction librarian together determine that students need more work in developing more sophisticated search strategies. Examples of iterative, expanded learning outcomes in this case might be:

5. Implements the search strategy in various information retrieval systems using different user interfaces and search engines, with different command languages, protocols, and search parameters
   a. Compares search results with expected results on a worksheet.
   b. Explains differences between search results and expected results to a peer.
   c. Resolves discrepancies under guidance of teacher, librarian, or peer.
   d. Writes criteria in research journal log for determining omissions or gaps in future search results.

Elements of constructivist learning outcomes are present in this example: a process of discovery or personalization for students; an adaptive "scaffolding" process by which the students come to know what is missing in the search strategy through the coaching of peers and instructors; and an explicit assignment in which students create their own understanding of "standards" for judging whether search results are acceptable. Unless learning objectives and outcomes address this level of understanding, internalization, and expertise in the student, they will perpetuate a lower level of skill and ability development. Hence learning objectives must be generative—they should point toward specific assignments, self-reflections, and "teachable moments" for students to gain control over their own learning. Without such generative, adaptive-learning outcomes, higher-order goals (such as those of information literacy programming) will continue only with traditional behaviorist learning objectives and lose opportunities for developing deeper learning in students.

GOALS AND OBJECTIVES AS PART OF THE INSTRUCTIONAL DESIGN PROCESS

Because library research and information literacy requires deeper learning, involving flexible reasoning, critical thinking, and adaptive strategies for negotiating the complexities and uncertainties of the current information environment, an instructional design approach that focuses on "essential understandings" is crucial.

The Backward Design Model (Wiggins and McTighe)

The well-known Backward Design Model of Wiggins and McTighe offers the best contemporary example of a constructivist approach to planning learning. The Backward Design template identifies six "facets of understanding": explanation, interpretation, application, perspective, empathy, and self-knowledge. (Wiggins and McTighe, 1998: 69) These elements are ideally suited for anyone attempting to become more fluent with information resources and information abilities, because such understandings necessarily involve an iterative process of deepening, more explicit metacognition over time.

What is worthy of understanding?
In this model, the instructional designer begins by considering the final outcome, "In other words, what are the fundamental concepts, strategies, and skills?" (Wiggins and McTighe, 1998: 18) Answers might be found by identifying elements which are core to a field or discipline, perhaps as outlined by professional organizations or experts within the organization. You might begin with a document such as the *ACRL Information Literacy Competency Standards* or the *AASL Information Power Standards*, but will almost certainly adapt, modify, or change them for local requirements.

What is evidence of understanding?
At the second stage, the instructional designer or librarian is called upon to identify criteria for student performances or activities that measure or assess understanding. Such criteria for designing an instructional unit can be thought of as "filters" that separate out genuine understanding in students from superficial or "verbalized understanding." Some criteria for evidence of understanding can include: "Valid. Reliable. Sufficient. Authentic Work. Feasible. Student friendly." (Wiggins and McTighe, 1998: 99) Such criteria need to be addressed explicitly in thinking through assignments or student self-assessments integrated with learning outcomes for information literacy; if assessment is not addressed at this stage of planning, any method of testing, evaluation, or assessment added on later will not likely measure the "understandings" envisioned as part of this design process. Learning outcomes must specify, insofar as possible, what the criteria are for demonstrating understanding or ability, and the acceptable evidence to meet those criteria.

What learning experiences and teaching promote understanding, interest, and excellence?
In the third stage, Wiggins and McTighe place the selection of learning experiences and teaching strategies—only after much work has been done in identifying the "core knowledge" or essential understandings of a discipline,

and in identifying what constitutes firm evidence of that knowledge or understanding on the part of students. Rather than the traditional skill-and-drill approach of traditional behaviorist lessons, Wiggins and McTighe place a high value on integrated understandings possible through alternative curriculum designs. For example, they focus on natural unfolding of content through such vehicles as narratives and stories, applications and scenarios, and even the spiral curriculum wherein topics or "essential understandings" are built into a course or tutorial in a circular, deepening matter. (Wiggins and McTighe, 1998: 134–156) Instructional designers and instructional librarians can take this stage of Backward Design to new levels with Web tutorials through story structures, case studies, unifying characters, real-life applications, and other means of embodying the content in engaging student interest.

Learning outcomes written for understanding, interest, and excellence will focus on those experiences that increase students' abilities cumulatively and gradually; return to concepts and abilities in different modules of a unit on deeper levels; and address the affective dimension of learning through presentation of material and engagement of student interest at a level appropriate to their interest and familiar to their concerns.

Implications for Web-based Instruction

This overview of goals and objectives has taken us from the traditional goals-and-objectives writing process of the behaviorists to the contemporary practices of constructivist teachers. Both approaches look for acceptable evidence or visible behavior that students are indeed learning. The major differences address what constructivists call "understandings" that students achieve through performances enabled and scaffolded by instructors as coaches and guides. Instead of moving through a prescribed set of skills requiring testing of recall and basic application, in the constructivist model students must have some ability to personalize learning by selecting goals appropriate for them. Additionally, assessment is built into the process on the front end, rather than as an afterthought, through pre-instruction in which students and instructors identify misconceptions early to prepare a customized set of learning objectives, assignments designed for the particular situation, and accompanying criteria for proof of learning.

Web-based instruction offers many opportunities for customization, personalization, narrative structures, alternative story options, simulations with database searching, immersive environments, conversations in real time with peers or teachers, and reflective experiences through journal writing. Writing learning objectives for online environments requires a great deal of adaptability combined with a focus on "essential understandings" that students are to develop.

Drawing from Laurillard and Wiggins and McTighe, a design process for this constructivist approach might resemble the following pattern:

1. *Identify the "core knowledge and abilities"*—the essential understandings—by consulting the *ACRL Information Literacy Competency Standards for Higher Education* or appropriate curricular planning materials from states and local institutions. Core knowledge and abilities might be organized by broad standards with more descriptive performance indicators for each as developed through local expertise and experience.

2. *Develop prototype set of goals and learning objectives* and try out these on the target audience through interviews, quizzes, pre-tests, and other methods, to learn about student misconceptions.

3. *Modify goals and objectives* (some omitted, some added or rewritten) as a result of "pre-instruction" process, which revealed the target audience's accurate knowledge and misconceptions.

4. *Identify methods of assessment* to determine evidence of student understanding and specify criteria for determining that such understanding has been achieved.

5. *Develop learning experiences* designed to provide students opportunities to achieve understandings identified in Step Three. Learning objectives are explicitly articulated or identified for students.

6. *Gather ongoing feedback through a "conversational framework" between learner-and-instructor, learner-and-learner, or learner-and-instruction* to evaluate the successes or challenges of the learning experience.
7. *Modify or adapt learning objectives to particular learning needs of students throughout the process.*
8. *Require student reflection, student self-monitoring, and student self-awareness within the learning objectives.*

CONCLUSION

In sum, learning objectives for Web-based instruction retain the classic measurable quality of the behaviorists, but they are linked to a design process that envisions learning environments that are iterative, personalized, and scaffolded. Learning objectives for Web-based instruction also are written to achieve an *experience*, a set of integrated abilities that are possible only through simulations, applications, scenarios, and practice, when combined with reflection. The reflective element is the most crucial component in advancing information literacy through Web-based instruction.

Our initial metaphor of goals and objectives as a "blueprint" may be entirely too static. With constructivist learning principles and a Web-based environment, we should think of goals and objectives as a "playbook" or repertoire of guiding plans for flexibly offered, dynamic, and evolving instructional experiences. For football players, a playbook offers strategies for action in unpredictable situations during a game. Athletes and learners alike must have access to a guiding plan, a template with a repertoire of possibilities. The successful person will adapt the strategies from that guiding plan to meet his or her needs. Students who are most successful at learning will use a varied repertoire for gaining and practicing information literacy abilities, adding and possibly developing their own playbook as they progress through their education.

REFERENCES

Bloom, Benjamin. 1956. *Taxonomy of Educational Objectives: The Classification of Educational Goals*. New York: David McKay.

Fry, Edward. 1963. *Teaching Machines and Programmed Instruction: An Introduction*. New York: McGraw-Hill.

Gagne, Robert M. 1977. *The Conditions of Learning*. New York: Holt, Rinehart, and Winston.

Green, Edward J. 1962. *The Learning Process and Programmed Instruction*. New York: Holt, Rinehart, and Winston.

Information Literacy Competency Standards for Higher Education. 2000. Chicago: Association of College and Research Libraries. Available: www.ala.org/ Content/NavigationMenu/ACRL/Standards_and_Guidelines/ standards.pdf.

Khan, Badrul H., ed. 1997. *Web-Based Instruction*. Englewood Cliffs, NJ: Educational Technology Publications.

Laurillard, Diana. 1993. *Rethinking University Teaching: A Framework for Effective Use of Educational Technology*. London: Routledge.

Mager, Robert. 1962. *Preparing Instructional Objectives*. Belmont, CA: Fearon.

Mager, Robert. 1988. *Making Instruction Work*. Belmont, CA: David S. Lake.

Wiggins, Grant, and Jay McTighe. 1998. *Understanding by Design*. Alexandria, VA: Association for Supervision and Curriculum Development.

Chapter 11

Interactivity

Susan Sharpless Smith

A significant factor in the design and development of Web-based instruction is deciding how best to integrate interactivity. Research has found that interaction is important for learner satisfaction and for the persistence of distance students. (Baker, 1997: 107–115) Research has also determined that students are more receptive to, and successful in, an environment that incorporates active learning. Active learning requires a learner to become a participant in their education, rather than simply a recipient of one-way delivery of information, by encouraging each individual to imbue information with personal meaning. In online instruction, the key to ensuring an active learning environment is through the incorporation of interactivity. Whether a course is being delivered strictly online, or has a Web-based component that supplements a traditional face-to-face class, integrating interaction via the Web can be an effective way to foster a setting that encourages self-directed study, communication, and collaboration.

In the context of Web-based instruction, interactivity is often defined as a dialog between a human and a computer program (the program responds to input by the human) or, in a broader interpretation, an exchange between two or more humans via a computer program. With the advent of the Web, interaction first became identified with the hyperlink, which allowed users to choose their own direction in navigating or exploring the information being presented. As the capabilities of the Web have evolved, however, hypertext can only be viewed as offering the most rudimentary type of interaction. To experience real interactivity, learners must be able to provide input, explore, make decisions, and receive feedback with the goal of deepening their understanding.

THEORIES AND MODELS THAT PROMOTE INTERACTIVITY

Many educational theories and models discuss the necessity of interactivity. Although they vary slightly in design or emphasis, all stress the importance of active learning and student engagement, and can be designed for online learning environments. Becoming familiar with a range of theories and strategies will assist you in developing instruction appropriate for your audience and learning objectives.

Authentic Learning

The term "authentic" is used loosely in educational literature and often means different things in various contexts. Authentic learning activities usually include portfolios, exhibitions, and performances. Shaffer and Resnick attempted to tie the various interpretations of the term into an umbrella characterization that they call "thick" authenticity. (1999: 195–199) They examined educational literature and identified four kinds of authentic learning, each of which is interdependent on the others:

- **Learning that is personally meaningful to the learner (personal authenticity)**
  Students' personal interests are a main determinant of an activity's worth.
- **Learning that relates to the world outside of school (real-world authenticity)**
  Students participate in solving problems or creating products that have real-life purposes.
- **Learning that provides an opportunity to think in the modes of a particular discipline (disciplinary authenticity)**

Students solve problems by using tools and methods established for a particular academic discipline, such as mathematics, science, or history.
- **Learning where the means of assessment reflect the learning process (authentic assessment)**
Students learn from assessment incorporated as an iterative part of the instruction.

Shaffer and Resnick believe that thick authenticity provides a useful framework for thinking about how to make effective use of computers to support learning. They provide examples of how three aspects of computational media—connectivity, modeling, and representational pluralism—can support the four different authenticities. (1999: 204–209)

Problem-Based and Project-Based Learning

Problem-based learning promotes active learning by using "real-world" problems as a context for students to develop critical thinking, practice problem-solving skills, and acquire knowledge of essential course concepts. Problem-based learning originated in the late 1960s at McMaster University as a method to change traditional medical education. Until then, the early stage of medical school involved students being exposed to large quantities of information, much of which had no real meaning to them at that point. Educators found that the students did not become excited about their medical education until residency training, when they were working with patients, trying to solve their problems. A decision was made to structure learning, from the beginning, around a series of medical problems presented to small groups with the faculty acting as guides. (Evensen and Hmelo, 2000: vii) Although problem-based learning is still identified with medical education, other disciplines are also finding it to be a useful approach.

In a problem-based learning program, groups are presented with a problem—often in a case-study format. As a group, learners organize their ideas and reflect on their prior knowledge as it relates to the given problem. As the discussion unfolds, they pose and record questions, called "learning points," on aspects

of the problem that they do not understand; thus they are recording both what they do and do not know. The learning
points are ranked and are assigned to individuals or to the
group as a whole. They also discuss what resources might be
appropriate to find the answers to the learning points. After researching aspects of the problem, the group reconvenes to explore the learning points, share what was learned, and integrate
this new knowledge into the context of the assignment.

Project-based learning offers a similar methodology, making learning more relevant to students by engaging them in authentic real-world tasks. Students are given or choose open-
ended projects that have more than one answer or approach,
and which can result in such outcomes as a finished product,
plan, or prototype. Project-based learning typically begins with
an end product in mind, the production of which requires specific content knowledge or skills and typically raises one or more
problems which students must solve. Through group work over
an extended period of time, students complete the project and
develop their collaborative skills. This method mirrors authentic real-world production activities that utilize students' ideas
and approaches to accomplish the tasks at hand. (Esch, 2000)

Both of these methods are instructional strategies that are
designed to engage students in real-world learning. They are
both student-centered approaches that utilize the instructor as
a facilitator or coach. Both foster cooperation and collaboration
through the use of groups.

Engagement Theory

Engagement theory, developed by Greg Kearsley and Ben
Shneiderman, incorporates elements of the previous models discussed but differs in that it relies on the belief that technology
can facilitate reaching these goals over other methods. With engaged learning "all student activities involve active cognitive
processes such as creating, problem-solving, reasoning, decision-
making, and evaluation." (1999) Three requirements for successful engaged learning include:

- Activities occur in a collaborative context.

- Activities are project-based.
- Activities emphasize learning outside the classroom.

Kearsley and Shneiderman emphasize that engagement theory differs from older models of computer-based learning that focused on individualized instruction and interactivity. It does encourage interactivity, but in the form of human interaction in the context of group activities rather than individual interaction with a computer program.

Experiential Learning

Carl R. Rogers' theory of learning focuses on the idea that learning is applied knowledge that addresses the needs and wants of the learner. Significant learning takes place to solve a problem or engage in a task meaningful to the student. Learning is initiated and controlled by the learner and thus is longer lasting and faster because it is taking place in a low-risk environment. The main qualities of experiential learning are: personal involvement, self-initiated, evaluated by learner, and pervasive effects on the learner. (Campbell, 1999; Kearsley, 2003)

Situated Learning

This theory, originated by Jean Lave, argues that learning that occurs is a function of the activity, context, and culture in which it occurs. Social interaction is a critical part of situated learning as learners become involved in a community of practice that embodies certain behaviors and beliefs. The learning that takes place is a gradual acquisition of knowledge as novices learn from experts in the context of everyday activities. This theory has been further developed by others to emphasize the idea of cognitive apprenticeship (Campbell, 1999; Kearsley, 2003), "a method designed to enculturate students into authentic practices through activity and social interaction, and based on the successful and traditional apprenticeship model." (Brown, Collins, and Duguid, 1989: 37) McLellan summarizes the key components of the situated learning model as: apprenticeship, collaboration, reflection, coaching, multiple practice, and articulation of learning skills. (1994: 7) Many of the researchers and teachers exploring the situated learning model have acknowledged that the computer can provide an alternative to the real-life setting, and can be used without forfeiting the authentic context (Herrington and Oliver, 1995: 3).

Social Development Theory

The basis of L. S. Vygotsky's social development theory is that social interaction is essential in the development of cognition. He believed that the range of skill that can be developed either through adult guidance or peer collaboration exceeds what can be attained alone. (Campbell, 1999; Kearsley, 2003)

Some common themes recur in these theories and will be important as you consider how to best use interactivity. These include the beliefs that: learning is enhanced through collaborative interaction with others, learning opportunities should be based on realistic tasks and environments, instructors should take the role of facilitator or coach, self-directed learning adds a sense of control to students, and activities work best when they have personal meaning for the student.

FRAMEWORKS FOR INTERACTIVE ACTIVITIES

In the previous section, various educational theories and models whose tenets invite the use of interactivity in an online environment were highlighted. These present a body of generalizations and principles that can provide broad ideas for interactive potential. However, in order to assemble the concepts into a structured, workable plan, a framework for interactive activities should be established. A few of the models discussed included frameworks, for example, Kearsley and Shneiderman's engagement theory is described by the authors as a framework for technology-based teaching and learning. In this section, you will be introduced to a few frameworks that can illustrate possibilities for the type that may work best for your instructional design. You will note that, while these frameworks specify a structure, they typically stop short of requiring any specific interactive technology. Once you have established the framework, the next step (addressed in the following sections) will be to determine specific types of interactions that are appropriate to your learning objectives.

Paulsen's framework of pedagogical computer-mediated communication techniques is helpful in categorizing the types of interactions that can be effective in different online settings. (2001) In this framework, Paulsen distinguishes four classes of techniques that use communication interactions to accomplish teaching objectives. One-alone techniques are characterized by retrieval of information from online resources and can be accomplished without communication with the instructor or other students. One-on-one techniques include those that can be accomplished via e-mail. One-to-many normally utilize bulletin boards or distribution lists to deliver information or lectures. Many-to-many might use discussion forums, conferencing software, or similar technologies to accomplish activities such as group discussion or collaboration.

Another framework comes from a model developed by Schank and Cleary that they call teaching architectures (1995). This architecture was developed with the goal of computer implementation of the model:

Incidental Learning

Much of what students need to learn can be boring. This model is based on the creation of tasks whose end results are appealing and which can be used to convey dull information. When an outcome is based on students memorizing facts, this model is appropriate.

Simulation-based Learning by Doing

As much as possible, new skills are best learned by doing. Working through the task helps prepare students to perform it in a real situation and so provides important practice for them. The nature of simulations requires participation by the student. This architecture would be used when subject matter is experiential.

Learning by Reflection

This strategy is used when the goal is to have students generate questions about what they are studying or working on. This model would help them to articulate the circumstances and create ways to move forward. This method is useful when self-assessment is expected.

Case-based Teaching

Many students learn best when they receive the information just in time to meet their needs. This model is used when students find they need further answers to progress and when the knowledge is presented by experts in the form of stories or case studies. It is a good approach when students are expected to learn from failure.

Learning by Exploring

When students become involved in what they are doing, they generate questions. This model answers questions as the student generates them and does it in a conversational format. This method can be used when the learner is put in the role of apprentice or the task is one where students enter another world or environment and are encouraged to explore it.

CATEGORIES OF INTERACTION

Each of the educational theories and frameworks presented can guide you toward selecting appropriate types of interactions to incorporate in your Web-based instruction. Some are synchronous (same time, different place) while others are asynchronous (different time, different place). It is useful to categorize these interactions according to the purposes they serve. Five major types of interaction that occur on the Web have been identified by Kathy Rutkowski (see below). (Smith, 2001: 136–140)

Social Interactions

The presence of social interaction is key to several of the educational theories and models presented. Social interactions include all of the various models of human-to-human communication that take place online, such as learner-to-learner, learner-to-instructor, learner-to-group, or instructor-to-group. In a Web-based environment, the importance of social interactions cannot be underestimated. There is always the fear that a student will feel isolated in an online situation where he or she has no person to approach. This type of interaction is the one used to exchange ideas, hold discussions, collaborate, and ask questions.

Information-Transfer Interactions

Information transfer encompasses all of the ways that data, information, and knowledge are shared. Transfer can occur with a one-way delivery of information or a two-way exchange of data between group members. This type of interaction may take the form of an online lecture, development of a project between learners, and feedback or evaluations from learners to instructors.

Remote-Access Interactions

The Web can be used to connect students to remote sites where they can interact with other systems. The interactions that occur in this category are those where a remote computer responds to input from a human; in return the human reacts to the response given by the computer. On the Web, learners might connect to a periodical database or library catalog to do research.

Knowledge-Building Interactions

Extending the focus of social interactions, knowledge building uses various approaches to address higher-level learning activities such as critical thinking. In the process of deepening their level of understanding, an individual might interact with a computer program, other group members, the instructor, or another subject expert. Knowledge-building activities can include such things as brainstorming, collaborations, debates, and group projects.

Virtual-Experience Interactions

Introducing a virtual experience interaction can be appropriate when you want a student to experience reality from a different perspective or simulate a real environment where the student can learn by doing. Elementary experiences can be created through a synchronous meeting, such as an online space where a study group schedules to meet at a certain time. More extensive virtual experiences can be designed via Virtual Reality Modeling Language (VRML). VRML allows for the construction of simulated, real, or imagined environments where the user is able to "walk" through a three-dimensional space, which may also provide real-time motion, sound, and possibly tactile or other forms of feedback.

The categories of interactions you choose to incorporate will depend on your project goals, audience, learning objectives, and the instructional design of your content.

TECHNOLOGIES FOR INTERACTIVITY

Once you have determined the types of interactions most appropriate for your instruction, the next step is selecting which technology will best accomplish your goals. When making that selection, it is important to assess the technical expertise of members of the project team, and select technologies that can be easily developed and maintained.

Communication and Collaboration Tools

Online communication is especially important for developing social interactions. Some common tools are packaged as part of learning management systems, while others are available as stand-alone applications from various vendors. The major types of communication technologies we will consider are e-mail, discussion forums, chat, and conferencing software.

E-mail
E-mail, an asynchronous technology, has become a common and convenient method for one-on-one communication. Using it as a tool for online interaction presents few obstacles even for learners who may be less experienced with the more advanced tools listed below. If members of your target audience do not have an e-mail address, they

can subscribe for a free account from a number of online services.

Discussion Forums

To facilitate information transfer, collaboration, idea sharing, knowledge building, and social interaction, consider a discussion forum. A forum can be set up for small groups or an entire class. After setting up a forum in a learning management system, such as Blackboard, one person establishes a discussion topic and, as others respond to a posting about that topic, a discussion thread is created. Discussion forums can be created through other groupware applications as well. A discussion forum is another asynchronous method of communication and, as such, may be a valuable way to allow students time for reflection before contributing responses. Examples of activities that could be used in a discussion forum are:

Electronic seminars
Students discuss topics, readings, or other assignments.

Debates
Two or more students are assigned to take different sides of an issue. Once their contributions are made, discussion is opened to input from others.

Case studies
The instructor poses a real-world problem or process, perhaps offering background information. Students discuss and contribute to aspects of the case.

Brainstorming
Students generate ideas about a topic or problem and then the instructor or another student creates a synthesis of ideas.

Delphi techniques
The instructor shares a document or idea, seeking input from all individuals, and progressively creating a consensus view.

Project groups
Students are grouped into teams to work on one or more projects. (Goodyear, 2001: 113–117)

Chat
A chat program provides a synchronous mode of communication where two or more people are simultaneously connected online and exchange text that is transmitted to the other person's computer screen instantly. This may be a good tool to use for real-time group communication, especially for younger target audiences (who seem to use it more than cellphones) and groups not located in close geographical proximity. Chat can also be useful for instructors offering virtual consulting or office hours. Another way chat can be used is modeled by the Wake Forest University's Physician Assistants program, which has an exclusively problem-based curriculum. Students are assigned to groups each semester and as they research learning points from their homes each evening, they maintain connection with other group members through a chat program. As they discover useful resources or have questions, they can share them immediately.

Conferencing
This synchronous method of communication is typically more sophisticated than a simple chat program. Often audio and video functionality is included in a conferencing application, which offers a richer range of experience for people with different learning styles. There may also be other tools to aid collaboration such as a whiteboard, shared control of applications between computers, and file transfer to a shared server.

Forms

Forms consist of a combination of an HTML interface accompanied by an underlying scripting that performs an action to handle the data input into the form. Forms can be used to gather and transmit information submitted on the form, as is the case with feedback, questionnaires and surveys, self-assessments, tests, and evaluations. Alternately, they can be used as a way to provide an interactive learning experience that takes place when a form is programmed to produce a simulation of a computer program for guided exercise purposes.

Interactive Animations

Some animation software applications, such as Flash and Shockwave, are capable of being programmed to offer an interactive experience to the student. Although they tend to be quite complicated to develop, when done well, these can go far in giving students an engaging learning experience. This type of software can be used to build simulations or to create activities that help teach concepts and critical thinking skills. It is becoming more common to find simulations that can be run over the Internet that are designed for group interactions. These allow everyone to see the model run and track the consequences of change. It is important to map out each piece of a planned interaction. A storyboard of the sequence the interaction will take depending on the input from the student is invaluable in making sure that you have considered all possibilities.

Connectivity to Live Resources and Systems

Providing connections to Web resources and databases can be a successful way to guide students in their quest to discover answers and solutions. By searching a live database, as opposed to a sample database, students will gain a more meaningful experience interacting with the size, structure, and complexity of the system. When developing this type of interaction, design your instruction in a way that the students do not get lost or disoriented, mistakenly leaving the instructional environment completely. Examples of resources and systems that can be valuable are online databases, library catalogs, online journal sites, and discussion lists.

Simulations and Modeling

Simulations and modeling represent real world environments, objects, or phenomenon. Modeling most often refers to three-dimensional objects. Development is accomplished with mathematical formulas written to represent the object on a computer. Simulations and models can be very complex to create and require behind-the-scenes programming to deduce the consequences of actions taken by students. If you have the expertise to develop and maintain them, these interactions can be valuable tools for providing students with a method to learn by doing in a controlled, nonthreatening way. Simulations are used in many fields such as medicine and aviation to teach vital skills.

QUESTIONS TO ASK

What skills do you want learners to develop through an interaction?

Interactivity should be integral to the instructional design of your site. It is important to revisit the learning objectives for your project. Some forms of interaction will be smaller segments within the larger context of a Web-based project; other forms will in fact become the entire construct of the site.

From a behaviorist approach, Bloom's *Taxonomy of Educational Objectives* (presented in Chapter 4 and Chapter 10) can provide a framework to distinguish between cognitive skills, which are categorized in six ascending levels: Knowledge, Comprehension, Application, Analysis, Synthesis, and Evaluation. If your aim is for students to be able to reach solutions to real problems, you will want to plan a much different task than if you want students to learn basic facts. Dupuis provides an illustration of using this framework in her Web presentation of interactions in TILT (Texas Information Literacy Tutorial), which teaches fundamental research skills to undergraduates. Bloom's hierarchy was used to move the tutorial in a linear format with increasingly complex concepts. Each concept includes an interaction that was designed to support one of Bloom's cognitive domains. (Dupuis, 1999)

From a constructivist approach, you might consider developing your Web-based instruction project around problem-based or project-based learning. Because the constructivist approach emphasizes the creation of new knowledge, these serve as good examples. In both, an inquiry model is used: students are presented with a problem or project. They begin by organizing previous knowledge, proceed by posing additional questions, identifying areas that require more knowledge, devise a plan to acquire that knowledge, do the necessary research, and reconvene to share and summarize the knowledge.

How will learners be accessing the interaction and what equipment will they use?

As you are planning interactions, consider what you know about your target audience and how they will be accessing your Web-based instruction. If designing a course that will be delivered at a distance, keep in mind that most of the students may not be accessing the instruction using a high-bandwidth connection. If the interaction requires a plug-in to view, consider whether the students have the necessary plug-in already installed, or the skills to be able to download it. What kind of hardware and software are the students using? Does their computer have enough RAM to play an interaction? Do they have the version of Web browser that is needed to view the interaction? If you have a diverse student group, consider offering a "low-tech" version along with the high-tech one.

It is worth noting that when planning interactive activities part of the process must include how to make these interactions accessible to those with disabilities. (Opitz, 2002) The inclusion of multimedia items such as interactive animations deserves special planning. If students cannot participate in a planned interactive activity because of a disability, their learning experience is being shortchanged. Part of the design process must include an alternative method that will allow all students to participate fully. Often, the solution is as simple as providing alternative text, captions, and auditory descriptions. As accessibility issues have become better recognized as barriers to Web content, many software companies have started to address how to make their technologies accessible to all. For example, the latest version of Flash now includes an accessibility panel so authors can include text equivalents that can be read by screen readers. Address the accessibility of your interactions during the planning stage, so it can be built into your interaction from the beginning rather than trying to deal with its inclusion after the fact.

Which interactions are suited for what they will be learning?

When you have determined the objectives you want to support with interaction, it is time to plan which interactions are suited for what you want your students to be doing. This can be best accomplished by matching your desired learning objectives and technological expectations with appropriate categories of interactions. Review the main components of the theory you are modeling and identify which categories support those components. For example, social interaction is specified as an important part of problem-based learning, engagement theory, situated learning, and the social development theory. Look at the technologies that can be used to accomplish social interactions, such as e-mail or chat, and select the one that matches a particular interaction activity goal.

How can you create the guidance and support needed for learning?

Having chosen the appropriate type of interaction, you will need to consider what instructional and functional design elements are needed to encourage productive contributions and to guide the direction and pace of the interchange. Some considerations include:

- How will you set the stage to welcome students?
- How will you establish a sense of group?
- How will you motivate students to participate?
- How will you model appropriate interaction behavior?
- How will contributions be assessed?
- What can students expect in the way of support and guid-

ance if technologically naïve or if an online learning environment is new to them? (Goodyear, 2001: 128–131)

These questions are very fundamental ones that should be considered from the very start of planning the interactions for your instruction. By anticipating the answers to them early in the development process you will help ensure that your interactive activities will be engaging and meaningful. The answers will become part of the instructional design's organization and development, which will be discussed in Chapter 12.

CONCLUSION

This chapter has endeavored to highlight some of the important issues to consider in designing interactive components for online instruction. We have identified educational theories and models that offer potential for interactivity, offered ideas for developing frameworks for selecting appropriate interactions, documented different categories of interactivity, presented methods to implement interactivity into Web-based instruction, and have offered some questions that should be asked when planning interactions. Incorporating interactive components into online instruction is a task that requires careful thought and planning. When executed successfully, interactivity will guarantee a sound active learning experience.

REFERENCES

Baker, Molly H. 1997. "Distance Teaching with Interactive Television: Strategies That Promote Interaction with Remote-site Students." In *Encyclopedia of Distance Education Research in Iowa*, 2nd Edition, edited by Nancy J. Maushak, Michael R. Simonson, and Kristen Egeland Wright, 107–115. Ames, IA: Technology Research and Evaluation Group, College of Education, Iowa State University.

Brown, John Seely, Allan Collins, and Paul Duguid. 1989. "Situated Cognition and the Culture of Learning." *Educational Researcher* 18, no.1 (January-February): 32–42.

Campbell, Katy. 1999. "The Web: Design for Active Learning." Alberta, Canada: Academic Technologies for Learning. Available: www.atl.ualberta.ca/articles/idesign/activel.cfm.

Dupuis, Elizabeth. 1999. "Designing Interactive Instructional Environments."

Berkeley, CA: The Library, University of California-Berkeley. Available: http://library.berkeley.edu/~edupuis/Interact/.

Esch, Camille. 2000. "Project-Based and Problem-Based: The Same or Different?" San Mateo, CA: The Challenge 2000 Multimedia Project. Available: http://pblmm.k12.ca.us/PBLGuide/PBL&PBL.htm.

Evensen, Dorothy H., and Cindy E. Hmelo. 2000. *Problem-Based Learning: A Research Perspective on Learning Interactions*. Mahwah, NJ: Lawrence Erlbaum.

Goodyear, Peter. 2001. "Effective Networked Learning in Higher Education: Notes and Guidelines." Lancaster, UK: Centre for Studies in Advanced Learning Technology, Lancaster University. Available: http://csalt.lancs.ac.uk/jisc/Advice.htm.

Herrington, Jan, and Ron Oliver. 1995. "Critical Characteristics of Situated Learning: Implications for the Instructional Design of Multimedia." Melbourne, Australia: Australian Society for Computers in Learning in Tertiary Education. Available: www.ascilite.org.au/conferences/melbourne95/smtu/papers/herrington.pdf.

Kearsley, Greg. 2003. "Explorations in Learning & Instruction: The Theory into Practice (TIP) Database." Available: http://tip.psychology.org.

Kearsley, Greg, and Ben Shneiderman. 1999. "Engagement Theory: A Framework for Technology-Based Teaching and Learning." Available: http://home.sprynet.com/~gkearsley/engage.htm.

McLellan, Hilary. 1994. "Situated Learning: Continuing the Conversation." Educational Technology 34, no.8: 7–8.

Opitz, Christine. 2002. "Online Course Accessibility: A Call for Responsibility and Necessity." *Educational Technology Review* 10, no.1 (June). Norfolk, VA: Association for the Advancement of Computing in Education. Available: www.aace.org/pubs/etr/issue2/optiz-x1.cfm.

Paulsen, Morten Flate. 2001. "The Online Report on Pedagogical Techniques for Computer-Mediated Communication." Chicago, IL: Berge Collins Associates. Available: http://www.emoderators.com/moderators/cmcped.html.

Schank, Roger, and Chip Cleary. 1995. "The Five Teaching Architectures." Chicago, IL: Engines for Education, Institute for the Learning Sciences. Available www.engines4ed.org/hyperbook/nodes/NODE-36-pg.html.

Shaffer, David W., and Mitchel Resnick. 1999. "Thick Authenticity: New Media and Authentic Learning." *Journal of Interactive Learning Research* 10, no.2: 195–215.

Smith, Susan Sharpless. 2001. *Web-Based Instruction: A Guide for Libraries*. Chicago, IL: American Library Association.

Chapter 12

Content Organization and Development

Sarah McDaniel

Content organization and development—the process of translating your planning documents into instructional materials that meet your goals for student learning—is the key to a successful project. Transforming insights about what learners should know, into instructional sequences that make learning happen, requires careful planning. The goal of instructional design is to manage a complex, iterative process in order to produce the best possible content for your project.

As you move instruction to the online environment, recall what you already know about sound instructional practice from traditional instruction. Dewald outlines the following characteristics, stating that good library instruction:

- Is course related.
- Incorporates active learning.
- Incorporates collaborative learning.
- Is delivered through more than one medium.
- Has clearly articulated educational objectives.
- Teaches concepts (not merely mechanics).
- Includes the option of following up with the librarian. (1999: 27–29)

Dewald examined online tutorials for evidence of these characteristics, and drew the conclusion that to maximize the potential of new technologies in instruction, the characteristics of good traditional instruction must be transferred to new environments. Chickering and Ehrmann drew parallel conclusions about undergraduate education: while research on learning in online environments is still being developed, we should rely on what we already know about instruction rather than discarding it in the rush to embrace new instructional technologies. (1996)

In this chapter, you will learn about methods of instructional design grounded in the best practices of traditional instruction and transferable to new online learning environments. By following these methods, you will create content pitched to meet your project goals and be able to measure the effectiveness of your content in fostering student learning.

TRADITIONAL INSTRUCTIONAL DESIGN

In *Principles of Instructional Design*, Gagne, Briggs, and Wager define instruction as "a set of events that affect learners in such a way that learning is facilitated." (1992: 3) Instruction is not just information we deliver through lecture or documentation, but all the events that learners encounter in a particular environment. The authors suggest an instructional design process consisting of the following clearly defined steps:

- Conduct needs assessment.
- Articulate and classify a hierarchy of learning objectives.
- Sequence instruction.
- Articulate performance objectives for each section.
- Plan delivery of instruction.
- Design assessment.
- Review. (1992: 15–16)

This approach, grounded in behaviorism, describes a process for creating instructional materials and environments that allow learners to meet clear and measurable learning outcomes. A systematic approach is useful in a complex enterprise such as developing a Web-based instruction project because the validity and soundness of each step can be confirmed through feedback collected during subsequent steps.

CONSTRUCTIVIST APPROACHES
TO INSTRUCTIONAL DESIGN

The preface to *Constructivism: Theory Perspectives and Practice* situates constructivism as a theory of knowledge and learning that suggests an approach to teaching "that gives learners the opportunity for concrete, contextually meaningful experience through which they can search for patterns, raise their own questions, and construct their own models, concepts and strategies." (Fosnot, 1996: ix)

Constructivist theories have had significant influence on instructional design. In practice, the development of goals and objectives for student learning remains central, but the process of writing objectives is more iterative, includes learner input, and emphasizes broader "understandings" over isolated skills. By moving away from a focus on discrete, sequential skills, constructivism can emphasize the development of complex, integrated abilities and "understandings" and foster independent thinking. A constructivist instructional design model could proceed as follows:

- Identify core knowledge and abilities.
- Develop prototype set of goals and learning objectives to try with audience.
- Modify goals and objectives as a result of "pre-instruction" process.
- Identify assessment methods and criteria to determine evidence of student understanding.
- Develop learning experiences.
- Gather ongoing feedback.
- Modify or adapt learning objectives to particular learning needs of students.
- Require student reflection and self-monitoring within the learning objectives.

Instructional design is a complex and iterative enterprise that should be informed by theories of learning and instruction and guided by instructional design methodologies that fit your project goals and philosophy. While "the specific combination of procedures often varies from one instructional design model to the next, most of the models include the analysis of instructional problems, and the design, development, implementation and evaluation of instructional procedures and materials intended to solve those problems." (Reiser, 2001: 60) The context and audience of your project will determine whether a traditional, constructivist, or combined approach is most appropriate. This chapter will outline the following procedures that are shared by most instructional design models:

- Needs assessment and pre-instruction.
- Refinement and sequencing of learning objectives.
- Selection and development of delivery of instruction or learning experience.
- Ongoing assessment or feedback.
- Reflection and review.

NEEDS ASSESSMENT AND PRE-INSTRUCTION

Previous chapters of this book have discussed critical elements that must be considered before you begin developing content. The information you have gathered will shape the product in important ways. Ideally, this needs assessment will include some type of pre-instruction where members of the target audience—through surveys, pre-tests, focus groups, or other methods—will influence what concepts are included in the final product. Review the planning documents and design decisions you have made so far to confirm that you are able to address the following questions:

- What is the purpose and scope of your project?
- Will the instruction have complementary segments online or in person?
- How much time will learners spend on your site, and how much can you cover in that time period?
- What are the demographics and interests of your audience?
- How would you describe the tone and style of your site?
- What metaphor or theme, if any, have you chosen for the site?
- What are the educational needs of your audience?

- What is the level of technological competence of your audience?
- What technologies are available to your audience and project?
- What categories of interactivity meet the needs of your instruction?
- What navigation and design elements are important for your project?

Clarity of purpose, voice, and design will assure your instructional project has coherence and usefulness for your users. As you consider purpose and scope, articulate relationships between your project and related classes or instructional modules. This review will help eliminate redundancy and bring focus to connections within the content. Based on how much time learners will spend on your site, decide how much you can cover in each lesson or module.

Review your educational technology selections to be sure these choices support your decisions about the instructional model, teaching goals, and level of interactivity. The completed site design, discussed in the next chapter, constitutes the shell that makes the instruction navigable by users. This shell will be filled out with the content you develop during the instructional design process.

Develop a governing metaphor or theme to organize the tutorial conceptually for users and provide coherence in examples provided. The metaphor or theme must be one that resonates with your audience and fits well with your content. University of Wisconsin, Madison's CLUE tutorial uses as its governing metaphor four hypothetical undergraduates who are unsuccessful doing research because they lack the skills and strategies covered in the tutorial. In a library session that follows completion of CLUE, students assist these hypothetical peers, applying skills they learned. While other metaphors seemed contrived to the project designers, this straightforward theme fits into the adopted instructional model, addresses the real-life complexity of students' research problems, and motivates students by showing them how the skills they gain from the tutorial will make them more effective information seekers. (Loomis and

Konrad, 1998) The metaphor or theme you select will permeate much of your content, so test it carefully on members of your target audience to be sure it will not become quickly dated.

REFINING AND SEQUENCING LEARNING OBJECTIVES

The objectives you articulate, discussed in Chapter 10, will determine what users learn from your tutorial and what conclusions you will be able to draw in your assessments of student learning. Consider cooperating with other stakeholders in the development of learning objectives. By incorporating language from an institutional strategic plan, local information skills standards, or national information literacy standards, you can get buy-in from stakeholders and greatly increase the usefulness and impact of your finished project.

Develop objectives iteratively by writing down things you'd like to measure about student learning, then creating prototype learning objectives that are precise and include action verbs that describe visible behaviors. Share or test your prototype learning objectives with members of the target audience. Refine and revise objectives based on learner feedback and data collected during subsequent steps in the instructional design process.

Each section or module of your Web-based instruction may address one or more of the target objectives you developed. Group target objectives into lessons that are coherent and represent a single idea. The number of objectives you can cover in each lesson or module will depend on your decisions about scope, the amount of time learners will spend on each lesson, and the complexity of the objectives you articulate.

In the traditional model, each of the target objectives is then described with more detailed, supporting objectives. Gagne proposed developing "learning hierarchies" by listing prerequisite or subordinate skills needed to master larger superordinate skills and abilities. (1985) This process would be conducted at progressively refined levels of granularity until you reach basic skills that are prerequisite. The objectives for each section should describe a range of behavior or cognition, from lower- to higher-order complexity, as well as target the active engagement of the learner. When written as objectives, the hierarchy of skills and abilities forms a rough outline for instruction. In the traditional model, finalized "performance objectives" are communicated to students and form the basis for assessment of student learning. In the constructivist model developed in Chapter 10, each target objective is described with "performance indicators" and "learning outcomes."

Sequence material logically so learners have the prerequisite knowledge to achieve each objective successfully. For each objective in the sequence you've outlined, list curriculum, or a comprehensive list of things learners will need to know to accomplish the objective. The objectives describe what you'd like learners to be able to do when they complete each section and the curriculum indicates the components they'll need to get there. If there are things you wanted to cover that cannot be included under your objectives, you'll need to revise the objectives or pare down your curriculum. You'll also need to identify areas where less advanced learners may need additional support.

To improve student learning, organize your content into "chunks," or a series of topics and subtopics. George Miller showed that the "span" of short-term memory, the amount of information people can "receive, process and remember" is generally fixed at five to nine topics. (1956) When content is organized "into several dimensions and successively into a sequence of chunks, we can manage to break (or at least stretch) this informational bottleneck." (Miller 1956: 97) Instructional designers have extrapolated that learning and retention are improved when curriculum, rather than being presented as a lengthy linear progression of items, is grouped into sections, topics, and "bits" of information.

Organizing content into chunks becomes all the more important in the inherently nonlinear Web environment. While you've grouped and sequenced objectives to facilitate learning, your site design may allow users to choose a variety of paths, linear or nonlinear, through the content. Users might select a particular path based on factors such as prior knowledge, need for remediation or review, and immediate learning needs. Plan for the coherence of every potential sequence through the material. Begin by making sure that each topic (consisting of one or more screens, addressing a single objective or answering a single question) stands on its own.

INSTRUCTION DELIVERY OR APPROACH

With your sequenced "chunks" of content, you are ready to select the appropriate approach to the delivery of instruction. The instructional plan you develop should be customized to the characteristics of the learners, the objectives you would like to achieve, and the instructional model you've chosen to adopt.

There are various taxonomies of instructional strategies. Wiggins and McTighe (1998) classify instruction as follows:

- **Didactic**
  Presenting textual or verbal information to provide background and present key concepts.
- **Coaching**
  Using interactions or exercises to guide learners through particular concepts while providing support and feedback on their performance.
- **Constructivist**
  Providing opportunities for guided, independent inquiry and peer interaction.

Didactic or direct instruction should be used to present information and examples, mostly for "enabling knowledge and skill." (Wiggins and McTighe, 1998: 163) Didactic instruction is most appropriate for orientations, processes, and procedures.

Alternative instructional strategies may be more appropriate for projects with objectives that target higher-order thinking such as Synthesis, Application, or Evaluation, and seek to emphasize authentic and active learning. From a cognitive standpoint, learners remember concepts by incorporating them into their own "cognitive schemata." (Morgan, 1996: 29) To allow learners to incorporate and remember new concepts, create a context for the new information, present the new information clearly and provide examples, then allow learners to practice or apply the information. Coaching and constructivist strategies implemented through sites developed around realistic problem solving will be better in these instances.

Coaching via interactions is particularly important for concepts that are "subtle; most prone to misunderstanding; and in need of personal inquiry, testing and verification." (Wiggins and McTighe, 1998: 163) Examples and interactions should progress from direct demonstration of the new concept to application in progressively more complex contexts. (Morgan, 1996) Use interactions to provide feedback and check for understanding during instruction, rather than just assessing learning at the end of a section. Consider what you want users to know as they complete one topic and before they move on to the next. Can you create an interaction that will have learners demonstrate mastery of a key concept before they move on? Will you provide some type of remediation or review for those who do not demonstrate mastery? While you may want to build interactions around these areas, avoid setting up frustrating loops that take control away from the learner.

Interactions can also be used as a constructivist strategy, where the learner "makes meaning" (Wiggins and McTighe, 1998: 161) of complex ideas rather than proceeding through a pre-set presentation of information. Constructivist strategies allow learners to use the information and concepts you've presented in new ways. While it's challenging to create these types of experiences online, some things to consider are having students answer open-ended questions, create peer interactions using online communication tools, build sites around realistic problem solving, or develop portfolios of their work.

Once you've decided on curriculum and approach to the delivery of instruction, it may be helpful to storyboard each section of the content. A storyboard "contains a sketch for each screen that includes text, information about the graphics (including placement, color, and size), design layout, color, font size and types, sounds (including narration), and audience interaction." (Smith, 2001: 20) The storyboard is a highly detailed flowchart, designed to guide team members as they develop the content for individual topics.

Cognitive Considerations

Through needs assessment and pre-testing you may have been able to identify what knowledge would be considered prerequisite and, thus, a good starting point for your instruction. While your project goals address learning for a large target audience, instruction focuses on the achievement of the individual learner.

Cognitive assessment is the measurement of individual learners' progressive growth in ability to understand concepts, and is performed in order to start learners at their current level and move them forward, whether or not they are exactly matched to the cognitive level of other members of your target audience. Cognitive assessment might range from a questionnaire on the learner's perceptions of his or her own learning to a pre-test at the beginning of a tutorial or section. You might create an initial review that all learners pass through. Alternatively, a pre-test can be used to create an individualized instruction program to diagnose gaps in individual learners' knowledge and pull out content to meet their needs. (Gagne, Briggs and Wager, 1992: 310–311) Ensuring every learner is prepared for the starting point you have chosen is key to success.

Scaffolding is a teaching methodology to allow less advanced learners in your target audience to achieve learning objectives. In the classroom model, an instructor or advanced peer provides support to less advanced peers in order to help them complete a learning task. The "cognitive apprenticeship model of instruction" includes a scaffolding phase where learners practice skills with a great deal of support and guidance; the support is gradually removed in later phases as they begin to function adequately at a higher level. With Web-based instruction, the learning environment, rather than a peer or instructor, must provide support for less advanced learners. This support might take the form of a glossary, context-specific help, tips or review for prerequisite concepts, and interactions that provide support and feedback as learners complete key tasks.

Affective Considerations

Affective, or emotionally based, issues directly relate to an individual's motivation, persistence through the instruction, and success. Learners may be motivated by external factors such as grades or course requirements, but there are strategies you can use to foster internal motivation as well. Communicate performance objectives clearly to allow learners to measure and take responsibility for their own progress through the material. Include assessments within the instruction that provide frequent, instructive feedback and include a variety of assessments and interactions, from simple to difficult, to allow learners to experience success and still feel challenged. Elements such as tone, style of graphics, use of language, and other design features all significantly impact an individual learner's receptivity to the instruction and should be considered during development and testing.

Fostering learner engagement is contingent on many elements of your instructional design. The strategies you'll use to keep learners engaged will vary depending on your audience characteristics, but generally you need to keep things moving quickly, even at the beginning. Make your content in all formats fun and engaging, particularly through the inclusion of multimedia and interactivity. Use what you know about the values, learning styles, feelings, and attitudes of your target population to make Web-based instruction a positive experience for them.

CONTENT DEVELOPMENT

Present your content in a way that engages learners and helps them assimilate the information. To maintain focus as you progress through the instructional design process, review content to determine if what you have written significantly contributes to the stated learning objectives; if not, move that content out of the primary path of instruction or remove it altogether. Throughout your writing, maintain a tone that is consistent, straightforward, and appropriate to your audience, keeping sentence structure and vocabulary simple and avoiding the use of jargon. Write each paragraph following the "inverted pyramid principle" (Nielsen, 2000: 111), presenting important material and conclusions up front in a clear topic sentence so users can see what they'll learn by reading the section.

Jakob Nielsen's *Designing Web Usability* offers guidelines for transferring the rules for writing good content to the Web environment (2000). Succinctness is all the more important online, as reading from computer screens is less pleasant and about 25 percent slower than reading from paper, particularly when users have to scroll to read all the text on a page. (2000: 101) Many learners have developed strategies to sift quickly through the vast amount of information available on the Web. Nielsen found that 79 percent of users tend to scan pages to pick out keywords and paragraphs that interest them, while only a few read word by word. (2000: 104) Anticipate the tendency to scan by keeping text precise and structuring content for scannability through effective use of meaningful headings, bulleted lists and bolding for emphasis, and use of the pyramid principle.

Hypertext affords the opportunity for learners to choose a variety of paths through the material. Apply Miller's (1956) findings about chunking, splitting long narratives into logical sequences of five to nine topics on a series of pages, rather than as a single long text on a sequence of continuous pages. Give each page or chunk a meaningful title that will define its focus for learners in a variety of contexts. Wherever possible, consider replacing text with graphics such as tables or diagrams, and interactions through which learners can gain their understanding through collaboration or practice.

Give some thought to the shelf life of your content. If you use screen shots from specific databases or examples from popular culture, content will be outdated very quickly as interfaces and learner interests change. Focus on concepts rather than specific tools, and choose examples with care to avoid frequent changes to maintain the accuracy of the content.

Above all, plan for copyediting to be part of your content development process in order to achieve a consistent voice and style in your site. This can be especially challenging if you have many content creators. Early in the content development process, create a style-specification sheet to include guidelines on topics such as amount of content per page, use of bullets or numbering, glossary of language to use, cross-references, punctuation, capitalization, and URLs. Be certain to edit extensively: spell checking and grammar checking are important, but you'll want to have text edited and proofread several times and by several members of your team to identify inconsistencies, make it usable, and avoid errors. Editing is perhaps most effective when the process is opened to include not only the project team, but also project partners, colleagues, and members of the target audience. Once content is sequenced, written and chunked, you'll also want to make revisions based on the way content looks online.

ONGOING ASSESSMENT AND REVIEW

Well-designed assessment within your site will help you measure the effectiveness of the instruction you've developed and learners' achievement of performance objectives. Begin assessing the effectiveness instruction with a review of the performance objectives or outcomes you've articulated. "The goal of formative evaluation is to help the development team recognize problems in the design of the tutorial so that those problems can be corrected prior to the completion of the project." (Smith, 2001: 175) Consider conducting a "cognitive walk-through" (2001: 175), where experts play the role of users and walk through the site in order to identify problems in the sequences of instruction, or conducting focus groups with learners at various stages of the content development process.

Summative assessment of student learning might take any number of forms, from traditional quizzes, to discussion and reflection elements, to products created and submitted in a portfolio. When designing quizzes, questions should always relate to concepts covered in the instruction, and some should be like those students will encounter in real life. Quiz questions might ask users to take information you've provided through text, examples, and interactions a step further, perhaps by transferring a concept to another topic or applying it to a real search. Even if the purpose of your quiz is to test an individual learner, either for credit or before he or she goes on to the next section of the instruction, the feedback you provide should always follow the questions immediately and foster further understanding and reflection.

You should also consider how you will provide users who have trouble with the quiz with review and remediation. Will you allow users to review particular topics before they go to the quiz? Will you recommend particular areas to review based on the quiz results? If you've grouped your content into freestanding "chunks," each answering a particular question, it will be easier to create review materials. Consider providing learners with the option of retaking quizzes until they are able to demonstrate mastery. If you've decided on a constructivist approach to instruction, activities and criteria for assessment should be designed to determine evidence of complex understandings. An example of this type of assessment would be assessing a portfolio of student work using a rubric, as discussed in Chapter 9.

Use the data you collect via assessment and evaluation to continuously review and revise the content you've created. If a quiz question causes problems for a disproportionate number of users, analyze the sequence of instruction for that topic and examine the wording of the question to locate and address the source of the problem. Also collect qualitative data on learners' experiences via open-ended questions, Web forms, or surveys and use their responses to inform revisions and improvements. Consider systematic and ongoing review to be an integral part of your project, in order to assure that your content continues to meet your goals and remains something of which you can be proud.

CONCLUSION

The instructional content is the link between planning and the success of the individual learner. This chapter outlines various instructional design models and guiding principles for the development of instructional materials. It is essential for you to select a framework that matches the context of your project and the needs of your audience. Adherence to an iterative sequence of steps—from needs assessment to reflection and review—is essential to effectively translate your ideas into instruction that addresses your goals, offers meaningful assessment of student learning, and leads to a successful project.

REFERENCES

Chickering, Arthur W., and Stephen C. Ehrmann. 1996. "Implementing the Seven Principles: Technology as Lever." *AAHE Bulletin* (October): 3–6. Available: www.tltgroup.org/programs/seven.html.

Dewald, Nancy. 1999. "Transporting Good Library Instruction Practices into the Web Environment: An Analysis of Online Tutorials." *Journal of Academic Librarianship* 25, no.1 (January): 26–31.

Fosnot, Catherine Twomey, ed. 1996. *Constructivism: Theory, Perspectives, and Practice.* New York: Teachers College Press.

Gagne, Robert M. 1985. *The Conditions of Learning and Theory of Instruction.* 4th Edition. New York: Holt, Rinehart and Winston.

Gagne, Robert M., Leslie J. Briggs, and Walter W. Wager. 1992. *Principles of Instructional Design.* 4th Edition. New York: Harcourt Brace Jovanovich.

Loomis, Abigail, and Lee Konrad. 1998. "Designing and Implementing CLUE. An Interactive, Multimedia Instruction Program." In *Theory and Practice: Papers and Session Materials Presented at the Twenty-fifth National LOEX Library Instruction Conference Held in Charleston, South Carolina, 8 to 10 May 1997,* edited by Linda Shirato and Elizabeth R. Bucciarelli. Ann Arbor, MI: Pierian Press.

Miller, George A. 1956. "The Magical Number Seven, Plus or Minus Two: Some Limits on Our Capacity for Processing Information." *Psychological Review* 63, no.2 (March): 81–97.

Morgan, Tom. 1996. "Changing the Chunks: Using Technology to Enhance Learning." *Learning and Leading with Technology* (February): 49–51.

Nielsen, Jakob. 2000. *Designing Web Usability.* Indianapolis, IN: New Riders.

Reiser, Robert G. 2001. "A History of Instructional Design and Technology, Part II: A History of Instructional Design." *Educational Technology, Research and Development* 49, no.2: 57–68.

Smith, Susan Sharpless. 2001. *Web-Based Instruction: A Guide for Libraries.* Chicago: American Library Association.

Wiggins, Grant, and Jay McTighe. 1998. *Understanding by Design.* Alexandria, VA: Association for Supervision and Curriculum Development.

Chapter 13

Site Design

Nancy O'Hanlon

An instructional Web site may contain one, several, or many lessons depending upon the goals for instruction. Regardless of the instructional approach chosen, your site must have a clear structure, or architecture, that is understandable to users so as not to obstruct their learning.

Web usability guru Jakob Nielsen notes that many Web sites evolve without any plan and end up as a chaotic collection of parts, with no apparent relationship to each other. (2000: 198) Without a well-designed site, learners will be forced to spend most of their time figuring out how to navigate and, consequently, will have less energy to devote to understanding the content. In the worst cases, they may become frustrated, tune out important information, or leave the site entirely.

Principles of good site design do not vary with the type of learner or the nature of instructional content. Whether you are creating a learning site for grade school students or senior citizens Nielsen tells us that "site design must be aimed at simplicity above all else, with as few distractions as possible and with a very clear information architecture and matching navigation tools." (2000: 164)

In this chapter, we will consider approaches for organizing and designing your Web-based instruction, both at the macro (overall site architecture) and micro (individual page) levels. Basic ground rules for creating navigation paths through the site, designing a consistent look for pages, and developing an easy to maintain "back-end" structure for your site will also be covered.

SITE ARCHITECTURE

All sites have a "homepage." The homepage introduces the user to the elements that will be present throughout the rest of the site—colors, fonts, labels, special features, and so on. Additionally, the homepage tells the target audience what the site purports to do and functions as a menu or jumping-off point for the subsections. Sites employ a number of techniques to establish the relationships between subsections. For example, each subsection might be designed in a different color or with a unique icon that is carried throughout the site to help users recognize the section they are in. Whatever technique you choose to present, it is important to be consistent.

Although there is general agreement on the characteristics of a good homepage, there is less consensus on the best structure for an instructional Web site. Three general choices are available when planning the macro or overall architecture of your site:

- Linear, or predetermined, paths chosen by the developer.
- Flexible paths chosen by the learner.
- Customized paths based on preferences or assessments.

Linear Paths

There is a synergy between the nature of the content and the architecture of a learning site. Alessi suggests providing more structure when teaching specific sequences or procedural skills. (2001: 52–53) For example, you may want to ensure that learners understand Boolean operators that can be used to combine search terms before addressing more advanced issues such as the use of parentheses to group compound searches together. If the content has a very structured sequence, then the organization and navigation features of the site should support this linear approach. In a linear scheme, forward and backward navigation and access to general help tools and glossaries are provided, but the learner is required to demonstrate completion of one component before progressing to a new task.

Learners bring different knowledge to all instruction. Some learners may be distracted or confused without overt direction and guidance through the content. Others will be ready to skip over some steps in a sequence. A strictly linear organization model works best when used along with a preassessment of the learner's skill level at the start of instruction, to avoid learners being presented with content they have already mastered. If your instruction will be designed such that it is likely a student will not be able to complete it in a single session, some method for exiting and returning easily to the stopping point must be provided. Cookies, addressed later in this chapter, provide one way to handle this.

Flexible Paths

A flexible organizational model for a learning site presumes that the content can be viewed in any order or sequence, depending upon learner choices. In this approach, all of the subsections, sometimes described as modules in educational sites, would be available from the homepage as well as easily accessible from other parts of the site. The learner can select samples from this buffet-style presentation, returning to the main menu on the homepage at will. This site architecture is suitable for most adult learners, and fits best with a constructivist model where learners control their learning environment. With a flexible architecture, it is not essential—although it may still be helpful—to provide tracking of where the user has been. To some extent, the native features of Web browsers (such as allowing visited links to be displayed a different color) can be used for this purpose. Figure 13–1 illustrates the flexible approach.

The WebMonkey site, a tutorial on information architecture, has a left-hand navigation panel that provides easy access to all five subsections of this tutorial. The outline-style panel is opened to a second level of detail at Lesson 4, showing the separate pages within this level. A user can move freely though the subsections and anyone who wished to jump out of this tutorial entirely could use the global navigation links (home/de-

**Figure 13–1. Example of the Flexible Model
of Site Architecture. URL: http://hotwired.lycos.com/
webmonkey/design/tutorials/tutorial1.html**

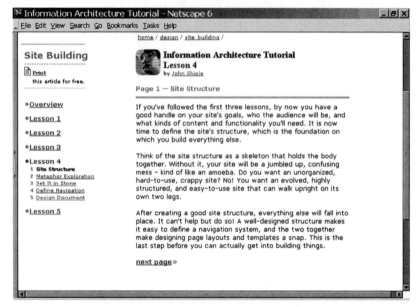

sign/site building) at the top of the window. Every page of this tutorial contains a similar navigation panel, allowing users to either follow the linear path suggested by the author (by using the "next" links at the bottom of each page) or to move around at will.

Customized Paths

A customized model takes the flexible approach a step further, allowing users to view different presentations of the same information or different variants of the same activity. For example, if your learning site must serve college undergraduates as well as graduate students, providing this sort of customization is essential. While the same principle, concept, or skill may be taught to both audiences, the examples and activities that are appealing to undergraduates will be quite different from those that have the most meaning for graduate students.

Similarly, customized paths allow for variations based on

personal preferences. Some learners prefer a visual approach to content presentation; in those cases, maps, graphs, charts, and illustrations may be most helpful. To accommodate learners who speak English as a second language, you might offer audio tracks in a range of languages. To develop a site with customized paths, you will need to prepare several variations of your lessons, such as a textual summary, a visual concept map that conveys the information graphically, and even pages with more remedial or more advanced discussions of the key ideas. Implementing a customized approach usually requires a learner profile be incorporated into the site design, so at the beginning of the instructional episode the user is presented with options to determine appropriate variants based on their needs and preferences.

NAVIGATION FEATURES

Regardless of the site architecture you design, general principles for providing navigation within the site apply. Users need cues to know where they are, where they have been, and where they can go. Features that appear in consistent locations on every page of the site form the global navigation system.

Title and Logo

The most fundamental global navigation aid is inclusion of a site title and/or logo. This "branding" easily conveys to users that they are still within your site, as opposed to somewhere else on the Web. Nielsen notes that when writing in languages that are read from left to right, this logo should be placed in the upper left corner and be made into a hyperlink, so that users can get home from anywhere by clicking on it. (2000: 191)

Toolbar

Another fundamental navigation aid is the toolbar. Although it may be constructed with text links, the toolbar is usually a graphic—either a series of small images displayed in a row, or

Figure 13–2. Example of Global and Local Navigation Schemes. URL: http://www.essentialmac.com/

one large Imagemap with various clickable zones that contain links to other sections of the site.

In addition to linking to the major site subsections, toolbars may provide access to features or tools that should be available to the user from any point in the site, such as "Home," "Help," "FAQ" (frequently asked questions), "Glossary," and "Search."

Figure 13–2 shows a tutorial about using the Macintosh computer that has a global navigation toolbar at the bottom of the page in a tabbed format, along with a "local" navigation scheme shown along the left side of the page. This local navigation scheme lists the pages within that particular tutorial, while the global toolbar allows users to jump back to the homepage of the site and choose a different lesson. Note that the "Customize" tab in the global toolbar is the same color as the background of the local menu. Here the use of corresponding colors provides another visual cue or placeholder to help users understand where they are in the site.

Figure 13–3. Example of Use of Breadcrumb Navigation.
URL: http://www.denison.edu/ohio5/infolit/

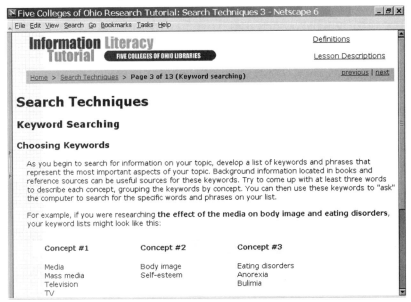

Hierarchical Menus

Users' "Where am I?" and "Where can I go?" questions may also be answered by employing a hierarchical menu, sometimes presented in a separate navigation frame. Hierarchical menus, or nested navigation, usually provide some visual symbol (such as a plus sign or small arrow) to indicate that a category in the hierarchy contains more information, which may be displayed by clicking on the symbol. In this way, users can expand or collapse the menu as needed. This device is familiar to most users, but may be overwhelming if more than five to seven items are included in a nested menu.

Hierarchical menus might also be displayed in drop-down lists, which appear when users either roll a mouse pointer over an image in a toolbar or click on a box to display a list of items hidden inside. Nielsen tells us that these kinds of menus may cause usability problems, because users cannot see the full set of options or choices without having to perform an action. (2000: 195)

Breadcrumbs are another device for helping users understand where they are and where else they can go. These text links list in a hierarchical fashion the major divisions above the page that users are viewing. Since the breadcrumb links are displayed in a vertical line, they don't consume much screen space, as shown in Figure 13–3.

Local Navigation

Local navigation devices—such as forward and backward arrows, or next and previous links—are incorporated into learning sites in various ways. Most importantly they should be handled in a consistent fashion and maximize efficiency for the user. For example, in Figure 13–3 the next and previous links are shown at both the top and bottom of the page. This saves time for users who are skimming content, because they do not need to scroll to the bottom of the display to move forward through the site.

Site Maps

Site maps may also function as a navigation aid. Nielsen reports that hypertext research studies show that overview diagrams help users find information faster. (2000: 221) Maps allows users to form a mental picture of the site as a whole, see the major (and often minor) subsections, and move about by clicking visible or embedded links. A site map may be a simple text listing of all the pages in a site in a hierarchical fashion, or a graphical depiction of the site contents such as the Imagemap shown in Figure 13–4. Simple navigation schemes such as breadcrumbs can be greatly enhanced without losing too much screen space by providing a link to a site map on each page.

External Links

Within your instruction you are likely to direct learners to resources and information available on sites other than your own. When designing these links you need to find a method that allows users to visit that site without leaving their place in your

Figure 13–4. Example of Use of Graphical Map for Navigation. URL: http://gateway.lib.ohio-state.edu/training/coursepack.html

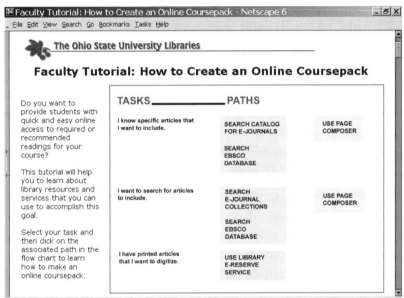

site. One common technique is to have links to external sites open in new browser windows. A factor in deciding whether to introduce additional windows is the skill level of your audience. When creating a site for those who may be inexperienced Web browsers or unfamiliar with routine computer operations, multiple windows can present problems. Some people, especially older or adult learners, may not know how to close new windows. Additionally, a new window may actually open underneath the one containing your instructional site content and cause confusion for those who do not understand how to bring the new window into view. If you do decide to open new windows, use Javascript code to control the size and placement of the new window as well as provide a "Close Window" button or link. If you decide against using additional windows, provide navigational support by reminding the user to use the browser's "BACK" function in order to return to the instruction.

PAGE DESIGN

In addition to providing a predictable navigation scheme throughout the site, you must also design a consistent look for individual pages. Here it is helpful to think in terms of page zones. Guenther notes "use of zones enhances the user experience by setting up consistent and expected areas where particular types of information can be found from page to page. This consistency goes a long way toward minimizing the cognitive overhead required by end-users as they navigate your site and allows the user to focus on the important part of your site, the content, without encountering a new design or new navigational path with every page they view." (2002: 83)

When planning your site design, list the types of pages you will present throughout the site such as: lesson content, help, interactions, assessments, and glossaries. For each type of page, list the recurring information and navigational features that should appear on or be accessible from it. For example, on a lesson page you may decide to include a sidebar containing definitions of new words, practice tasks or examples, in addition to the main text and illustrations. Learners will be able to make efficient use of these features if they are consistent in appearance and placement on the page.

Templates

Templates are especially helpful when you wish to create consistent page displays. A template is a pattern or grid, with some recurring information contained in it, so that you do not need to repeatedly redesign pages from scratch. Web development tools, such as Macromedia Dreamweaver, make template development easy. First, you create a page design using the Web editor, placing any recurring graphics (such as logos and toolbars) and display features (such as menus, sidebar text boxes, headers, and footers). When you save this page design as a template, you can specify which parts of the page should not change and which will be editable. Then when you want to create a new page based on your template, you can add content and make changes in the editable areas, while other parts of the page are locked and remain static. When updating the template, all pages that use it are also changed. For a large site, this saves considerable maintenance time. For example, if your logo or footer must be edited, simply update the template files and these changes are made everywhere. Templates can also help to maintain consistent site design when many different people are contributing pages to the learning site.

FLOWCHARTS

The development of instructional Web sites is a complex process that may be facilitated by the development of a flowchart. The flowchart, a diagram providing an overview of the structure of the site, portrays the ways a user may move through various steps in the instructional process, such as presentation of lesson content, practice or application, review, and mastery testing. The elements of the process (actions, decision points, inputs/outputs, and flow) are represented in the flowchart by standard symbols (circles, rectangles, diamonds, and arrows).

Alessi notes that flowcharts show structure and sequence, the big picture of an instructional program, while storyboards are used to show the visual details, what learners will see on site pages (2001: 503). Flowcharts provide a blueprint to use in the building of a prototype for an instructional Web site. They help us plan what we are going to do and they keep us focused on the final goal. Various software programs for easily creating flowcharts are available. One application, SmartDraw, offers many examples of flowcharts on its Web site (www.smartdraw.com/resources/centers/flowcharts/).

BACK-END STRUCTURE

Ideally, you should consider how to manage the many different kinds of files on your site at the outset of the project. Creating an efficient "back-end" structure for the site, by organizing directories and naming files logically, facilitates both the initial design and ongoing maintenance. Some ground rules include:

- **Organize files of the same type together**
  Create separate directories for file types such as images
  and scripts. Doing so will make it easier to locate them
  when you need to make changes to those files, and when
  you wish to create links to them from multiple pages.
  Similarly, consider creating directories for each subsection
  of your project so the back-end is generally consistent
  with the organization that users see. These techniques will
  make creation and maintenance more efficient, especially
  once new staff become responsible for oversight of the
  project.
- **Create logical names for files and directories**
  Choose a standard naming convention for similar pages
  within the site and subsections. When possible, restrict
  names to one word. If you must include more than one
  word, connect them with an underscore, rather than
  spaces or other characters which may not be recognized
  by servers trying to access the file. It is best for names and
  extensions (such as ".html" and ".gif") to remain in lowercase letters. Some Web servers differentiate between
  upper and lowercase; by using only one form consistently,
  you won't make mistakes when creating links in your
  content.
- **Set up "working" directories to use for development
  and revision of pages**
  This allows the developer to build pages away from public view and to test them with various browsers, to make
  sure that they work properly, before going "live." Some
  Web development tools, such as Macromedia Dreamweaver, allow you to maintain separate sites for development and production use and to upload files from the
  development site to the main production server when
  ready. Dreamweaver provides some other controls, such
  as requiring content authors to "check out" files to work
  on, thus preventing confusion when multiple people are
  working on a project. If a group maintains your site and
  you don't use a Web editor that offers this type file management, you must develop ground rules for maintaining various parts of the site and set up ownership and ac-

cess rights of various pages, so that one person doesn't undo someone else's work.

QUESTIONS TO ASK

Decisions about site architecture, navigation, page design, and back-end structure are common to all types of Web sites. However, there are also some additional considerations specific to designing a learning site.

Do you want to track learners' progress through the site or provide customization?

As discussed earlier, cookies are one common method for adding personalization to your site. Cookies are small text files sent to a learner's computer, with which your Web site can communicate. The developer determines what information will be saved to the cookie and, hence, will be available to a Web site to identify the user (for example, to recall their profile of preferences), to track a user's progress (for example, to return them to the place in the instruction where they left), and to provide customized information (such as examples relevant to their class, discipline, educational level, occupation, or interest). Bonner provides this example: " . . . if you offer two versions of your site, one with frames and one without, there's no need to make the user choose each time they visit. Instead, you can save their selection in a cookie, and then the next time they come to your door, your server can read the cookie and automatically deliver the preferred site type." (Bonner, 2002)

Do you need users to register?

Registration can provide useful information to the site developers and instructors. By tracking the overall profile of visitors to the site and which site features they employ, you can collect useful data that will guide your site revisions. On the other hand, registration discourages many users from taking advantage of casual learning opportunities, and inhibits browsing of your site by those who want to determine if the content is relevant to their needs. If you choose to require learners to register, you must provide a data collection form and maintain a database to store the user information for authentication purposes or use learning management software, such as WebCT or Blackboard, that has these capabilities. Learning management software handles user registration, authentication, usage tracking, grading functions, and collection of statistics. The drawback is that these applications can be prohibitively expensive for smaller organizations to purchase and manage. Some Web authoring software, such as Dreamweaver enhanced with the free Learning Site extension, provides similar registration and grade tracking features. Homegrown systems developed with a data collection form and database, such as SQL or LDAP, will require significant programming and technical expertise.

Are you designing tests or other assessments of learners' progress?

If your site needs to identify students and confirm that the responses are their own, you will need some method for secure authentication. This is particularly important when the learners are being credited with a grade or other performance assessment of their work. In some cases, you may be able to offer open access to instructional content and only require authentication at the point before the test or other assessment is introduced. Many scripts developed by others are available online and can be adapted to your needs. For more informal learning situations where you simply wish to provide feedback without collecting scores, Javascript can be used to create simple interactions. For example, Builder.com (http://builder.com/) is a good source for quiz and other types of scripts that can be adapted for your site. Other library learning site developers may also be willing to share their scripts upon request.

Is your site accessible to all types of learners?

Last, but certainly not the least of considerations, is the need to make sure that learners of varying abilities, especially those with physical or cognitive impairments, can make full use of your site's features. Generally speaking, taking the time to make content easily accessible for the most challenged learners results in improvements that will benefit everyone who uses the site. As you develop images, multimedia (such as Flash), and scripts to manage various site functions, you must be aware of the ways that those using alternative browsing techniques (special adaptive browsers or programs like screen readers) to access content are impacted by design decisions. Before beginning development, take time to review the accessibility guidelines and other support materials provided by the Web Accessibility Initiative (WAI, www.w3.org/WAI/). Use Bobby or one of the other tools identified on the WAI site to evaluate your Web pages for accessibility problems and get pointers on how to repair any problems. Additionally, the Center for Applied Special Technologies (CAST) site presents a variety of strategies and examples for making Web learning content available to those with physical and learning disabilities (www.cast.org/teachingeverystudent/).

CONCLUSION

To enhance the learner's experience, you must consider the general structure or architecture of your site, the global and local navigation paths, and the specific look-and-feel of various types of pages. You must consider instruction-specific issues related to user registration, authorization, testing, and grades in order to determine whether additional development software or programming is needed to make the site functional as a virtual classroom. And to streamline maintenance and development, you must also create an efficient back-end structure. This may seem like an intimidating list of tasks. As you plan your Web-based instruction, take time to explore a variety of other instructional sites, consider the ways that designers have implemented the elements discussed in this chapter, and use the best sites as models for your own.

REFERENCES

Alessi, Stephen M. 2001. *Multimedia for Learning: Methods and Development.* 3rd Edition. Boston: Allyn and Bacon.

Bonner, Paul. 2002. "Adding Cookies to Your Site." *Builder.com*. Available: http://builder.cnet.com/webbuilding/0–3882–8–5235849–1.html.

Guenther, Kim. 2002. "Web Site Management." *Online* 26 (September/October): 82–85.

Nielsen, Jakob. 2000. *Designing Web Usability: The Practice of Simplicity*. Indianapolis, IN: New Riders Publishing.

Chapter 14

Putting Content Online

Dennis Glenn

Web publishing presents issues concerning content presentation that must be addressed with a new mindset, not simply a reliance on principles historical to print publishing. Similarly, Web-based instruction is not simply putting instructional products online, but developing an environment that allows for the transfer and discovery of knowledge. Through Web sites we can activate multiple levels of learning and encoding of information into long-term memory. John Seely Brown elaborates:

> . . . with the Web, we suddenly have a medium that honors multiple forms of intelligence—abstract, textual, visual, musical, social, and kinesthetic. As educators, we now have a chance to construct a medium that enables all young people to become engaged in their ideal way of learning. The Web affords the match we need between a medium and how a particular person learns. (2000: 12)

This chapter discusses concepts that will assist you in producing a dynamic Web-based instruction product based upon your audience, site architecture, instructional approach, and content. To be effective, your product must attract attention. Product design is a set of rules, or road maps, that leads the producer in the right direction. Oftentimes, rules contradict one another. A good designer knows when to follow the rules and when to break them. Areas to be discussed in this chapter include economy of space, proximity, emphasis, balance, shape, color, typography, and incorporation of multimedia.

AN ENGAGING MEDIUM

Citing psychological studies, Jerome Bruner claimed that people remember approximately 30 percent of what they read and about 10 percent of what they hear, but when hearing and sight are both required, the retention rate jumps to 80 percent. (Tannenbaum, 1998: 67) Psychologists refer to this phenomenon as "dual coding." Dual-code theory presupposes that language and knowledge are represented in separate verbal and nonverbal memory systems: the verbal system specializes in linguistic information and the nonverbal system deals with perceptual information. (Mandler, 1991) This theory suggests that words and pictures are cognitively processed in different ways. Pictures offer additional information about the world allowing for more elaborate encoding than words alone. (Paivio, Rogers and Smythe, 1968) Within your instruction, consider ways to engage learners through multiple senses. Text, graphics, videos, and animation engage our visual sense; audio clips activate our aural sense; and online interactions require touch and physical motion. (Smell and taste are left to the future.)

You can also create a richer effect by creating depth on your site. QuickTime VR, headers with drop shadows, and multi-layered images are a few techniques for enhancing an interface. "We were born into a world of three dimensions yet our visual displays portray a world of two dimensionality. Escaping this flatland is the essential task of envisioning information." (Tufte, 1990: 12) Escaping the flatland of our computer screens may also be an important component for many interactive elements within your site. Not only do three-dimensional images attract users' attention, some implementations through simulations, modeling, and virtual environments might also engage users' imaginations. By developing sites that employ various techniques for communicating with the users, you address various learning styles, engage multiple senses, and aid long-term retention of the information.

PRINCIPLES OF DESIGN

To develop an effective instructional site, consider basic design principles. The mantra is "keep it simple." Form does follow function—let the information propel your visitor deeper into the site. A word of caution: don't be dazzled by technology. We all have waited for a Flash animation to finish and then discovered that the information was lacking or buried so deep by poor navigation that it was not worth the effort to continue. A single design approach that appeals to broad audiences is simply not the case. Experiment; test your ideas with focus groups. Don't be locked into your first idea. The difference between Web design and most other product design is the impermanence of the object. Nobody believes that a Web design will last more than a few years at most. In fact, most designers try to introduce new material every time you visit the site. For example, every time you visit the Northwestern University School of Communication site (www.communication.northwestern.edu/) a new student greets you at the top of the page, as shown in Figure 14–1.

**Figure 14–1. Index Page for School of Communication.
URL: http://www.communication.northwestern.edu/**

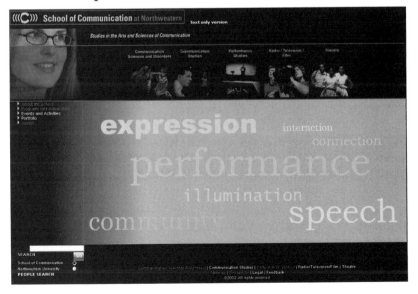

Economy of Space

The browser window is approximately 700 x 600 pixels—an unfortunately small canvas. Within this limited space, you must be frugal about the elements you incorporate, choosing to include the type and quantity of information that will be most valuable to the learner. Many Web sites have an overwhelming number of elements in their design, only ensuring that everything is lost in the minutiae. Gestalt psychologists describe a basic law of visual perception as "any stimulus pattern to be seen in such a way that the resulting structure is as simple as the given conditions permit." (Alley and Jansack, 2001: 53) Simplicity demands that the site be structured to include only the most relevant elements needed at each level or page, while placement of those elements will be consistent so users can easily detect a pattern. Viewers should have all the necessary information to discern the basic structure of the site and, ideally, be only one click away from meeting their need.

What is the optimal number of elements to be placed on a given page? In the 1950s, George Miller developed the theory positing that the optimum number of elements the short-term memory can process is seven, plus or minus two. Though very few designers adhere to it today, this is a handy rule. "There is a severe limit on how much information we can process. The estimate is that adults can handle about seven independent items of information at one time . . . It also seems reasonable that the more one has a *sense of the structure of a subject* [emphasis added], the more densely packed and longer a learning episode one can get through without fatigue." (Bruner, 1960: 51)

Since computer screen real estate is so precious, refer to the Theory of Small Multiples as coined by Edward Tufte: "For a wide range of problems in data presentation, small multiples are the best design solution . . . Small multiples reveal, all at once the scope of alternatives, a range of options." (1990: 67–68)

Consider whether the same, or supplementary, information could be conveyed through a well-crafted image or series of images. For example, on Northwestern University's School of Communication Web site, graphic icons (shown in Figure 14–2) represent each of the five departments in the school, with each

**Figure 14–2. Video Gallery for School of Communication.
URL: http://www.communication.northwestern.edu/
portfolio/video/**

icon supported by a Flash animation that defines the department visually.

Proximity

It is also imperative to consider how to structure the content,
juxtaposing all forms of media to create a coherent whole. The
concept of "chunking," discussed in Chapter 12, encourages you
to break larger pieces of text into smaller paragraphs and man-
ageable pages. Having constructed your text in this manner, you
will also need to consider how to position relevant images and
other links with that text. Consider the "Contiguity Principle,"
which argues for placement of text and graphics near each other.
(Clark, 2002) For example, in your design, make sure the graph-

ics are small enough that the text is paired with and scrolls with them.

When the viewer runs her mouse over a selected graphic in Figure 14–2, another graphic and word description appears in a designated place. The viewer can then quickly compare large amounts of information without clicking to a new page.

Emphasis

In Western culture, the eye enters the frame at the top left and moves in a clockwise direction. For this reason, many Web sites have navigation along the left side, and people have come to expect to find it there. But, the display of the content is the heart of the design process. Headings and graphics are the most obvious methods to attract attention. Graphic images do not have to be big to have a big impact. The most effective images use the "Z" axis to create depth.

Renaissance painters first developed perspective in their images about the time that the camera obscura was discovered. Representing objects as they appeared to the human eye demanded new techniques. Their paintings also incorporated "chiaroscuro" lighting techniques to enhance the realism gained by perspective drawing. I mention these concepts because the Renaissance painters faced the same problem we have today in trying to break out of the flatness of our two-dimensional computer displays (see Figure 14–3).

Text headings give structure to the space. Adding a drop shadow to text headers that you create in Photoshop will greatly enhance the visual depth of the page and draw attention to the text fields that sit near the header. If you refer to Figure 14–4, you can see that I used drop shadows to separate the title from the complex background image.

Balance and White Space

Balance is an equality of forces. A physicist would describe the potential energy within the system at a minimum—it is where all action stops. Not a good condition when we need to direct a viewer's attention to objects within the frame of your site.

Figure 14–3: Example of Image with Perspective.

Figure 14–4. Index Page for The Last Expression.
URL: http://lastexpression.northwestern.edu/

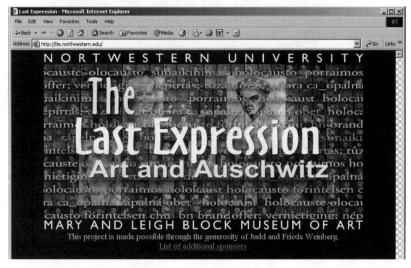

What is important to achieve is a frame loaded with potential energy. Potential energy is tension within the frame. (I might have a different view if I was designing a Web site for a mental health organization.) As designers, we assign objects of differing weights, shape, and color to places within the frame. All objects are connected to one another. It is our job to make sense of those connections. Use objects or vectors to lead, push, or pull the eye of the viewer to the material at hand.

Another issue is the amount of negative or white space in the frame. Balance and white space go hand in hand. Less white space creates tension and anxiety. Multiple elements fight for attention within the frame. Inclusion of greater or lesser amounts of white space will contribute to affective issues of your site design. Over the years we have associated large amounts of space with class or wealth and small space with the poor and disadvantaged. Compare the design in Figure 14–4— heavily layered with images to create a sense of the confinement prisoners experienced—to the essays section of the site shown in Figure 14–5, which uses larger portions of space to highlight individuality.

White space does not have to be white. There is a tendency

Figure 14–5. Exhibition Essay Page from The Last Expression. URL: http://tle.nwu.edu/exhibition_fr_e_milart.html

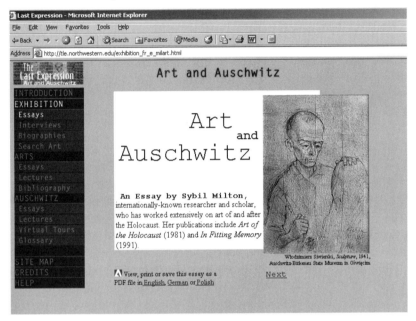

to use black as a background color for the page. I avoid black because white text on black background is difficult to discern in large amounts of body copy. I often use pastel colors to identify sections and create a sense of space.

ELEMENTS OF DESIGN

Two important elements of a work of art are shape and color. For our discussion on Web design, I have added a third, typography, because text headings enhance "readability" in our design. Readability is the combination of techniques that aids viewers to quickly perceive your message. Most often people come to your site seeking information. Statistically, you have a few seconds to impress upon visitors that the information they seek is contained somewhere in your site.

With some care, these elements can be used to develop the affective connection with your target audience. Even though I have listed them separately, they work together to create the wholeness of design. The Germans called it "gestalt," meaning shape or form. It also refers to a set of scientific principles about sensory perception that were developed in the first half of the twentieth century. These theories demonstrated that any element in a design is dependent on its place and function within the whole. An artist's vision is not just a physical record of elements but recognition of the beauty of the structural patterns contained within the frame.

Shape

In his seminal book, *Art and Visual Perception*, Rudolf Arnheim posited this thought on shapes: "For the purposes of everyday life, seeing is essentially a means of practical orientation, of determining with one's eyes that a certain thing is present at a certain place and that it is doing a certain thing." (1974: 42) "Our perception relies primarily on the structural features of objects— perception starts with the grasping of outstanding structural features." (1974: 43–44) What are the structural patterns that the viewer will discern from your design? The viewer is looking for recognizable elements from his or her past to create their own personal construct of your material. Shapes are the basic building blocks of those constructs.

Somewhere in my past, I was told that everything is made up of three basic shapes: the circle, square, and triangle. Shapes have connotations influenced by our past experiences with objects. Circles imply peace, warmth, and nurturing. The square is solid and strong, but also dull and predictable. The triangle connotes conflict and tension and, by its nature, has action associated with its ability to point to other objects. A graphical vector acts in a similar way by guiding our eye from a stationary element in a specific direction. In the School of Communication Web site we placed a student in the upper left-hand corner so that the student's eyes form a triangle and point to the theme line of our school. Conceptually, this is the vision statement articulated for the School of Communication. The eyes act as directional vectors that lead the viewer to focus attention on this critical area within the interface.

Color

The Scotch physicist, James Clerk Maxwell, wrote, "The science of color must . . . be regarded as essentially a mental science." (Birren, 1986: 24) Any discussion of color must contain numerous caveats. First and foremost, is consistency of monitor calibration. The designer's screen may have been color calibrated for Web authoring, but it is anyone's guess what the viewer "sees." As Josef Albers observed: "If one says 'Red' (the name of a color) and there are 50 people listening, it can be expected that there will be 50 reds in their minds. And one can be sure that all these reds will be very different." (1975: 3) Albers' book illustrates this concept, showing how a black versus a white background color influences our perception of the same shade of red.

So where does one look to for good advice for color interactions? "Nature has given man an innate sense of normalcy in his perception of the world." (Birren, 1986: 50) It was the Impressionists, in the second half of the nineteenth century, who moved their canvases out of musty studios to where the light was clear and strong. It was from their canvases that we finally got a sense of how "natural light" would affect color in the scenes they painted. Nature provides infinite color combinations to emulate. We often view natural scenes and ascribe an emotion to them. Scenes—like a beautiful sunset, a foggy morning at the shore, or a field of flowers in bright sun—evoke emotional feelings.

The psychological and emotional state of the viewer is dramatically impacted by the color interactions the designer chooses. During focus group testing of *The Last Expression* site, I discovered that the initial designs that contained the colors red and black caused a negative reaction from Holocaust survivors. I quickly moved from primary colors to pastels. The color red appears larger and nearer in a scene due to red focusing at a point behind the retina whereas blue has the opposite effect. Red and yellow are considered hard colors while blue and green are soft.

When shapes are near one another or share visual properties like color, the brain visually groups or unifies these forms into cohesive forces. Segregating forces tend to repel these forms. Warm colors segregate better than cool ones. According to David Katz, "Color, rather than shape, is more closely related to emotion." (Birren, 1986: 50) One last comment about color: you don't need a lot. The eye simplifies colors into small bunches of wavelengths of red, orange, yellow, green, blue, and violet.

Typography

There are two general classifications of font typefaces: serif, in which small strokes extend from each letter, and sans serif, which lack flourishes. Most computers have the typefaces Times New Roman, a serif font, and Arial, a sans serif font, preloaded. Josef Albers said, "We do not read letters but words, words as a whole, as a word picture." (1975: 4) The typeface the designer selects sends the viewer a message *about* the message. Information about the site's message is conveyed even before the content is read. (Tannenbaum, 1998: 89)

Designing for the Web, you should distinguish between body text and headings. These two categories serve different functions and require different solutions. Researchers have determined that the greater difference in the letters, the greater the comprehension. "Sans serifs were designed as letters not for text but as captions." (Albers, 1975: 4) If you expect your audience will be printing large quantities of text from your site, use serif fonts for all your body copy and consider making those pages available as PDF files. Serif fonts used on the Web have a problem with "hinting," the uniform spacing between letters is often too close, especially in 9 point or smaller. I try to use 12-point type for all body text. I equate reading large amounts of text on the computer screen with trying to read a book on a subway. Yes, it is possible, but why suffer through all that pain. Readability of your site will improve if the text is placed in narrow columns.

Another consideration is the availability of your chosen typeface on the computers used to view your site. Users must have that same font loaded on their machine to display the material as you intended. If you design a site with an uncommon typeface, it is likely that their computer will instead display a default font such as Times or Arial. In those cases, all of your hard work will be for naught. There are a number of solutions to this problem. For example, you might limit your selection to common fonts, or design your pages to use any of a "family" of fonts that are similar in the hopes of finding at least one of those types on the user's computer. I like to create graphic images of headings, which ensures the font will be the one I have chosen.

INCORPORATING MEDIA

Multimedia is what makes the Web a great communications tool. The ability to add sound, video, animation, and virtual reality is the differentiating factor on why interest in using the Web expands exponentially year after year. "Motion is the strongest visual appeal to attention . . . Motion implies a change in condition of the environment, and change may require reaction." (Arnheim, 1974: 372) Our cognitive development was predicated on refining one's attention and reaction to short-term changes, allowing us to hone our survival skills. Interaction with the material enhances learning and comprehension. I use video and virtual reality extensively to create interactive learning environments.

Audio and Video

If you have access to streaming media servers, you can offer audio and video clips. Media should be provided in two streams: a 300k file for faster connections such as DSL and cable modems, and a 56k file for dial-up connections. While video is inappropriate for people with lower bandwidth connectivity, audio tracks will still play reasonably well. Many sites deliver Real Video because it will stream to both Macs and PCs, but the cost of serving hundreds of simultaneous viewers on large sites could be problematic. Windows Media is a good choice since it is loaded on most PC machines and does not charge by the number of simultaneous viewers served. As one example, the OYEZ Project (www.oyez.org/) is a multimedia database that includes aural recordings of cases brought before the U.S. Supreme Court.

Virtual Reality

QuickTime VR (QTVR) is another vehicle to display a large amount of visual information about a specific site or location. Cognitively, QTVR works on various levels by letting viewers direct their vision over the photographic material. This permits them to explore a "master shot" of the location at their pace and interest. Additionally, unlike a photograph that has frame lines and has been edited by the maker, viewers are free to see the location as if they are standing there. You can also imbed links to other images or even sites to enlarge the scope of the inquiry. This multimedia approach is particularly useful if you are emphasizing familiarity with a physical space or want to create a simulation of the place for online visitors.

CONCLUSION

Putting your content online is the synthesis of all your prior work from planning through development. To succeed, you will need to develop a new mindset, a mindset informed by understanding your audience, drawing creative ideas from a range of sources, and employing design principles wisely. Development of Web-based instruction is a collaborative project, akin to producing a major motion picture without the budget. It takes a special talent and a lot of hard work—not just once, but continually. Using the tools outlined above will add depth and interactivity to your site. Arnheim summed it up best: "Language (alone) cannot do the job directly because it is no direct avenue for sensory contact with reality; it serves only to name what we have seen or heard or thought." (1974: 2) Multimedia gets us closer to reality.

REFERENCES

Albers, Josef. 1975. *Interaction of Color*. New Haven, CT: Yale University Press.
Alley, Lee R., and Kathryn E. Jansack. 2001. "The Ten Keys to Quality Assur-

ance and Assessment in Online Learning." *Journal of Interactive Instruction Development*, 13, no.3 (Winter): 3–18.

Arnheim, Rudolf. 1974. *Art and Visual Perception: A Psychology of the Creative Eye*. Berkeley, CA: University of California Press.

Birren, Farber. 1986. *Color Perception in Art*. West Chester, PA: Schiffer Publishing.

Brown, John Seely. 2000. "Growing Up Digital: How the Web Changes Work, Education, and the Ways People Learn." *Change Magazine* (March/April): 11–20.

Bruner, Jerome S. 1960. *The Process of Education*. Cambridge, MA: Harvard University Press.

Clark, Ruth. 2002. "Six Principles of Effective e-Learning: What Works and Why." *The eLearning Developers' Journal* (September 10): 1–8.

Mandler, G. 1991. "Your Face Looks Familiar But I Can't Remember Your Name: A Review of Dual Process Theory." In *Relating Theory and Data: Essays on Human Memory in Honor of Bennet B. Murdock*, edited by William E. Hockley and Stephan Lewandowsky. Hillsdale, NJ: L. Erlbaum Associates, 207–225.

Paivio, Allan, T. B. Rogers, and Padric C. Smythe. 1968. "Why Are Pictures Easier to Recall than Words?" *Psychonomic Science*, 11, no.4: 137–138.

Tannenbaum, Robert S. 1998. *Theoretical Foundations of Multimedia*. New York: W. H. Freeman.

Tufte, Edward R. 1990. *Envisioning Information*. Cheshire, CT: Graphic Press.

Appendix A

Project Proposals

During the planning process, it is useful to develop a written project proposal. Elements of this proposal may seem obvious, but codifying your ideas will make it easier for others to understand, endorse, and support the project, and will be necessary if you choose to seek grant funding. The document should be written for administrators and other potential stakeholders, but it will also serve as an important guide for the project team throughout the development process. A well-written proposal is clear, succinct, organized, and informative. Through it the reader should learn what your product will accomplish, how it compares to similar initiatives, and how it will positively impact your organization. Drafting a physical document to share and discuss with others is the first necessary milestone for project success.

Project proposals vary widely in length and detail. If the project is similar to others your institution has recently supported, then a briefer proposal will likely be successful. Alternately, the more complex and unique the project you propose, the more complete and clear your proposal must be. If your project proposal is lengthy, you might select the most important points and place them in bold or in an executive summary. Consider including the following sections in your written project proposal.

PROJECT NAME

If your project will be a stand-alone instruction project or tutorial, do not underestimate the difficulty in selecting a title or name. In the initial stages of project planning your team may offer many suggestions. Undoubtedly those that appeal most to some will be unacceptable to others. Your final selection should be timeless, memorable, and appropriate for the project scope. Consider these questions:

- Is your project name easy to say and remember?
- Will your selection remain viable over the next few years?
- Is this name appropriate for your audience and institution?
- Does this name complement the spirit and intent of the project?
- Do other projects have similar names or acronyms, which may be confusing?
- Does your institution wish to pursue copyright for this name?

BRIEF DESCRIPTION

A quality proposal will include a succinct statement, perhaps just two or three sentences, which adequately describes the project. Carefully select the terms you use in this description as many people may read only this excerpt rather than the fuller description. This description will also be useful in short press releases or announcements. Within this statement, include the project's scope, approach, and audience. Consider these questions:

- What is the topic or focus of the project?
- How will this project be implemented or accessed?
- Who is the primary audience?
- What are the anticipated results or benefits of the project?

COMPLETE DESCRIPTION

The complete description may also be considered a project summary. Within this section worry less about brevity than clarity. By thoroughly considering these issues and documenting your intent, this summary will act as an invaluable foundation for the team throughout project development. Much of the content for this section will come from your increased familiarity with the audience, technology, and programmatic needs of your organization. Consider these questions:

- What are the major elements of the project?
- What current problems will the project alleviate?
- What are the goals and objectives?
- What are the needs of the target audience?
- What are the format, philosophy, and design of the project?
- How will the product be utilized and integrated into other programs?
- What are some of the assumptions of the project?
- What limitations or givens are you working with?
- How does this relate to or differ from similar projects?
- What are the intended results?
- How will the project continue to be sustained after initial development?

IMPACT

This segment can be particularly important to your colleagues and administrators. In this section, synthesize your conclusions from an analysis of your organization's strengths and opportunities. Consider these questions:

- How does this project relate to the organization's mission?
- What people or groups will be affected by the completed project?
- What effect might this project have on related processes and programs?
- What experience and previous success do you bring as expertise?
- How will you assess the success and utility of the final product?

TIMELINE

Your schedule should take into account initial preparation, other staff commitments, and testing. If applicable, explain what products or reports will be created at certain intervals throughout the process. Consider these questions:

- What is the estimated start date and completion date?
- What related initiatives are happening in the organization?
- When would it be valuable to test a prototype or pilot?
- When do you need a completed product?
- How will you know when the project is ready to go public?
- When will evaluation and assessment take place?
- How frequently will you handle ongoing maintenance and review?

REQUIREMENTS

In the final section list succinctly all resources necessary to undertake the project. This section should include an estimated budget for all equipment, staff, facilities, testing, and means of communication. If you have conducted a cost/benefit analysis of the project, key findings might be integrated into this section as well. Consider these questions:

- What resources are available within the organization at no additional cost?
- What equipment, including hardware, software and upgrades, are needed?
- What finances are needed for human resources, including benefits, contracts, and pay scales for appropriate job titles?
- How will facilities need to be allotted, upgraded, or remodeled?
- What resources are needed for testing?
- What resources are needed for publicity and awareness?
- What is the total estimated budget?

Appendix B
Related Readings

These readings, selectively chosen by the editor and contributing authors, offer various perspectives on, approaches to, and levels of granularity of the concepts discussed in this book. Rather than segmenting the list by chapter titles, the following six categories—project and team management, pedagogies and technologies, instructional design and development, cognitive and learning assessment, Web design and development, and evaluation and usability testing—were created to logically group resources on similar issues. While some sources are also found in the "References" section of an individual chapter, many of these sources were recommended for this list because they offer more concentrated discussion on a topic or a particular type of learning environment not addressed in detail.

PROJECT AND TEAM MANAGEMENT

Culp, Gordon L., and Anne Smith. 1992. *Managing People (Including Yourself) for Project Success*. New York: Van Nostrand Reinhold.

Dupuis, Elizabeth A., Clara S. Fowler, and Brent Simpson. 2001. "Avoiding Culture Shock: Strategies for Successful Partnerships in Library Instruction." In *Library User Education in the New Millennium: Blending Tradition, Trends, and Innovation*, edited by Julia K. Nims and Ann Andrew. (Library Orientation Series No. 31) Ann Arbor, MI: Pierian Press.

Frame, J. Davidson. 1999. *Project Management Competence: Building Key Skills for Individuals, Teams, and Organizations*. San Francisco: Jossey-Bass.

Hall, Brendon. 1997. *Web-based Training Cookbook: Everything You Need to Know for Online Training*. New York: Wiley.

Katzenbach, Jon R., and Douglas K. Smith. 1999. *The Wisdom of Teams: Creating the High-Performance Organization*. New York: Harper Business.

Laufer, Alexander, and Edward J. Hoffman. 2000. *Project Management Success Stories: Lessons of Project Leaders.* New York: Wiley.

Pinto, Jeffrey K., ed. 1998. *Project Management Institute Project Management Handbook.* San Francisco: Jossey-Bass.

Raspa, Dick, and Dane Ward, eds. 2000. *Collaborative Imperative: Librarians and Faculty Working Together in the Information Universe.* Chicago: Association of College and Research Libraries.

Taylor, James. 1998. *A Survival Guide for Project Managers.* New York: AMACOM.

PEDAGOGIES AND TECHNOLOGIES

Anglin, Gary J., ed. 1995. *Instructional Technology: Past, Present, and Future.* 2nd Edition. Englewood, CO: Libraries Unlimited.

Chickering, Arthur W., and Stephen C. Ehrmann. 2002. "Implementing the Seven Principles: Technology as Lever." Washington, DC: TLT Group. Available: www.tltgroup.org/programs/seven.html.

Cook, E.K., and E.J. Kazlauskas. 1993. "The Cognitive and Behavioral Basis of an Instructional Design: Using CBT to Teach Technical Information and Learning Strategies." *Journal of Educational Technology Systems* 21, no.4: 287–302.

Educational Technology Development Group. 2002. "Catalyst Planning Considerations: Desktop Web Editor Comparison." Seattle, WA: University of Washington. Available: http://catalyst.washington.edu/catalyst/planning/desktools.html.

Getty, Nancy K., Barbara Burd, Sarah K. Burns, and Linda Piele. 2000. "Using Courseware to Deliver Library Instruction via the Web." *Reference Services Review* 28, no.4: 349–359.

Herrington, Jan, and Peter Standen. 2000. "Moving from an Instructivist to a Constructivist Multimedia Learning Environment." *Journal of Educational Multimedia and Hypermedia* 9, no.3: 195–205.

Jayne, Elaine, and Patricia Vander Meer. 1997. "The Library's Role in Academic Instructional Use of the World Wide Web." *Research Strategies* 15, no.3: 123–150.

Kearsley, Greg. 2002. "Is Online Learning for Everybody?" *Educational Technology* 42, no.1 (January): 41–44. Available: http://home.sprynet.com/~gkearsley/everybody.htm.

Khan, Badrul H., ed. 1997. *Web-Based Instruction.* Englewood Cliffs, NJ: Educational Technology Publications.

Maricopa Center for Learning and Instruction. 2002. "Web Courseware Comparisons and Studies." Tempe, AZ: Maricopa Center for Learning and Instruction. Available: www.mcli.dist.maricopa.edu/ocotillo/courseware/compare.html.

Stephenson, John, ed. 2001. *Teaching and Learning Online: Pedagogies for New Technologies.* London: Kogan Page.

Weiss, Renee E., Dave S. Knowlton, and Bruce W. Speck, eds. 2000. *Principles of Effective Teaching in the Online Classroom*. New Directions for Teaching and Learning 84. San Francisco: Jossey-Bass.

Wilson, Brent G., ed. 1996. *Constructivist Learning Environments: Case Studies in Instructional Design*. Englewood Cliffs, NJ: Educational Technology Publications.

INSTRUCTIONAL DESIGN AND DEVELOPMENT

Association of College and Research Libraries, Instruction Section. 2002. "Writing Measurable Objectives." Available: www.ala.org/Content/ContentGroups/ACRLI/IS/Organization9/Planning4/SMART_Objectives/Writing_Measurable_Objectives.htm.

Battersby, Mark, and the Learning Outcomes Network. 1999. "So, What's a Learning Outcome Anyway?" Vancouver, BC: Centre for Curriculum, Transfer and Technology. ERIC Document ED430611.

Dewald, Nancy, Ann Scholz-Crane, Austin Booth, and Cynthia Levine. 2000. "Information Literacy at a Distance: Instructional Design Issues." *Journal of Academic Librarianship* 26, no.1 (January): 33–44.

Dick, Walter, and Robert A. Reiser. 1989. *Planning Effective Instruction*. Englewood Cliffs, NJ: Prentice-Hall.

Driscoll, Marcy P. 1994. *Psychology of Learning for Instruction*. Boston: Allyn and Bacon.

Foote, Chandra J., Paul J. Vermette, and Catherine F. Battaglia. 2001. *Constructivist Strategies: Meeting Standards and Engaging Adolescent Minds*. Larchmont, NY: Eye on Education.

Furst, Edward J. 1981. "Bloom's Taxonomy of Educational Objectives for the Cognitive Domain: Philosophical and Educational Issues." *Review of Educational Research* 51, no.4 (Winter): 441–453.

Gagne, Robert M., and M. David Merrill. 1990. "Integrative Goals for Instructional Design." *Educational Technology, Research and Development* 38, no.1: 23–30.

Gagne, Robert M., and Marcy Perkins Driscoll. 1988. *Essentials of Learning for Instruction*. 2nd Edition. Englewood Cliffs, NJ: Prentice-Hall.

Mager, Robert F. 1997. *Preparing Instructional Objectives: A Critical Tool in the Development of Effective Instruction*. 3rd Edition. Atlanta: Center for Effective Performance.

Reichel, Mary, and Mary Ann Ramey. 1987. *Conceptual Frameworks for Bibliographic Education: Theory into Practice*. Littleton, CO: Libraries Unlimited.

Veldof, Jerilyn R., and Karen Beavers. 2001. "Going Mental: Tackling Mental Models for the Online Library Tutorial." *Research Strategies* 18, no.1: 3–20.

West, Charles K., James A. Farmer, and Phillip M. Wolff. 1991. *Instructional Design: Implications from Cognitive Science*. Englewood Cliffs, NJ: Prentice Hall.

Wiles, Jon, and Joseph Bondi. 1998. *Curriculum Development: A Guide to Practice*. 5th Edition. Upper Saddle River, NJ: Merrill.

COGNITIVE AND LEARNING ASSESSMENT

Angelo, Thomas A., and K. Patricia Cross. 1993. *Classroom Assessment Techniques: A Handbook for College Teachers*. 2nd Edition. San Francisco: Jossey-Bass.

Ash, Linda E. 2000. *Electronic Student Portfolios*. Arlington Heights, IL: SkyLight Training and Publishing.

Barton, James, and Angelo Collins, eds. 1997. *Portfolio Assessment: A Handbook for Educators*. Menlo Park, CA: Addison-Wesley.

Chase, Clinton I. 1999. *Contemporary Assessment for Educators*. New York: Longman.

Gillespie, Cindy S., et al. 1996. "Portfolio Assessment: Some Questions, Some Answers, Some Recommendations." *Journal of Adolescent & Adult Literacy* 39, no.6 (March): 480–491.

Herman, Joan L., Pamela R. Aschbacher, and Lynn Winters. 1992. *A Practical Guide to Alternative Assessment*. Alexandria, VA: Association for Supervision and Curriculum Development.

Jacobs, Lucy Cheser, and Clinton I. Chase. 1992. *Developing and Using Tests Effectively: A Guide for Faculty*. San Francisco: Jossey-Bass.

Lockhart, Marilyn. 2002. "The Use of Student Journals to Increase Faculty and Learner Inquiry and Reflection." *Academic Exchange Quarterly* 6, no.1 (Spring) 2002: 21–27.

Lynn, Laurence E., Jr. 1999. *Teaching and Learning with Cases: A Guidebook*. New York: Chatham House.

Muilenburg, Lin Y., and Zane L. Berge. 2002. "Designing Discussion for the Online Classroom." In *Designing Instruction for Technology-Enhanced Learning*, edited by Patricia L. Rogers. Hershey, PA: Idea Group, 100–113.

Naumes, William, and Margaret J. Naumes. 1999. *The Art & Craft of Case Writing*. Thousand Oaks, CA: Sage Publications.

Romance, Nancy R., and Michael R. Vitale. 1999. "Concept Mapping as a Tool for Learning: Broadening the Framework for Student-Centered Instruction." *College Teaching* 47, no.2 (Spring): 74–79.

Schrock, Kathy. 2002. "Kathy Schrock's Guide for Educators: Assessment and Rubric Information." Available: http://school.discovery.com/schrockguide/assess.html.

Taggart, Germaine L., Sandra J. Phifer, Judy A. Nixon, and Marilyn Wood, eds. 1998. *Rubrics: A Handbook for Construction and Use*. Lancaster, PA: Technomic.

Taplin, Margaret, and Olugbemiro Jegede. 2001. "Gender Differences in Factors Influencing Achievement of Distance Education Students. *Open Learning* 16, no.2 (June): 133–154.

Williams, Janet L. 2000. "Creativity in Assessment of Library Instruction." *Reference Services Review* 28, no.4: 323–334.

WEB DESIGN AND DEVELOPMENT

Builder.com. 1995. "Programming and Scripting." San Francisco: CNET Networks. Available: http://builder.cnet.com/webbuilding/0–3882.html.

Instone, Keith. 2000. "Information Architecture and Personalization. Ann Arbor, MI: Argus Center for Information Architecture. Available: http://argus-acia.com/white_papers/personalization.html.

Instone, Keith. 1995. "Usable Web." Available: http://usableweb.com/.

Krug, Steve. 2000. *Don't Make Me Think! A Common Sense Approach to Web Usability.* Indianapolis, IN: New Riders Publishing.

Li, Xiaodong. 2000. "Designing an Interactive Web Tutorial with Cross-Browser Dynamic HTML" *Library Hi Tech* 18, no.4: 369–382.

National Cancer Institute. "Research-Based Web Design and Usability Guidelines." Bethesda, MD. Available: http://usability.gov/guidelines/.

Nielsen, Jakob. 2000. *Designing Web Usability: The Practice of Simplicity.* Indianapolis, IN: New Riders Publishing.

Rosenfeld, Louis and Peter Morville. 1998. *Information Architecture for the World Wide Web.* Sebastopol, CA: O'Reilly.

Smith, Susan Sharpless. 2001. *Web-Based Instruction: A Guide for Libraries.* Chicago: American Library Association.

Spyridakis, Jan H. 2000. "Guidelines for Authoring Comprehensible Web Pages and Evaluating Their Success. *Technical Communication* 47, no.3 (August): 359–382.

Suarez, Doug. 2002. "Designing the Web Interface for Library Instruction Tutorials Using Dreamweaver, Fireworks, and Coursebuilder." *Information Technology and Libraries* 21 (September): 129–134.

Tufte, Edward R. 1997. *Visual Explanations: Images and Quantities, Evidence and Narrative.* Cheshire, CT: Graphics Press.

Tufte, Edward R. 1990. *Envisioning Information.* Cheshire, CT: Graphics Press.

Van Duyne, Douglas K., James A. Landay, and Jason I. Hong. 2003. *The Design of Sites: Patterns, Principles, and Processes for Crafting a Customer-Centered Web Experience.* Boston: Addison-Wesley.

Weinman, Lynda. 2003. *Designing Web Graphics 4.* Indianapolis, IN: New Riders Publishing.

EVALUATION AND USABILITY TESTING

Bloor, Michael, Jane Frankland, Michelle Thomas, and Kate Robson. 2001. *Focus Groups in Social Research.* London: Sage Publications.

Campbell, Nicole, ed. 2001. *Usability Assessment of Library-Related Web Sites: Methods and Case Studies: LITA Guide #7.* Chicago: American Library Association.

Dickstein, Ruth, and Victoria A. Mills. 2000. "Usability Testing at the University of Arizona Library: How to Let the Users in on the Design." *Information Technology and Libraries* 19, no.3 (September): 144–151.

Edmunds, Holly. 1999. *The Focus Group Research Handbook.* Lincolnwood, IL: NTC Business Books.

Glitz, Beryl. 1998. *Focus Groups for Libraries and Librarians.* New York: Forbes Custom Publishing.

Greenbaum, Thomas L. 1998. *The Handbook for Focus Group Research.* 2nd Edition. Thousand Oaks, CA: Sage Publications.

Hom, James. 1996. "The Usability Methods Toolbox." Available: http:// jthom.best.vwh.net/usability/.

Kliem, Ralph L., and Irwin S. Ludin. 1998. *Project Management Practitioner's Handbook.* New York: AMACOM.

Merton, Robert K., Marjorie Fiske and Patricia L. Kendall. 1990. *The Focused Interview: A Manual of Problems and Procedures.* 2nd Edition. New York: Free Press.

Morgan, David L., Richard A. Krueger, and Jean A. King. 1998. *The Focus Group Kit (Vols. 1–6).* Thousand Oaks, CA: Sage Publications.

Nielsen, Jakob. 1995. "The Alert Box: Current Issues in Web Usability." Fremont, CA: Nielsen Norman Group. Available: www.useit.com/alertbox/.

Norlin, Elaina, and CM! Winters. 2002. *Usability Testing for Library Websites: A Hands-on Guide.* Chicago: American Library Association.

Rubin, Jeffrey. 1994. *Handbook of Usability Testing: How to Plan, Design, and Conduct Effective Tests.* New York: Wiley.

Shonrock, Diana D. 1996. *Evaluating Library Instruction: Sample Questions, Forms, and Strategies for Practical Use.* Chicago: American Library Association.

Veldof, Jerilyn R., Ruth Dickstein, and Vicki Mills. 1999. "Chauffeured by the User: Usability in the Electronic Library." *Journal of Library Administration* 26, no.3/4: 115–140.

About the Contributors

SUSAN CAROL CURZON, Ph.D., is Dean of the University Library at California State University, Northridge. Prior to that she was with the City of Glendale where she was the Director of Libraries, and with the County of Los Angeles Public Library where she held various positions including, as a Regional Administrator, supervising eleven branches. She started her career as special librarian. Her Ph.D. is in Public Administration from the University of Southern California and her M.L.S. from the University of Washington. She is the author of two books and a variety of articles. In 1993, she was *Library Journal*'s Librarian of the Year. Sue was the Chair of the California State University Information Competence Initiative from its inception in 1995 until 2002.

NANCY H. DEWALD has been an academic reference and instruction librarian for over eighteen years. She has written articles and given presentations on Web-based library instruction, and her article "Web-Based Library Instruction: What Is Good Pedagogy?" published in *Information Technology & Libraries*, was selected by the American Library Association Library Instruction Round Table as one of the "Top 20 Library Instruction Articles" for 1999. She is currently at the Pennsylvania State University's Berks Campus in Reading, PA.

ELIZABETH A. DUPUIS is currently the Head of Instructional Services for the Doe and Moffitt Libraries at the University of California, Berkeley. The nine years preceding this position she spent as an instruction librarian and Head of the Digital Information Literacy Office at the University of Texas at Austin. She was the project manager and instructional designer of TILT (Texas Information Literacy Tutorial, http://tilt.lib.utsystem.edu/), a Web-based tutorial covering basic library and research skills developed for first-year students of the University of Texas System. Over a two year period, she led a small team to plan, design, and evaluate the three-module tutorial. In 2000 the site was released under an Open Publication License, allowing other institutions to download and customize the site to meet the needs of their audiences. She is active within state and national professional organizations and serves on the editorial boards for *Research Strategies* and *PSQ: Public Services Quarterly*.

CLARA S. FOWLER has been the Coordinator of Library Instruction for the University of Houston Libraries since 2001. Prior to this, she was an instruction librarian at the University of Texas at Austin. As content leader for TILT (Texas Information Literacy Tutorial, http://tilt.lib.utsystem.edu), she worked with a small development team and honed her skills for the effective delivery of online content. The TILT team was honored with the Association of College and Research Libraries Instruction Section award in 2000 for "Innovation in Instruction". Clara's current research interests include integrating the library instruction program into course management systems and instructional leadership.

CRAIG GIBSON is Associate University Librarian for Public Services at George Mason University, where he is responsible for reference and instruction, interlibrary loan and document delivery, government documents, and access services in the main library. His article, "Critical Thinking: Implications for Instruction," won the Reference Press Service Award in 1997 for best article in *RQ*. He was selected to be a participant in the ACRL Instruction Section's Think Tank III, and he has held several ACRL Instruction Section committee memberships and offices. In 1999, he was selected to join the Institute for Information Literacy's Immersion Program Faculty, and in that same year, he served on the ACRL Task Force on Information Literacy Competency Standards. Craig teaches a course on information literacy for The Catholic University's graduate program in library and information science, and he has consulted with the

TLT Group (Teaching and Learning with Technology Group) on instruction-related initiatives and projects. He has given numerous presentations and workshops on critical thinking and research skills, staff development, and the concept of the learning library, and has written articles on assessment and distance learning.

DENNIS GLENN is currently Assistant Dean for Distributed Education in the School of Communication at Northwestern University. Mr. Glenn builds interactive learning environments that individualize instruction over broadband networks and Distance Learning Courseware. His previous position at Northwestern University was Visual and Curriculum Design Specialist in the Information Technology Department and Manager of the Advanced Media Production Studio. Dennis has been a professional photographer, film director, and educator.

TRUDI BELLARDO HAHN, as Manager of User Education Services for the University of Maryland Libraries, coordinates a program of information literacy instruction aimed at 40,000 students and faculty on the College Park campus. She works closely with teaching faculty and library staff in developing, monitoring, and assessing library instruction that supports the University curriculum and serves the needs of various precollege students and other outside groups. She is also an adjunct faculty in the College of Information Studies at the University of Maryland. She has published books and articles, made conference presentations, and conducted workshops on the topics of online retrieval, indexing, interface design, databases, World Wide Web searching, information literacy issues, history of information science, and education and training for the information profession. She is currently serving as president of the American Society for Information Science & Technology. She earned a Ph.D. in Information Systems at Drexel University and an MSLS and a BA in Linguistics from the University of Kentucky.

TRUDI E. JACOBSON is the Coordinator of User Education Programs at the University at Albany, SUNY, and an adjunct faculty member at the School of Information Science and Policy at the same institution. She coordinates and teaches the undergraduate Information Literacy course, UNL 205, which reaches approximately 1,000 freshmen and sophomores each year. Web-based tutorials offered by the University Library form a key component of the University at Albany's campus-wide information literacy program. Her professional interests include the use of critical thinking and active learning activities. She is the co-editor of *Teaching the New Library to Today's Users* and *Teaching Information Literacy Concepts: Activities and Frameworks from the Field*, and editor of *Critical Thinking and the Web: Teaching Users to Evaluate Internet Resources*. She has published articles in a number of journals, including *Portal, The Journal of General Education, College & Research Libraries, Journal of Academic Librarianship, Research Strategies, College Teaching, The Teaching Professor*, and *Education*.

Scott Macklin, formerly the Associate Director of UWired, now directs the Program for the Educational Transformation through Technology at the University of Washington. PETTT seeks to enhance the effectiveness of the educators at University of Washington, and thus of the institution itself, by creating a campus framework to promote the thoughtful exploration, development, assessment, and dissemination of next-generation technologies and strategies for teaching and learning. In 2000, his co-authored article, *The Catalyst Project: Supporting Faculty Uses of the Web . . . with the Web*, won the EDUCAUSE contribution of the year award. Scott serves as Vice President of Education on the executive board of the Society of Information Managers. He also serves on the EDUCAUSE Systemic Progress in Teaching and Learning Award committee and is a member of the Society of the Learning Sciences.

Pat Davitt Maughan has been User Research Coordinator at the Teaching Library, University of California at Berkeley, since 1993. She has conducted a wide range of quantitative and qualitative research, including focus groups, user surveys, and usability studies involving Berkeley's librarians, faculty and students. Formerly Head of the Science Libraries at Berkeley, she was also a 2001–2002 Fellow at UC Berkeley's Townsend Center for the Humanities. She serves as a consultant to the California Digital Library and Library Solutions Institute and Press. Recent areas of research focus on assessing information literacy and library service quality. She has published the results of her research in *The Journal of Academic Librarianship* and *College & Research Libraries*. Pat has taught information literacy and library research skills to thousands of students, and has lectured at UC Berkeley's School of Information Management and Systems, the Colegio de Estudios Superiores de Administracion in Colombia, the University of Helsinki, and the Summer School on the Digital Library in the Netherlands.

Sarah McDaniel currently works as the Humanities Librarian at the University of California, Berkeley. Prior to this position, she worked as Instructional Services Coordinator for the Information Services Division at the University of Southern California. She has led a variety of instructional initiatives including InfoMasters, a summer technology-training program for K–12 teachers in Los Angeles, and a new initiative to work with Graduate Student Instructors at UC Berkeley to integrate research into the undergraduate curriculum. She received her MLIS and MA in Foreign Languages and Literatures from the University of Wisconsin, Milwaukee.

Deborah A. Murphy is Coordinator of Instructional Services at the University of California, Santa Cruz McHenry Library since 1987. Prior to this, she was Online Coordinator at Stanford University's Meyer Library, where as a member of the Faculty Software Developer's Program she authored "BiblioMania," one of the first interactive library instruction programs for the Macintosh computer. She has published and spoken at national conferences on instructional software design and development of online teaching resources. At UCSC, she continues developing instructional and information literacy resources integrating new technologies. She and her team are currently working on revision of the nationally recognized "UCSC NetTrail" (http://nettrail.ucsc.edu), an interactive Web-based online literacy course developed by a cross campus team.

NANCY O'HANLON is an Instruction Librarian and Associate Professor at Ohio State University Libraries. She is the project manager and designer of net.TUTOR (http://gateway.lib.ohio-state.edu/tutor), a Web-based program providing instruction on use of Internet tools, searching skills, and research techniques. During the past five years, more than 150 classes at Ohio State University have used net.TUTOR to teach Internet and information literacy skills to students. Nancy is also currently leading a group to redesign the OSU Libraries Web site.

SUSAN SHARPLESS SMITH, technology team leader for the Z. Smith Reynolds Library at Wake Forest University in Winston-Salem, NC, leads the planning, development, implementation, maintenance, and evaluation of the library's technology activities. Her interest in Web-based instruction emerged when studying for her MA in Educational Technology Leadership at George Washington University, where her focus of study was on the development of educational Web sites. She is the author of *Web-Based Instruction: A Guide for Libraries*.

JERILYN R. VELDOF is the User Education Coordinator at the University of Minnesota Libraries in the Twin Cities. Prior to this position, she was the University of Minnesota's Distance Learning Instruction Librarian and a Social Sciences & Undergraduate Services Librarian at the University of Arizona. Jerilyn has been involved in the user-centered design process for a number of Web sites at the University of Minnesota and the University of Arizona including a tutorial, OPAC, pathfinder tools, University homepage and several library homepages. She has given numerous presentations and one-day workshops on usability testing and has co-authored usability related articles for *The Journal of Library Administration, Research Strategies*, and *Internet Reference Services Quarterly*. Jerilyn's MLS is from the State University of NY at Buffalo.

Index

Access (Microsoft software program), 98
Accessibility, 39, 99, 103, 205-206, 231, 238-239
  and computer issues, 39, 99, 103
  and user issues, 205-206, 231, 238-239
Analog, 98
Andragogy, 47-49, 56, 64-65, 160, 166
  see also Educational theories and approaches; Pedagogy
Animations, 51, 61, 203
Assessment, 61, 79-83, 87-91, 147-152, 162, 185, 192-193, 218, 221-222
  examples of uses, 61, 81-83
  methods for, 148-149, 155-161
  of educational technology, 80
  of student learning, 79, 147-148, 153-155, 185
  rubrics, 81, 83, 150-152, 161
  types of, 149-152, 192-193, 218
  see also Needs assessment; Quizzes
Assignments, 55, 56, 61, 63, 76, 78-79, 149
Audience, 11, 37-42, 47-49, 64, 73-74, 103-104, 129-130, 166-167, 205-206, 219
  characteristics of, 38-42

  design related to, 47-49, 64, 103-104, 129-130, 166-167, 219
  technological considerations for, 11, 39, 41-42, 73-74, 205-206
Audio, 51, 83, 229, 253

Backward Design Model, 184-186
Balance, 246, 248-249
Behaviorism, 49-50, 54, 65, 171-178, 210
Benchmarking, 21, 99-100, 139-140
Blackboard. *See* Learning management systems
Bloom, Benjamin, 49-50, 65, 173-174
Briggs, Leslie, 210
Budget, 1-3, 7, 11, 19-22, 260

Caching, 100
Catalyst, 82
Center for Applied Special Technologies, 239
Center for Instructional Design and Research, University of Washington, 77, 81-83
Chat, 39, 41, 51, 55, 166, 202
Chunking, 215-216, 222, 245
Cleary, Chip, 197-198
CLUE (tutorial), 213